London Bus
& Allocat
2015

PAUL JORDAN & PAUL SMITH

London United buses lined up in the bus station outside **Hounslow Bus Garage** (AV) on
September 27th, 2014.

NOSTALGIA ROAD

THIS BOOK IS DEDICATED TO
TIIU JORDAN

Stagecoach London bus **17814** parked outside **Leyton Bus Garage** (T) on September 20th, 2014.

First published by Crécy Publishing 2015

© Paul Jordan & Paul Smith 2015

A CIP record for this book is available from the British Library

ISBN 9781908347343

Printed in Malta by Melita Press

Crécy Publishing Limited
1a Ringway Trading Estate
Shadowmoss Road
Manchester M22 5LH

www.crecy.co.uk

Front Cover: Stagecoach London Bus **17873** in the yard at **West Ham Garage** (WH) on July 26th, 2014.

Back Cover Top: Metroline Bus **VW1366** exiting from **Alperton Garage** (ON) on July 27th, 2014.

Back Cover Bottom Left: Arriva London buses **LT173, LT214** and **LT226** at **Clapton Garage** (CT) on August 5th, 2014.

Back Cover Bottom Right: Arriva London Bus **LT4** parked inside **Ash Grove Garage** (AE) on August 5th, 2014.

CONTENTS

LIST OF GARAGES
IN ALPHABETICAL ORDER

INTRODUCTION

Arriva London buses **LT173**, **LT214** & **LT226** at **Clapton Bus Garage** on August 5th, 2014.

This volume is specifically dedicated to those 77 garages that supplied buses for Transport for London routes as at January 1st, 2015 and the information includes a photograph of the depot, location map, address with postcode, operator, nearest station and some of the bus routes that either pass it or are reasonably adjacent.

There are also NG and OS co-ordinates as well as a list of the routes that are supplied by the garage. In all instances we have endeavoured to be as up to date and accurate as we are able, and none more so than in the allocation lists for each garage. These are correct to at least September 1st, 2014 and any last minute amendments or new buses supplied following this date and prior to going to press may be found on Page 112.

Commencing on Page 107 is a short section dealing with the three bus garages that currently are not supplying buses to routes but are active in maintenance or storing vehicles. Also, although technically not within our remit, the three garages that maintain and supply the tour buses are covered.

All the garages were visited between June 2013 and November 2014 and, unless stated, all the photographs were taken by the authors. Except for where authorization was sought and given, all the photographs were taken from public places.

Needless to say, using this book does not give any authority to enter any of the establishments and permission to do so must be sought from the appropriate bus operator.

WITH MANY THANKS TO

Leon Daniels *(Managing Director Surface Transport, TfL)*, Lisa Taylor *(Chief of Staff to MD, Surface Transport, TfL)*, Bob Pennyfather and Ken Robinson *(Arriva London)*, Mark Threappleton, David Jones, Colin Wright and Steve Harrison *(Stagecoach London)*, Scott Crowder, Yvonne Dawson, Raj Chadha and Matt Larkin *(Metroline)*, Eugene Clarke, Glenn Woodman and Graham Oliver *(Go-Ahead London)*, Richard Hall, Ray Clapson and Joanna Munns *(London United)*, Adam Leishman *(Tower Transit)* and David Hillas.

CHANGES FROM 2014

Apart from the regular change of buses, 2014 saw the closure of one garage and opening of two. **Lee Valley** (LV) closed on February 28th, 2014 when the site was compulsory purchased by the National Grid and **Edmonton** (EC) was reinstated as a service depot on March 1st, 2014. Tellings Golden Miller took over route E10 with buses from their **Heathrow** Depot

Paul Jordan, **Walsall** and Paul Smith, Kings Heath, **Birmingham**

The Ealing Road exit from **Alperton Garage** viewed on July 26th, 2014 with Metroline bus **VW1366** parked in the main doorway.

ALPERTON (ON)
Ealing Road, Alperton, Wembley, Middlesex HA0 4LL
Operated by: Metroline
Location: TQ17988375 [51.540372, -0.300206]
Nearest Tube Station: Alperton (100 yards)
Nearest Bus Routes: 245 & 487 - Alperton, Alperton (Stop C)
Bus Routes Serviced: 83/223/224/245 & 487

The garage was built by the London Passenger Transport Board and opened in June 1939. It was one of three depots built by the LPTB and the only modern-day survivor. The garage was extended on the north west side during the period 1976 to 1978 when part of a London Transport railway site was taken over.

VEHICLE ALLOCATION

DE1647	YX58 HVA	DE1964	YX12 DKL	VW1367	LK62 DLJ	VW1395	LK62 DVC	VW1766	LK59 CXD
DE1665	YX09 AEU	DE1965	YX12 DKN	VW1368	LK62 DLO	VW1396	LK62 DVF	VW1767	LK59 CXE
DE1666	YX09 AEV	DE1966	YX12 DKO	VW1369	LK62 DLV	VW1397	LK62 DVG	VW1768	LK59 CXF
DE1667	YX09 AEW	DE1967	YX12 DKU	VW1370	LK62 DLX	VW1752	LK59 CWN	VW1769	LK59 CXG
DE1668	YX09 AEY	DE1968	YX12 DKV	VW1371	LK62 DMV	VW1753	LK59 CWO	VW1770	LK59 CXH
DE1669	YX09 AEZ	DE1969	YX12 DKY	VW1372	LK62 DND	VW1754	LK59 CWP	VW1771	LK59 CXJ
DE1670	YX09 AFA	DEM1912	YX61 EKR	VW1373	LK62 DNE	VW1755	LK59 CWR	VW1772	LK59 CXL
DE1671	YX09 AFE	DEM1913	YX61 EKT	VW1374	LK62 DNU	VW1756	LK59 CWT	VW1773	LK59 CXM
DE1672	YX09 AFF	DEM1914	YX61 EKU	VW1375	LK62 DNO	VW1757	LK59 CWU	VW1774	LK59 CXN
DE1673	YX09 AFJ	DEM1915	YX61 EKV	VW1376	LK62 DNX	VW1758	LK59 CWV	VW1775	LK59 CXO
DE1674	YX09 AFK	DEM1916	YX61 EKW	VW1377	LK62 DOH	VW1759	LK59 CWW	VW1776	LK59 CXP
DE1958	YX12 DKA	DEM1917	YX61 EKY	VW1389	LK62 DTZ	VW1760	LK59 CWX	VW1777	LK59 FCO
DE1959	YX12 DKD	DEM1918	YX61 EKZ	VW1390	LK62 DUA	VW1761	LK59 CWY	VW1778	LK59 FCP
DE1960	YX12 DKE	VW1249	LK12 ABX	VW1391	LK62 DUH	VW1762	LK59 CWZ	VW1779	LK59 FCU
DE1961	YX12 DKF	VW1251	LK12 ACO	VW1392	LK62 DUJ	VW1763	LK59 CXA	VW1780	LK59 FCV
DE1962	YX12 DKJ	VW1365	LK62 DKN	VW1393	LK62 DUU	VW1764	LK59 CXB	VW1781	LK59 FCX
DE1963	YX12 DKK	VW1366	LK62 DKV	VW1394	LK62 DVB	VW1765	LK59 CXC		

Ash Grove Depot on August 5th, 2014. The piers in the foreground straddling the entrance carry the ex-GE Hackney Fields to London Liverpool Street line. Visible through the bridge is the entrance to the depot.

ASH GROVE (AE)
Mare Street, South Hackney, London E8 4RH
Operated by: Arriva London
Location: TQ34718363 [51.536072, -0.059181]
Nearest Station: Cambridge Heath (0.3 miles)
Nearest Bus Routes: 26/48/55/106/254/D6/N26/
N55 & N253 - St Josephs Hospice (Stop LH)
Bus Routes Serviced: 38/78/106/168 & 254

For historical notes regarding this depot see Page 7.

NB This depot is also used by CT Plus and is coded as HK Ash Grove (See Page 7)

VEHICLE ALLOCATION

DW412	LJ11 AEC	LT5	LTZ 1005	T169	LJ60 AUU	VLW136	LJ03 MHM	VLW157	LJ03 MPX
DW413	LJ11 AED	LT6	LTZ 1006	T170	LJ60 AUV	VLW137	LJ03 MHN	VLW158	LJ03 MPY
DW516	LJ13 CCX	LT7	LTZ 1007	T171	LJ60 AUW	VLW138	LJ03 MFN	VLW159	LJ03 MPZ
DW517	LJ13 CCY	T66	LJ59 ACY	T172	LJ60 AUX	VLW139	LJ03 MFP	VLW160	LJ03 MRU
DW518	LJ13 CCZ	T67	LJ59 ACZ	T173	LJ60 AUY	VLW140	LJ03 MFU	VLW161	LJ03 MRV
DW519	LJ13 CLZ	T68	LJ59 ADO	T174	LJ60 AVB	VLW141	LJ03 MFV	VLW162	LJ03 MRX
DW520	LJ13 CME	T69	LJ59 ADV	T175	LJ60 ATZ	VLW142	LJ03 MEV	VLW163	LJ03 MRY
DW521	LJ13 CMF	T70	70 CLT	T176	LJ60 AUA	VLW143	LJ03 MFA	VLW164	LJ03 MSU
DW522	LJ13 CMK	T71	LJ59 ADZ	T177	LJ60 AUC	VLW144	LJ03 MFE	VLW165	LJ03 MSV
DW523	LJ13 CDE	T72	LJ59 AEA	T178	LJ60 AUE	VLW145	LJ03 MFF	VLW166	LJ03 MSX
DW524	LJ13 CDF	T73	LJ59 ABF	T179	LJ60 AUF	VLW146	LJ03 MFK	VLW167	LJ03 MMU
DW525	LJ13 CDK	T74	LJ59 ABK	VLW126	LF52 UPA	VLW147	LJ03 MBF	VLW168	LJ03 MMV
DW526	LJ13 CDN	T75	LJ59 ABN	VLW127	LF52 UPB	VLW148	LJ03 MBU	VLW169	LJ03 MMX
DW527	LJ13 CDO	T76	LJ59 ABO	VLW128	LF52 UPC	VLW149	LJ03 MBV		
DW528	LJ13 CDU	T77	LJ59 ABU	VLW129	LG52 DAA	VLW150	LJ03 MBX		
DW529	LJ13 CKU	T78	LJ59 ABV	VLW130	LJ03 MGZ	VLW151	LJ03 MBY		
DW530	LJ13 CKV	T79	LJ59 ABX	VLW131	LJ03 MHA	VLW152	LJ03 MDE		
DW531	LJ13 CKX	T80	LJ59 ABZ	VLW132	LJ03 MHE	VLW153	LJ03 MDF		
DW532	LJ13 CKY	T81	LJ59 ACF	VLW133	LJ03 MHF	VLW154	LJ03 MDK		
DW533	LJ13 CLF	T82	LJ59 ACO	VLW134	LJ03 MHK	VLW155	LJ03 MDN		
LT4	LTZ 1004	T83	LJ59 AAE	VLW135	LJ03 MHL	VLW156	LJ03 MDU		

The north end of **Ash Grove Depot** viewed on August 5th, 2014. There is an additional parking area for buses and another entrance gate at the far end of the yard off Sheep Lane. The building incorporates offices and a multi storey staff car park.

NB This depot is also used by Arriva London and is coded as AE Ash Grove (See Page 6)

ASH GROVE (HK)
Mare Street, South Hackney, London E8 4RH
Operated by: CT Plus
Location: TQ34718363 [51.536072, -0.059181]
Nearest Station: Cambridge Heath (0.3 miles)
Nearest Bus Routes: 26/48/55/106/254/D6/N26/ N55/N253 - St Josephs Hospice (Stop LH)
Bus Routes Serviced: 153/212/309/385/388/394/ 675/W5/W12 & W13

Ash Grove was opened by London Buses on April 25th, 1981 and, following the split of the company into eleven separate entities, was used by London Forest until it was wound up in 1991.

The depot was re-opened in 1994 by Kentish Bus, but this itself became defunct in 1997 and Ash Grove was not re-opened again until 2000 when East Thames Buses took it over. On October 13th, 2005 the company moved out to Mandela Way (See Page 57) but was subsequently replaced by CT Plus, part of the HCT Group, supporting community transport.

VEHICLE ALLOCATION

DA 2	YX62 DHC	DCS5	HX03 MGV	HTL 2	LR52 LTN	OS 3	YJ59 NRO	OS22	YJ12 GVU
DA 3	YX62 DHD	DCS6	HX03 MGU	HTL 3	LR52 LTJ	OS 4	YJ10 EYF	OS23	YJ12 GVV
DA 4	YX62 DHY	DCS7	HX03 MGJ	HTL 4	LR52 LTF	OS 5	YJ10 EYG	OS24	YJ12 GVW
DA 5	YX62 DKD	DCS8	HX03 MGY	HTL 5	LR52 LWE	OS 6	YJ10 EYH	OS25	YJ12 GVX
DA 6	YX62 DKE	DCS9	HX03 MGZ	HTL 6	LR52 LTK	OS 7	YJ10 EYG	OS26	YJ12 GVY
DA 7	YX62 DKL	DE1	PN07 KPY	HTL 7	LR52 LWF	OS 8	YJ10 EYL	OS27	YJ12 GVZ
DA 8	YX62 DMU	DE2	PN07 KPZ	HTL 8	LR52 LWH	OS 9	YJ60 PFA	SD 1	YR59 NPA
DA 9	YX62 DPF	DE3	PN07 KRD	HTL 9	LR52 LWJ	OS10	YJ60 PFD	SD 2	YR59 NPC
DA10	YX62 DSZ	DE4	PN07 KRE	HTL10	PF52 TFX	OS11	YJ60 PFE	SD 3	YR59 NPD
DA11	YX62 DTV	DE5	PN07 KRF	HTL11	PF52 TGZ	OS12	YJ60 PFF	SD 4	YR59 NPF
DA12	YX62 DTY	DE6	PN07 KRG	HTL12	LR52 LYC	OS13	YJ60 PFG	SD 5	YR59 NPG
DAS1	SN57 DWE	DP1	SN53 EUD	HTL13	LR52 LYJ	OS14	YJ60 PFK	SD 6	YR59 NPJ
DAS2	SN57 DWF	DPS2	BU05 HFG	HTP3	PN03 UMB	OS15	YJ60 PFN	SD 7	YR59 NPN
DCS1	E8 NJB	DPS4	BX54 DLK	HTP4	PN03 UMK	OS16	YJ60 PFO	SD 8	YR59 NPE
DCS2	KV03 ZFF	EO1	PN08 SWJ	HTP5	LR52 KWG	OS19	YJ61 MKA	SD 9	YR59 NPK
DCS3	KV03 ZFG	HEA1	SN62 DND	HTP6	PN03 ULY	OS20	YJ12 GVR	SD10	YR59 NPO
DCS4	KV03 ZFH	HTL 1	LR52 LTO	OS 2	YJ59 NRN	OS21	YJ12 GVT		

7

Atlas Road Bus Garage on May 10th, 2014. It was opened on October 1st, 2011 when part of Westbourne Park Depot (See Page 100) was closed to accommodate construction work on the Crossrail project. *Allison Smith*

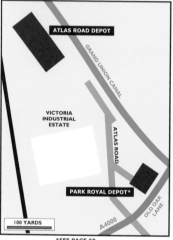

*SEE PAGE 69

ATLAS ROAD (AS)
Atlas Road, Harlesden, London NW10 6DN
Operated by: Tower Transit
Location: TQ21418261 [51.531674, -0.254199]
Nearest Station: Willesden Junction (0.5 miles)
Nearest Bus Routes: 228 & 266 - Old Oak Common, Old Oak Common Lane (Stop J)
Bus Routes Serviced: 28/31/266/328/N28 & N31

The entrance to **Atlas Road Bus Garage** viewed on May 10th, 2014. *Allison Smith*

VEHICLE ALLOCATION

TN33185	LR02 LZE	VN37975	BG61 SYK	VNW32374	LK04 HZD	VNW32397	LK54 FNO	VNW32420	LK04 JCV
TN33187	LT52 WVC	VN37976	BN61 MYA	VNW32375	LK04 HZE	VNW32398	LK54 FNP	VNW32421	LK04 JCX
TN33198	LT52 XAJ	VN37977	BN61 MYB	VNW32376	LK04 HZF	VNW32399	LK04 HXH	VNW32422	LK04 HYZ
TN33199	LT52 XAK	VN37978	BG61 SXJ	VNW32377	LK04 HZG	VNW32400	LK04 HXJ	VNW32423	LK04 JCZ
VN36291	BX12 CVO	VN37979	BG61 SXM	VNW32378	LK04 HZH	VNW32401	LK04 HXL	VNW32424	LK04 HYB
VN36292	BX12 CVM	VN37980	BG61 SXL	VNW32379	LK04 HZJ	VNW32402	LK04 HXM	VNW32425	LK04 HYC
VN36293	BX12 CVK	VN37981	BG61 SXN	VNW32380	LK04 HZL	VNW32403	LK04 HXN	VNW32426	LK04 HYF
VN36294	BX12 CVL	VN37982	BG61 SXO	VNW32381	LK04 HZM	VNW32404	LK04 HXP	VNW32427	LK04 HYG
VN36295	BX12 CVP	VN37983	BG61 SXP	VNW32382	LK04 HZN	VNW32405	LK04 HXR	VNW32428	LK04 HYH
VN37960	BN61 MXG	VN37984	BG61 SXR	VNW32383	LK04 JBU	VNW32406	LK04 HXS	VNW32429	LK04 HYJ
VN37962	BN61 MXK	VNW32361	LK04 HYN	VNW32384	LK04 HZS	VNW32407	LK04 HXT	VNW32430	LK04 HYL
VN37963	BN61 MXJ	VNW32362	LK04 HYM	VNW32385	LK04 HZT	VNW32408	LK04 HXU	VNZ32495	LK54 FLA
VN37964	BN61 MXP	VNW32363	LK04 HYW	VNW32386	LK04 HZU	VNW32409	LK04 HXV	VNZ32496	LK54 FLB
VN37965	BN61 MXM	VNW32364	LK04 HYT	VNW32387	LK04 HZV	VNW32410	LK04 HXW	VNZ32497	LK54 FLC
VN37966	BN61 MXO	VNW32365	LK04 HYX	VNW32388	LK04 HZW	VNW32411	LK04 HXX	VNZ32498	LK54 FLD
VN37967	BN61 MXR	VNW32366	LK04 HYY	VNW32389	LK04 HZX	VNW32412	LK04 JBE	VNZ32499	LK54 FLE
VN37968	BN61 MXS	VNW32367	LK04 HYA	VNW32390	LK04 HZY	VNW32413	LK04 HZP	VNZ32500	LK54 FLF
VN37969	BN61 MXT	VNW32368	LK04 HYS	VNW32391	LK04 HZZ	VNW32414	LK04 JBV	VNZ32501	LK54 FLG
VN37970	BN61 MXU	VNW32369	LK04 HYU	VNW32392	LK04 HXA	VNW32415	LK04 JBX	VNZ32502	LK54 FLH
VN37971	BN61 MXY	VNW32370	LK04 HYV	VNW32393	LK04 HXB	VNW32416	LK04 JBY	WN35001	LK58 EDO
VN37972	BN61 MXX	VNW32371	LK04 HZA	VNW32394	LK04 HXC	VNW32417	LK04 JBZ	WN35002	LK58 EDP
VN37973	BN61 MXW	VNW32372	LK04 HZB	VNW32395	LK04 HXD	VNW32418	LK04 JCJ	WN35003	LK58 EDR
VN37974	BN61 MXV	VNW32373	LK04 HZC	VNW32396	LK04 HXE	VNW32419	LK04 JCU	WN35004	LK09 CZS

Arriva London bus T13 standing in front of the maintenance building at **Barking Bus Garage** on September 20th, 2014.

MAPLESTEAD ROAD

CASTLE ROAD

MAPLESTEAD ROAD

A13 — RIPPLE ROAD

BARKING DEPOT

100 YARDS

RIPPLE ROAD INDUSTRIAL AREA

BARKING (DX)
Ripple Road, Barking IG11 0SL
Operated by: Arriva London
Location: TQ46678358 [51.532288, 0.113521]
Nearest Tube Station: Upney (1.3 miles)
Nearest Bus Routes: 173/287/673 & 687 - Lodge Avenue (Stop P)
Bus Routes Serviced: 128/135/150/173/325/647 & 678

Arriva London bus T181 in the wash plant at **Barking Bus Garage** on September 20th, 2014.

The depot was opened by Grey-Green in 1992 and consists simply of a main yard and a few ancillary buildings within Ripple Road Industrial Area. Grey-Green was subsumed into the Cowie Group in the mid-1990s and, subsequently, Arriva London.

VEHICLE ALLOCATION

ENL10	LJ58 AVT	ENL64	LJ60 AYG	T17	217 CLT	T186	LJ60 ASZ	VLA132	LJ05 GPX
ENL49	LJ10 CSF	ENL65	LJ60 AYH	T18	LJ08 CVO	T187	LJ60 ATF	VLA133	LJ05 GPY
ENL50	LJ10 CSO	ENL66	LJ60 AYK	T19	519 CLT	T188	LJ60 ATK	VLA134	LJ05 GPZ
ENL51	LJ10 CSU	ENL67	LJ60 AYL	T20	LJ08 CVR	T189	LJ60 ATN	VLA135	LJ05 GRF
ENL52	LJ59 LVL	ENL68	LJ60 AYM	T21	LJ08 CUU	T190	LJ60 ATO	VLA136	LJ05 GRK
ENL53	LJ59 LVM	ENL69	LJ60 AYN	T22	LJ08 CUV	T191	LJ60 ATU	VLA137	LJ05 GRU
ENL54	LJ59 LVN	ENL70	LJ60 AYO	T23	LJ08 CUW	T192	LJ60 ATV	VLA138	LJ05 GRX
ENL55	LJ10 CSV	ENL71	LJ60 AYP	T24	324 CLT	T193	LJ60 ATX	VLA139	LJ05 GRZ
ENL56	LJ10 CSX	ENL72	LJ60 AYS	T25	LJ08 CUY	VLA124	LJ05 BJE	VLA140	LJ05 GSO
ENL57	LJ10 CSY	ENL73	LJ60 AXV	T26	LJ08 CVA	VLA125	LJ05 BJF	VLA141	LJ05 GSU
ENL58	LJ10 CSZ	ENL74	LJ60 AXW	T180	LJ60 AUH	VLA126	LJ05 BJK	VLA142	LJ55 BTE
ENL59	LJ10 CTE	T12	LJ08 CVG	T181	LJ60 AUK	VLA127	LJ05 BJO		
ENL60	LJ10 CTF	T13	LJ08 CVH	T182	LJ60 AUL	VLA128	LJ05 BJU		
ENL61	LJ10 CTK	T14	LJ08 CVK	T183	LJ60 AUM	VLA129	LJ05 GLZ		
ENL62	LJ60 ATY	T15	LJ08 CVL	T184	LJ60 AUN	VLA130	LJ05 GME		
ENL63	LJ60 AYF	T16	LJ08 CVM	T185	LJ60 ASX	VLA131	LJ05 GMF		

Barking Bus Garage on September 18th, 2013 with Stagecoach London bus 19795 passing on a Route 145 service to Dagenham.

BARKING (BK)
205 Longbridge Road, Barking IG11 8UE
Operated by: Stagecoach London
Location: TQ45288516 [51.518865, 0.143123]
Nearest Tube Station: Upney (0.7 miles)
Nearest Bus Routes: 5/145/387 & N15 - Barking Bus Garage, Faircross (Stop BC)
Bus Routes Serviced: 5/15/62/101/145/169/366/387/396/687 & N15

When the garage was opened by the London General Omnibus Company in January 1924 the entrance was on the corner of South Park Drive and Longbridge Road. The depot was extended eastwards in 1931 and again more recently when two adjoining dwellings were purchased and demolished to create more parking for vehicles.

Looking northeast towards **Barking Bus Garage** on August 20th, 2014 with Stagecoach London bus 19856 passing on a Route 5 service to Canning Town. The original entrance, now filled-in and used as offices, can be seen on the corner of South Park Road and Longbridge Road,

Barking Bus Garage on August 20th, 2014 with Stagecoach London buses, including 18216, parked at the east end of the site on the additional space created when the dwellings were demolished.

VEHICLE ALLOCATION

17581	LV52 HFO	17896	LX03 ORJ	19773	LX11 BFO	19849	LX12 CZC	36279	LX11 AWU
17582	LV52 HFP	17897	LX03 ORK	19774	LX11 BFP	19850	LX12 CZD	36280	LX11 AWV
17583	LV52 HFR	17898	LX03 ORN	19775	LX11 BFV	19851	LX12 CZE	36281	LX11 AWW
17585	LV52 HFT	17899	LX03 ORP	19776	LX11 BFW	19852	LX12 CZF	36282	LX11 AWY
17587	LV52 HFV	17900	LX03 ORS	19777	LX11 BFY	19853	LX12 CZG	36283	LX11 AWZ
17788	LX03 BWB	17901	LX03 ORT	19778	LX11 BFZ	19854	LX12 CZH	36284	LX11 AXA
17856	LX03 NEY	17902	LX03 ORU	19779	LX11 BGE	19855	LX12 CZJ	36285	LX11 AXB
17857	LX03 NFA	17904	LX03 ORW	19780	LX11 BGF	19856	LX12 CZK	36286	LX11 AXC
17858	LX03 NFC	18216	LX04 FXD	19781	LX11 BGK	19857	LX12 CZL	36287	LX11 AXD
17859	LX03 NFD	18217	LX04 FXE	19782	LX11 BGO	19858	LX12 CZM	36288	LX11 AXF
17860	LX03 NFE	19756	LX11 BDF	19783	LX11 BGU	25301	LX58 CHF	36289	LX11 AXG
17861	LX03 NFF	19757	LX11 BDO	19784	LX11 BGV	25302	LX58 CHG	36290	LX11 AXH
17862	LX03 NFG	19758	LX11 BDU	19785	LX11 BGY	25303	LX58 CHH	36291	LX11 AXJ
17863	LX03 NFH	19759	LX11 BDV	19794	LX11 BHN	25304	LX58 CHJ	36292	LX11 AXK
17878	LX03 NGH	19760	LX11 BDY	19795	LX11 BHO	25305	LX58 CHK	36293	LX11 AXM
17880	LX03 NGU	19761	LX11 BDZ	19796	LX11 BHP	25306	LX58 CHL	36294	LX11 AXN
17881	LX03 NGV	19762	LX11 BEJ	19797	LX11 BHU	25307	LX58 CHN	36295	LX11 AXO
17882	LX03 NGY	19763	LX11 BEO	19798	LX11 BHV	25308	LX58 CHO	36296	LX11 AXP
17883	LX03 NGZ	19764	LX11 BEU	19799	LX11 BHW	25309	LX58 CHV	36297	LX11 AXR
17884	LX03 NHA	19765	LX11 BEY	19800	LX11 BHY	25310	LX09 AAE	36298	LX11 AXS
17885	LX03 OPT	19766	LX11 BFA	19801	LX11 BHZ	25311	LX09 AAK	36299	LX11 AXT
17886	LX03 OPU	19767	LX11 BFF	19802	LX11 BJE	25312	LX09 AAJ		
17887	LX03 OPV	19768	LX11 BFJ	19803	LX11 BJF	25313	LX09 AAF		
17888	LX03 OPW	19769	LX11 BFK	19804	LX11 BJJ	25314	LX09 AAN		
17893	LX03 ORF	19770	LX11 BFL	19805	LX11 BJK	36276	LX11 AWO		
17894	LX03 ORG	19771	LX11 BFM	19847	LX12 CZA	36277	LX11 AWP		
17895	LX03 ORH	19772	LX11 BFN	19848	LX12 CZB	36278	LX11 AWR		

The exit from **Battersea Bus Garage** on September 6th, 2014 with Abellio buses 2433 & 9544 departing.

BATTERSEA (QB)
Silverthorne Road, Battersea, London SW8 3HE
Operated by: Abellio
Location: TQ28877644 [51.473148, -0.145334]
Nearest Station: Queenstown Road (0.4 miles)
Nearest Bus Routes: 137/156/452 & N137 - Battersea, Silverthorne Road (Stop T)
Bus Routes Serviced: 3/49/156/211/344/414/452/ C2/C3/C10 & N3

Opened on May 17th, 2010 by the Mayor of London, Boris Johnson, Battersea Depot occupies part of the site of the former Longhedge Works which were built by the London Chatham & Dover Railway in 1862 and closed by BR in the mid-50s. Most of the works was demolished in 1957 but part of it still remains at the rear of Stewarts Lane Depot.

The entrance to **Battersea Bus Garage**, at the north east end of the site, on September 6th, 2014 with the wash plant in view in the centre of the picture.

Abellio buses **2484**, **2474**, **2482** & **2469** lined up in the yard at **Battersea Bus Garage** on September 6th, 2014.

VEHICLE ALLOCATION

2414	SN61 DGX	2464	SL14 DFC	9403	LJ56 VTC	9484	LJ09 OKT	9526	SN12 AAY
2415	SN61 DGY	2465	SL14 LOA	9404	LJ56 VTD	9485	LJ09 OKU	9527	SN12 AAZ
2416	SN61 DGZ	2466	SL14 LOD	9405	LJ56 VTE	9486	LJ09 OKV	9528	SN12 ABF
2417	SN61 DHA	2467	SN64 OER	9406	LJ56 VTF	9487	LJ09 OKW	9529	SN12 ABK
2418	SN61 CXX	2468	SN64 OES	9407	LJ56 VTG	9488	LJ09 OKX	9530	SN12 ABO
2419	SN61 CXY	2469	SN64 OET	9408	LJ56 VTK	9489	LJ09 OKY	9531	SN12 ABU
2420	SN61 CXZ	2470	SN64 OEU	9409	LJ56 VTL	9490	LJ09 OLA	9532	SN12 ABV
2421	SN61 CYA	2471	SN64 OEV	9410	LJ56 VTM	9491	LJ09 OLB	9533	SN12 ABX
2422	SN61 CYC	2472	SN64 OEW	9411	LJ56 VTN	9492	LJ09 OLC	9534	SN12 ABZ
2423	SN61 CYE	2473	SN64 OEX	9412	LJ56 VTO	9493	LJ09 OLE	9535	SN12 ACF
2424	SN61 CYF	2474	SN64 OEY	9413	LJ56 VTP	9494	LJ09 OLG	9536	SN12 ACJ
2425	SN61 CYG	2475	SN64 OEZ	9414	LJ56 VTT	9495	LJ09 OLH	9537	SN12 ACO
2426	SN61 CYH	2476	SN64 OFA	9415	LJ56 VTU	9496	LJ09 OLK	9538	SN12 ACU
2427	SN61 CYJ	2477	SN64 OFB	9416	LJ56 VTV	9497	LJ09 OLM	9539	SN12 ACV
2428	SN61 CYK	2478	SN64 OFC	9417	LJ56 VTW	9499	LJ09 OLN	9540	SN12 ACX
2429	SN61 CYL	2479	SN64 OFD	9418	LJ07 OPE	9499	LJ09 OLO	9541	SN12 ACY
2430	SN61 CYO	2480	SN64 OFE	9419	LJ56 VTY	9500	LJ09 OLP	9542	SN12 ACZ
2431	SN61 CYP	2481	SN64 OFG	9420	LJ07 OPF	9501	LJ09 OLR	9543	SN12 ADO
2432	SN61 CYS	2482	SN64 OFH	9421	LJ07 OPG	9502	LJ09 OLT	9544	SN12 AUO
2433	SN61 CYT	2483	SN64 OFJ	9422	LJ07 OPH	9503	LJ09 OLU	9545	SN12 AOS
2434	SN61 CYU	2484	SN64 OFK	9423	LJ07 OPK	9504	LF59 XDZ	9546	SN12 AOT
2435	SN61 CYV	2485	SN64 OFL	9424	LJ56 VUD	9505	SN59 AVR	9547	SN12 AOU
2436	SN61 CYW	2486	SN64 OFM	9425	LJ07 OPL	9506	SN59 AVT	9548	SN12 AOV
2437	SN61 CYX	8437	RX51 FGM	9426	LJ56 VUF	9507	SN59 AVU	9549	SN12 AOW
2438	SN12 AUE	8501	LJ56 ONN	9427	LJ07 OPM	9508	SN59 AVV	9550	SN12 AOX
2439	SN12 AUF	8552	YX11 AEA	9467	LJ09 OJZ	9509	SN59 AVW	9551	SN12 AOY
2440	SN12 AUH	8553	YX11 AEB	9468	LJ09 OKA	9510	SN59 AVX	9552	SN12 AOZ
2441	SN12 AUJ	8554	YX11 AEC	9469	LJ09 OKB	9511	SN59 AVY	9553	SN12 APF
2442	SN12 AUK	8555	YX11 AED	9470	LJ09 OKC	9512	SN59 AVZ	9554	SN12 APK
2443	SN12 AUL	8556	YX11 AEE	9471	LJ09 OKD	9513	SN59 AWA	9555	SN12 APO
2452	SL14 DDF	8557	YX11 AEF	9472	LJ09 OKE	9514	SN59 AWC	9556	SN12 APU
2453	SL14 DDJ	8558	YX11 AEG	9473	LJ09 OKF	9515	SN59 AWF	9557	SN12 APV
2454	SL14 DDK	8559	YX11 AEJ	9474	LJ09 OKG	9516	SN59 AWG	9558	SN12 APX
2455	SL14 DDN	8560	YX11 AEK	9475	LJ09 OKH	9517	SN59 AWH	9757	YN51 KVP
2456	SL14 DDO	8561	YX11 AEL	9476	LJ09 OKK	9518	SN59 AWJ	9759	YN51 KVS
2457	SL14 DDU	8562	YX11 AEM	9477	LJ09 OKL	9519	SN59 AWM	9812	LG52 HWN
2458	SL14 DDV	8563	YX11 AEN	9478	LJ09 OKM	9520	SN59 AWO	9817	LG52 XYM
2459	SL14 DDX	8564	YX11 AEO	9479	LJ09 OKN	9521	SN59 AWP	9821	LG52 XYY
2460	SL14 DDY	8565	YX11 AEP	9480	LJ09 OKO	9522	SN59 AWR		
2461	SL14 DDZ	8566	YX11 AET	9481	LJ09 OKP	9523	SN59 AWU		
2462	SL14 DEU	9401	LJ56 VSZ	9482	LJ09 OKR	9524	SN12 AAV		
2463	SL14 DFA	9402	LJ56 VTA	9483	LJ09 OKS	9525	SN12 AAX		

Abellio bus 9816 parked outside of **Beddington Depot** on August 19th, 2014.

*SEE PAGE 30

BEDDINGTON (BC)
Unit 10, Beddington Cross, Beddington Farm Road,
Croydon CR0 4XH
Operated by: Abellio
Location: TQ29826653 [51.383058, -0.135957]
Nearest Tram Station: Therapia Lane (0.5 miles)
Nearest Bus Route: 455 - Beddington,
Beddington Cross (Southbound)
Bus Routes Serviced: 152/157/201/322/407/455/
931/P13 & T33

The west end of **Beddington Depot** on August 19th, 2014 with Abellio bus 8016 standing in the drive. The depot was opened by Connex in 2000.

VEHICLE ALLOCATION

8013	BX54 DLZ	8062	Y38 YVV	8497	KX04 HRF	8776	YX61 ELH	9030	BX55 XMC
8014	BX54 DME	8065	SK02 TZN	8498	KX04 HRG	8777	YX12 DLD	9031	BX55 XMD
8015	BX54 DMF	8338	YX11 AHL	8502	LJ56 ONO	8778	YX12 DLE	9032	BX55 XME
8016	BX54 DMO	8339	YX11 AHN	8503	LJ56 ONP	8779	YX12 DLF	9033	BX55 XMG
8017	BX54 DMU	8434	RX51 FGG	8504	LJ56 ONR	8780	YX12 DLJ	9066	BX55 XNV
8018	BX54 DMV	8435	RG51 FGJ	8505	LJ56 ONS	8781	YX12 DLK	9067	BX55 XNW
8019	BX54 DMY	8436	RG51 FGK	8506	LJ56 ONT	8782	YX12 DLN	9068	BX55 XNY
8020	BX54 DMZ	8471	HX04 HTY	8516	YX59 BYJ	8783	YX12 DLO	9071	LF06 YRD
8024	BU05 HDY	8472	HX04 HTZ	8517	YX59 BYK	8784	YX12 DLU	9072	LF06 YRE
8025	BU05 HEJ	8473	LF06 YRJ	8518	YX59 BYL	8785	YX12 DLV	9073	LF06 YRG
8026	BU05 HFA	8474	LF06 YRK	8519	YX59 BYM	8786	YX12 DLY	9739	YN51 KUU
8027	BU05 HFB	8475	LF06 YRL	8520	YX59 BYN	8787	YX12 DLZ	9740	YN51 KUV
8028	BU05 HFC	8476	LF06 YRM	8521	YX59 BYO	9021	BX55 XLS	9742	YN51 KUX
8029	BU05 HFD	8477	LF06 YRN	8522	YX59 BYP	9022	BX55 XLT	9750	YN51 KVG
8031	BU05 HFK	8488	KX03 HZF	8523	YX59 BYR	9023	BX55 XLU	9751	YN51 KVH
8035	BU05 HFV	8491	KX03 HZT	8524	YX59 BYS	9024	BX55 XLV	9752	YN51 KVJ
8036	BU05 HFW	8492	KX03 HZV	8525	YX59 BYT	9025	BX55 XLW	9753	YN51 KVK
8037	BU05 HFX	8493	KX03 HZY	8526	YX59 BYU	9026	BX55 XLY	9819	LG52 XYO
8044	V304 MDP	8494	KX03 HZZ	8527	YX59 BYV	9027	BX55 XLZ	9823	LG52 XZA
8054	X314 KRX	8495	KX04 HRD	8528	YX59 BYW	9028	BX55 XMA		
8061	X322 KRX	8496	KX04 HRE	8775	YX61 ELC	9029	BX55 XMB		

Go-Ahead London bus **VWL13** exiting from the service road between the two sections of **Belvedere Bus Garage** on September 7th, 2013. The vehicle is operating on Route 180 which terminates at Crabtree Manorway North and turns around in the depot.

BELVEDERE (BV)
Burts Wharf, Crabtree Manor Way, Kent DA17 6LJ
Operated by: Go-Ahead London
Location: TQ50208043 [51.502829, 0.162525]
Nearest Station: Belvedere (1.3 miles)
Nearest Bus Routes: 180 - Crabtree Manorway North (Alighting Stop)
Bus Routes Serviced: 180/244/669 & N1

The garage was purchased by Harris Buses in 1998 and used by that company until it folded in 2000. It was then taken over by East London Buses (an operating name for London Buses) and subsequently sold to Go-Ahead London in October 2009.

The office and amenities block at **Belvedere Bus Garage** on September 7th, 2013.

Go-Ahead London buses parked up at **Belvedere Bus Garage** on September 7th, 2013.

VEHICLE ALLOCATION

PVL370	PJ53 SRU	SE62	YX60 EPO	SE76	YX60FCF	VWL13	LB02 YXL	VWL21	LF52 TGY
SE55	YX60 DXT	SE63	YX60 FSU	SE78	YX60FCL	VWL14	LB02 YXM	VWL22	LF52 TGZ
SE56	YX60 FSN	SE64	YX60 EPP	SE82	YX60FCU	VWL15	LB02 YXN	VWL23	LF52 THG
SE57	YX60 DXU	SE65	YX60 EPU	SE84	YX60FCY	VWL16	LF52 TGN	VWL24	LF52 THK
SE58	YX60 FSO	SE66	YX60 EOP	VWL6	LB02YXD	VWL17	LF52 TGO	VWL25	LF52 THN
SE59	YX60 FSP	SE67	YX60 FCZ	VWL 9	LB02 YXG	VWL18	LF52 TGU	VWL26	LF52 THU
SE60	YX60 FSS	SE68	YX60 FDA	VWL11	LB02 YXJ	VWL19	LF52 TGV		
SE61	YX60 DXW	SE74	YX60FCD	VWL12	LB02 YXK	VWL20	LF52 TGX		

Go-Ahead London bus **SE82** departing from **Bexleyheath Bus Garage** on August 20th, 2014 to take up duties on Route B11 to Thamesmead.

BEXLEYHEATH (BX)
Erith Road, Bexleyheath, Kent DA7 6BX
Operated by: Go-Ahead London
Location: TQ49727566 [51.460206, 0.153714]
Nearest Station: Barnehurst (0.6 miles)
Nearest Bus Routes: 89/229/422/602/B11/B16 &
N89 - Bexleyheath, Bexleyheath Bus Garage
(Stop NW)
Bus Routes Serviced: 89/132/229/401/422/486/
625/658/661/669/B11/B16/N21 & N89

Bexleyheath is unique in that it was the only depot specifically built for trolleybuses by the London Passenger Transport Board. It was opened on November 10th, 1935 and suffered from bomb damage during WWII. Trolleybuses ceased on March 3rd, 1959 and it closed as an omnibus garage in 1986 but reopened in 1988.

VEHICLE ALLOCATION

E39	LX06 FKO	E202	SN61 BKJ	LDP202	SN51 UAR	SE71	YX60 FBZ	WVL361	LX60 DWM
E40	LX56 ETD	E203	SN61 BKK	LDP209	SN51 UAY	SE72	YX60 FCA	WVL362	LX60 DWN
E41	LX56 ETE	E204	SN61 BKL	PVL154	X554 EGK	SE73	YX60 FCC	WVL363	LX60 DWO
E42	LX56 ETF	E205	SN61 DCV	PVL160	X616 EGK	SE75	YX60 FCE	WVL364	LX60 DWP
E43	LX56 ETJ	E206	SN61 DCX	PVL161	X561 EGK	SE77	YX60 FCG	WVL365	LX60 DWU
E44	LX56 ETK	E207	SN61 DCY	PVL162	X562 EGK	SE79	YX60 FCM	WVL366	LX60 DWV
E45	LX56 ETL	E229	YX61 DSE	PVL163	X563 EGK	SE80	YX60 FCO	WVL367	LX60 DWW
E46	LX56 ETO	E230	YX61 DSO	PVL164	X564 EGK	SE81	YX60 FCP	WVL368	LX60 DWY
E47	LX56 ETR	E231	YX61 DSU	PVL165	X656 EGK	SE83	YX60 FCV	WVL369	LX60 DWZ
E48	LX56 ETT	E232	YX61 DSV	PVL166	X566 EGK	VWL3	LB02 YWZ	WVL370	LX60 DXA
E49	LX56 ETU	E233	YX61 DSY	PVL167	X567 EGK	VWL6	LB02 YXB	WVL371	LX60 DXB
E50	LX56 ETV	E234	YX61 DSZ	PVL215	Y815 TGH	WVL272	LX06 ECF	WVL372	LX60 DXC
E51	LX56 ETY	E235	YX61 DTF	PVL229	Y729 TGH	WVL273	LX06 ECJ	WVL373	LX60 DXD
E52	LX56 ETZ	E236	YX61 DTK	PVL362	PJ53 SOE	WVL350	LX60 DVY	WVL374	LX60 DXE
E53	LX56 EUA	E237	YX61 DTN	PVL363	PJ53 SOH	WVL351	LX60 DVZ	WVL375	LX60 DXF
E54	LX56 EUB	E238	YX61 DPF	PVL364	PJ53 SOU	WVL352	LX60 DWA	WVL376	LX60 DXG
E55	LX56 EUC	E239	YX61 DPK	PVL365	PJ53 SPU	WVL353	LX60 DWC	WVL377	LX60 DXH
E56	LX56 EUD	E240	YX61 DPN	PVL366	PJ53 SPV	WVL354	LX60 DWD	WVL378	LX60 DXJ
E62	LX57 CHV	E241	YX61 DPO	PVL367	PJ53 SPX	WVL355	LX60 DWE	WVL379	LX60 DXK
E63	LX57 CHY	E242	YX61 DPU	PVL368	PJ53 SPZ	WVL356	LX60 DWF	WVL455	LJ61 GVP
E64	LX57 CHZ	E243	YX61 DPV	PVL369	PJ53 SRO	WVL357	LX60 DWG	WVL456	LJ61 GVT
E65	LX57 CJE	E244	YX61 DPY	PVL370	PJ53 SRU	WVL358	LX60 DWJ		
E66	LX57 CJF	E245	YX61 DPZ	SE69	YX60 FBU	WVL359	LX60 DWK		
E67	LX57 CJJ	LDP193	SN51 UAF	SE70	YX60 FBY	WVL360	LX60 DWL		

Bow Bus Garage on September 20th, 2014 with Stagecoach bus 12331 leaving to take up duties on Route 205 to Paddington. The depot was built on the site of a mental asylum and was opened as an electric tram shed by London County Council between 1908 and 1910. It was closed to trams by London Transport on November 5th, 1939 and used as a trolleybus garage until August 18th, 1959, at which point it was utilized solely for omnibuses.

BOW (BW)
Fairfield Road, Bow, London E3 2QP
Operated by: Stagecoach London
Location: TQ37418311 [51.530099, -0.020788]
Nearest DLR Station: Bow Church (0.3 miles)
Nearest Bus Routes: 8/205/276 & 488 - Bow Bus Garage (C)
Bus Routes Serviced: 5/8/15/205/277/N8 & N15

VEHICLE ALLOCATION

12128	LX61 DFD	12151	LX61 DCY	12324	SL14 LRO	15110	LX09 FZG	61251	LTZ 1251
12129	LX61 DFE	12152	LX61 DCZ	12325	SL14 LNP	15111	LX09 FZH	61252	LTZ 1252
12130	LX61 DFF	12153	LX61 DDA	12326	SL14 LNR	15112	LX09 FZJ	61253	LTZ 1253
12131	LX61 DFG	12304	SN14 TXZ	12327	SL14 LNT	15113	LX09 FZK	61254	LTZ 1254
12132	LX61 DFJ	12305	SN14 TYA	12328	SL14 LNU	15114	LX09 FZL	61255	LTZ 1255
12133	LX61 DFK	12306	SN14 TYB	12329	SL14 LNV	15115	LX09 FZM	61256	LTZ 1256
12134	LX61 DFL	12307	SN14 TYC	12330	SL14 LNW	15116	LX09 FZN	61258	LTZ 1258
12135	LX61 DFN	12308	SN14 TYD	12331	SL14 LNX	15117	LX09 FZO	61259	LTZ 1259
12136	LX61 DFO	12309	SN14 TYF	12332	SL14 LNY	15118	LX09 FZP	61260	LTZ 1260
12137	LX61 DFP	12310	SN14 TYG	12333	SL14 LNZ	15119	LX09 FZR	61261	LTZ 1261
12138	LX61 DDL	12311	SN14 TYH	15097	LX09 FYS	15120	LX09 FZS	61263	LTZ 1263
12139	LX61 DDN	12312	SN14 TYK	15098	LX09 FYT	61239	LTZ 1239	61264	LTZ 1264
12140	LX61 DDO	12313	SN14 TYO	15099	LX09 FYU	61240	LTZ 1240	61265	LTZ 1265
12141	LX61 DDU	12314	SN14 TYP	15100	527 CLT	61241	LTZ 1241	61266	LTZ 1266
12142	LX61 DDV	12315	SN14 TYS	15101	LX09 FYW	61242	LTZ 1242	61267	LTZ 1267
12143	LX61 DDY	12316	SN14 TYT	15102	LX09 FYY	61243	LTZ 1243	61268	LTZ 1268
12144	LX61 DDZ	12317	SN14 TYU	15103	LX09 FYZ	61244	LTZ 1244	61269	LTZ 1269
12145	LX61 DEU	12318	SN14 TYV	15104	LX09 FZA	61245	LTZ 1245	61270	LTZ 1270
12146	LX61 DFA	12319	SK14 CSX	15105	LX09 FZB	61246	LTZ 1246	61271	LTZ 1271
12147	LX61 DFC	12320	SK14 CSY	15106	LX09 FZC	61247	LTZ 1247	61272	LTZ 1272
12148	LX61 DCO	12321	SK14 CSZ	15107	LX09 FZD	61248	LTZ 1248		
12149	LX61 DCU	12322	SK14 CTE	15108	LX09 FZE	61249	LTZ 1249		
12150	LX61 DCV	12323	SK14 CTU	15109	LX09 FZF	61250	LTZ 1250		

Brentford Bus Garage on September 27th, 2014 with Metroline buses **VW1043**, **TP433**, **VW1052** & **DE997** in view. It was originally the coach depot for Armchair Passenger Transport and became a bus garage in 1998 when the company won the franchise to operate Route 260.

BRENTFORD (AH)
Armchair House, Commerce Road, Brentford TW8 8LZ
Operated by: Metroline
Location: TQ17037755 [51.484694, -0.315841]
Nearest Station: Syon Lane (0.8 miles)
Nearest Bus Routes: 235/237/267/635/E2/E8 & N9 (Brent Lea)
Bus Routes Serviced: 190/209/237/609/E2 & E8

The Metroline office block and bus stop at **Brentford Bus Garage** on August 17th, 2013.

Metroline bus **DE1002** approaching **Brentford Bus Garage** on September 27th, 2014.

VEHICLE ALLOCATION

DM961	LK58 CRF	DE1000	LK09 EOB	TP413	LK03 CFG	VW1044	LK10 BXN	VW1060	LK60 AEE
DM962	LK09 EKJ	DE1001	LK09 EOC	TP415	LK03 CFL	VW1045	LK10 BXO	VW1061	LK60 AEF
DM963	LK09 EKL	DE1002	LK09 EOD	TP433	LK03 GFZ	VW1046	LK10 BXP	VW1062	LK60 AEG
DM964	LK58 CRV	DE1003	LK09 EOE	TP440	LK03 GGX	VW1047	LK10 BXR	VW1063	LK60 AEJ
DM965	LK58 CRX	DE1004	LK09 ENT	TP446	LK03 GHF	VW1048	LK10 BXS	VW1064	LK60 AEL
DM966	LK58 CRZ	DE1005	LK09 ENU	TP453	LK03 GHX	VW1049	LK10 BXU	VW1065	LK60 AEM
DM967	LK58 CSF	DE1006	LK09 ENV	VW1034	LK59 JJU	VW1050	LK10 BXV	VW1066	LK60 AEN
DM968	LK09 EKM	DE1007	LK09 ENW	VW1035	LK10 BXC	VW1051	LK10 BXW	VW1067	LK60 AEO
DM969	LK58 CSU	DE1008	LK09 ENX	VW1036	LK10 BXD	VW1052	LK10 BXX	VW1068	LK60 AEP
DM970	LK09 EKN	DE1009	LK09 ENY	VW1037	LK10 BXE	VW1053	LK10 BXY	VW1069	LK60 AET
DE993	LK09 ENC	DE1010	LK09 ENM	VW1038	LK10 BXF	VW1054	LK10 BXZ	VW1070	LK60 AEU
DE994	LK09 ENE	DE1011	LK09 ENN	VW1039	LK10 BXG	VW1055	LK10 BYA	VW1071	LK60 AEV
DE995	LK09 ENF	DE1012	LK09 ENO	VW1040	LK10 BXH	VW1056	LK60 AEA	VW1072	LK60 AEW
DE996	LK09 ENH	DE1013	LK09 ENP	VW1041	LK10 BXJ	VW1057	LK60 AEB		
DE997	LK09 ENJ	DE1014	LK09 ENR	VW1042	LK10 BXL	VW1058	LK60 AEC		
DE998	LK09 ENL	TP411	LK03 CFE	VW1043	LK10 BXM	VW1059	LK60 AED		

Metroline bus **VW1043** passing **DE1002** as it exits from **Brentford Bus Garage** on September 27th, 2014.

The north end of the yard at **Brentford Bus Garage** on August 17th, 2013, showing the additional bus parking available and the wash plant.

Brixton Bus Garage on September 6th, 2014 with Arriva London bus **DW288** parked on the main road, and Arriva London buses **DLA371** and **DW244** in view on the exit road. Brixton Bus Garage was originally known as Telford Avenue and re-named in 1950.

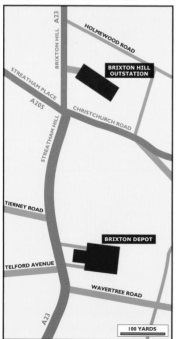

BRIXTON (BN)

39 Streatham Hill, London, SW2 4TB
Operated by: Arriva London
Location: TQ30547317 [51.442471, -0.123635]
Nearest Station: Streatham Hill (0.5 miles)
Nearest Bus Routes: 57/133/137/333/417/N133 & N137 - Streatham Hill/Telford Avenue (Stop TA)

Opened as a tram depot by the London Tramways Company Ltd on December 7th, 1892, closed to trams by London Transport on April 7th, 1951 and subsequently utilized as an omnibus garage. (Buses had first operated from January 7th, 1951.) It was extended in 1993.

BRIXTON HILL (OUTSTATION)

219 Brixton Hill, SW2 1NR
Operated by: Arriva London
Location: TQ30507352 [51.445957, -0.123727]
Nearest Station: Streatham Hill (0.6 miles)
Nearest Bus Routes: 45/59/109/118/133/159/250/ 333/N109 & N133 - Holmewood Road (Stop BT)

Opened as a tram depot by London County Council on March 6th, 1924 and closed by London Transport on April 7th, 1951. It was sold for commercial use but subsequently reinstated as an omnibus depot to cater for increased bus services introduced by Ken Livingstone when he was Mayor of London.

Bus Routes Serviced: 50/59/109/137/159/319 & N109

Arriva bus **HV146** departing from **Brixton Bus Garage (Outstation)**, originally the Brixton Tram Depot, on September 6th, 2014.

VEHICLE ALLOCATION									
DLA298	Y498 UGC	DW54	LJ04 LEF	DW119	319 CLT	DW284	LJ59 LWM	VLA147	LJ55 BTX
DLA312	Y512 UGC	DW55	LJ04 LEU	DW120	LJ05 BMZ	DW285	LJ59 LWN	VLA148	LJ55 BTY
DLA313	Y513 UGC	DW56	656 DYE	DW121	LJ05 BNA	DW286	LJ59 LWO	VLA149	LJ55 BTZ
DLA314	Y514 UGC	DW57	LJ04 LFB	DW122	LJ05 BNB	DW287	LJ59 LWP	VLA150	LJ55 BUA
DLA322	LG52 DAO	DW58	LJ04 LFD	DW123	LJ05 BND	DW288	LJ59 LWR	VLA151	LJ55 BUE
DLA323	LG52 DAU	DW59	LJ04 LFE	DW124	LJ05 BNE	DW289	LJ59 LVU	VLA152	LJ55 BPZ
DLA324	LG52 DBO	DW60	LJ04 LFF	DW125	LJ05 BNF	DW290	LJ59 LVV	VLA153	LJ55 BRV
DLA325	LG52 DBU	DW61	LJ04 LDA	DW126	LJ05 BNK	DW291	LJ59 LVW	VLA154	LJ55 BRX
DLA326	LG52 DBV	DW62	LJ04 LDC	DW127	LJ05 BNL	DW292	LJ59 LVX	VLA155	LJ55 BRZ
DLA328	LG52 DBZ	DW63	LJ04 LDD	DW128	LJ05 GKX	DW293	LJ59 LVY	VLA156	LJ55 BSO
DLA329	LG52 DCE	DW64	WLT 664	DW129	LJ05 GKY	DW294	LJ59 LVZ	VLA157	LJ55 BSU
DLA330	LG52 DCF	DW65	LJ04 LDF	DW130	LJ05 GKZ	DW295	LJ59 LWA	VLA158	LJ55 BSV
DLA331	LG52 DCO	DW66	LJ04 LDK	DW131	LJ05 GLF	DW296	LJ10 CUH	VLA159	LJ55 BSX
DLA332	LG52 DCU	DW68	LJ04 LDN	DW132	LJ05 GLK	DW297	LJ10 CUK	VLA160	LJ55 BSY
DLA333	LG52 DCV	DW69	LJ04 LDU	DW133	LJ05 GLV	HV132	LT63 UHR	VLA161	LJ55 BSZ
DLA334	LG52 DCX	DW70	WLT 970	DW230	LJ59 AEZ	HV133	LT63 UJO	VLA162	LJ55 BVP
DLA335	LG52 DCY	DW71	LJ04 LGF	DW231	LJ59 AFA	HV134	LT63 UJP	VLA163	LJ55 BVR
DLA336	LG52 DCZ	DW72	LJ04 LGG	DW232	LJ59 AEB	HV135	LT63 UJR		
DLA337	LJ03 MFX	DW73	LJ04 LGK	DW233	LJ59 AEC	HV136	LT63 UJS		
DLA338	LJ03 MFY	DW74	LJ04 LGL	DW234	LJ59 AED	HV137	LT63 UJU		
DLA339	LJ03 MFZ	DW75	LJ04 LGN	DW239	LJ59 AEL	HV138	LT63 UJV		
DLA340	LJ03 MGE	DW76	WLT 676	DW240	LJ59 AEM	HV139	LT63 UJW		
DLA341	LJ03 MGU	DW77	LJ04 LGV	DW241	LJ59 AEN	HV140	LT63 UJX		
DLA342	LJ03 MGV	DW78	LJ04 LGW	DW242	LJ59 ACU	HV141	LT63 UJY		
DLA343	LJ03 MDV	DW79	LJ04 LGX	DW243	LJ59 ACV	HV142	LT63 UJZ		
DLA344	LJ03 MDX	DW80	LJ04 LGY	DW244	LJ59 ACX	HV143	LT63 UJD		
DLA345	LJ03 MDY	DW81	LJ04 LFU	DW245	LJ59 AAF	HV144	LT63 UJE		
DLA346	LJ03 MDZ	DW82	LJ04 LFV	DW246	LJ59 AAK	HV145	LT63 UJF		
DLA347	LJ03 MEU	DW83	LJ04 LFW	DW247	LJ59 AAN	HV146	LT63 UJG		
DLA371	LJ03 MVC	DW84	LJ04 LFX	DW248	LJ59 AAO	HV147	LT63 UJH		
DLA372	LJ03 MVD	DW85	WLT 385	DW249	LJ59 AAU	HV148	LT63 UJJ		
DW45	LJ53 NHN	DW86	LJ04 LFZ	DW250	LJ59 AAV	HV149	LT63 UJK		
DW46	LJ53 NHO	DW87	LJ04 LGA	DW251	LJ59 AAX	HV150	LT63 UJL		
DW47	LJ53 NHP	DW88	LJ04 LGC	DW277	LJ59 LXA	HV151	LT63 UJM		
DW48	WLT 348	DW89	LJ04 LGD	DW278	LJ59 LXB	HV152	LT63 UJN		
DW49	LJ53 NGU	DW90	LJ04 LGE	DW279	LJ59 LWF	VLA102	LJ54 BCU		
DW50	LJ53 NGV	DW91	LJ04 LFG	DW280	LJ59 LWG	VLA103	LJ54 BCV		
DW51	LJ04 LDX	DW92	LJ04 LFH	DW281	LJ59 LWH	VLA144	LJ55 BTO		
DW52	LJ04 LDY	DW93	LJ04 LFK	DW282	LJ59 LWK	VLA145	LJ55 BTU		
DW53	LJ04 LDZ	DW118	LJ05 BMV	DW283	LJ59 LWL	VLA146	LJ55 BTV		

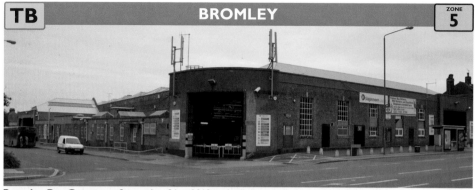

TB — BROMLEY — ZONE 5

Bromley Bus Garage on September 21st, 2013 with all three exits and entrances in view.

BROMLEY (TB)
111 Hastings Road, Bromley, Kent BR2 8NH
Operated by: Stagecoach London
Location: TQ42416611 [51.375785, 0.044762]
Nearest Station: Bromley South (2.7 miles)
Nearest Bus Routes: 261/261/336/358 & 402 - Bromley Common, Bromley Bus Garage (Stop BN)
Bus Routes Serviced: 61/208/227/246/261/269/ 314/636/637/638/664/R5/R7 & R10

Stagecoach London bus 36313 receiving attention on Lower Gravel Road alongside **Bromley Bus Garage** on September 21st, 2013.

Stagecoach London buses allocated to **Bromley Bus Garage** are also accommodated in a compound on the north side of Lower Gravel Road and on August 21st, 2014 buses 10148, 17968 & 10187 were amongst those parked here.

VEHICLE ALLOCATION

10139	LX12 DFU	10188	SN63 NBJ	17965	LX53 JZH	19138	LX56 EAW	36312	LX58 CAE
10140	LX12 DFV	10189	SN63 NBK	17966	LX53 JZJ	19139	LX56 EAY	36313	LX58 CAO
10141	LX12 DFY	10190	SN63 NBL	17967	LX53 JZK	19140	LX56 EBA	36541	LX12 DJE
10142	LX12 DFZ	10191	SN63 NBM	17968	LX53 JZL	19835	LX61 DDE	36542	LX12 DJF
10143	LX12 DGE	10192	SN63 NBO	17969	LX53 JZM	23101	LX12 DKK	36543	LX12 DJJ
10144	LX12 DGF	10193	SN63 NBX	17970	LX53 JZN	23102	LX12 DKL	36544	LX12 DJK
10145	LX12 DGO	10194	SN63 NBY	17971	LX53 JZO	23103	LX12 DKN	36545	LX12 DJO
10146	LX12 DGU	10195	SN63 NBZ	17972	LX53 JZP	23104	LX12 DKO	36546	LX12 DJU
10147	LX12 DGV	17779	LX03 BVR	17973	LX53 JZR	23105	LX12 DKU	36547	LX12 DJV
10148	LX12 DGY	17780	LX03 BVS	17974	LX53 JZT	23106	LX12 DKV	36548	LX12 DJY
10149	LX12 DGZ	17795	LX03 BWJ	17975	LX53 JZY	23107	LX12 DKY	36549	LX12 DJZ
10150	LX12 DHA	17831	LX03 BYF	18213	LX04 FXA	23108	LX12 DLD	36550	LX12 DKA
10151	LX12 DHC	17832	LX03 BYG	18214	LX04 FXB	23109	LX12 DLE	36551	LX12 DKD
10152	LX12 DHD	17833	LX03 BYH	18215	LX04 FXC	23110	LX12 DLF	36552	LX12 DKE
10153	LX12 DHE	17841	LX03 BYT	19131	LX56 EAF	23111	LX12 DLJ	36553	LX12 DKF
10154	LX12 DHF	17842	LX03 BYU	19132	LX56 EAG	23112	LX12 DLK	36554	LX12 DKJ
10164	SN63 JVM	17843	LX03 BYV	19133	LX56 EAJ	23113	LX12 DLN	36581	YX63 LGA
10184	SN63 NBD	17844	LX03 BYW	19134	LX56 EAK	34366	LV52 HGC	36582	YX63 LGC
10185	SN63 NBE	17845	LX03 BYY	19135	LX56 EAM	36309	LX58 BZW	36583	YX63 LGD
10186	SN63 NBF	17864	LX03 NFJ	19136	LX56 EAO	36310	LX58 BZY		
10187	SN63 NBG	17866	LX03 NFL	19137	LX56 EAP	36311	LX58 CAA		

Stagecoach buses 17843 & 17788 departing from the Compound at **Bromley Bus Garage** on August 21st, 2014.

An interior view of **Bromley Bus Garage** on August 21st, 2014 with Stagecoach buses 17864 & 36581 parked inside.

The Camberwell New Road entrance to **Camberwell Bus Garage** on August 31st, 2013. The depot was built in 1914 but did not come into commercial use until 1919 due to requisitioning for the war effort.

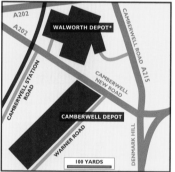

*SEE PAGE 94

CAMBERWELL (Q)
Warner Road, London SE5 9LU
Operated by: Go-Ahead London
Location: TQ32317666 [51.474136, -0.095157]
Nearest Station: Denmark Hill (0.7 miles)
Nearest Bus Routes: 36/185/436 & N136 -
Warner Road (Stop H)
Bus Routes Serviced: 12/42/45/68/185/345/355/
360/468/N68/P5 & X68

The entrance at the south end of **Camberwell Bus Garage** on September 12th, 2014. The garage suffered from some bomb damage during WWII and was modernized during the 1950s.

24

Go-Ahead London buses lined up in the yard at the south end of **Camberwell Bus Garage** on September 12th, 2014.

VEHICLE ALLOCATION

DWL37	FJ54 ZDC	LDP250	SN53 KKG	SE93	YX11 CPZ	WVL141	LX53 AYO	WVL250	LX06 EAP
E100	LX09 EZU	LDP251	SN53 KKH	VWL10	LB02 YXH	WVL142	LX53 AYP	WVL251	LX06 EAW
E101	LX09 EZV	LDP252	SN53 KKJ	WHV1	LJ61 GVW	WVL143	LX53 AYT	WVL252	LX06 EAY
E102	LX09 EZW	LDP253	SN53 KKL	WHV2	LJ61 GVX	WVL144	LX53 AYU	WVL253	LX06 EBA
E103	LX09 EZZ	LDP254	SN53 KKM	WHV3	LJ61 GVY	WVL145	LX53 AYV	WVL254	LX06 EBC
E104	LX09 FAF	LDP255	SN53 KKO	WHV4	LJ61 GVZ	WVL146	LX53 AYW	WVL255	LX06 EBD
E105	LX09 FAJ	LDP256	SN53 KKP	WHV5	LJ61 GWA	WVL147	LX53 AYY	WVL256	LX06 EBF
E106	LX09 FAK	LDP257	SN53 KKR	WHV6	LJ61 GWC	WVL148	LX53 AYZ	WVL257	LX06 EBG
E107	LX09 FAM	LDP258	SN53 KKT	WHV7	LJ61 GXE	WVL149	LX53 BJK	WVL258	LX06 EBJ
E108	LX09 FAO	LDP259	SN53 KKU	WHV8	LJ61 GXF	WVL151	LX53 BJU	WVL259	LX06 EBK
E109	LX09 FAU	LDP260	SN53 KKV	WHV9	LJ61 GXG	WVL212	LX06 DYS	WVL260	LX06 EBL
E110	LX09 FBA	LDP261	SN53 KKW	WHV10	LJ61 GXH	WVL213	LX06 DYT	WVL261	LX06 EBM
E111	LX09 FBB	LDP262	SN53 KKX	WHV11	LJ61 GXK	WVL214	LX06 DYU	WVL262	LX06 EBN
E112	LX09 FBC	PVL151	X551 EGK	WHV12	LJ61 GXL	WVL215	LX06 DYV	WVL263	LX06 EBO
E113	LX09 FBD	PVL272	PN02 XBW	WHV13	LJ61 GXM	WVL216	LX06 DYW	WVL264	LX06 EBP
E114	LX09 FBE	PVL298	PJ02 RFK	WHV14	LJ61 GXN	WVL217	LX06 DYY	WVL265	LX06 EBU
E115	LX09 FBF	PVL299	PJ02 RFL	WHV15	LJ61 GXO	WVL218	LX06 DZA	WVL266	LX06 EBV
E116	LX09 FBG	PVL300	PJ02 RFN	WHV16	LJ61 GXP	WVL219	LX06 DZB	WVL267	LX06 EBZ
E117	LX09 FBJ	PVL301	PJ02 RFO	WHY1	LX06 ECN	WVL220	LX06 DZC	WVL268	LX06 ECA
E118	LX09 FBK	PVL302	PJ02 RFX	WHY2	LX55 EAC	WVL222	LX06 DZE	WVL269	LX06 ECC
E119	LX09 FBN	PVL303	PJ02 RFY	WHY3	LX55 EAE	WVL223	LX06 DZF	WVL270	LX06 ECD
E120	LX09 FBO	PVL304	PJ02 RFZ	WHY4	LX55 EAF	WVL224	LX06 DZG	WVL271	LX06 ECE
E121	LX09 FBU	PVL305	PJ02 RGO	WHY5	LX55 EAG	WVL225	LX06 DZH	WVL380	LX60 DXM
E122	LX09 FBV	PVL306	PJ02 RGU	WHY6	LX55 EAJ	WVL226	LX06 DZJ	WVL381	LX60 DXO
E123	LX09 FBY	PVL307	PJ02 RGV	WHY7	LX57 CLZ	WVL227	LX06 DZK	WVL382	LX60 DXP
E124	LX09 FBZ	PVL308	PJ02 TVN	WHY8	LX11 DVA	WVL228	LX06 DZL	WVL383	LX60 DXR
E125	LX09 FCA	PVL309	PJ02 TVO	WHY9	LX11 DVB	WVL229	LX06 DZM	WVL384	LX60 DXS
E126	LX09 FCC	PVL310	PJ02 TVP	WHY10	LX11 DVC	WVL230	LX06 DZN	WVL385	LX60 DXT
E127	LX09 FCD	PVL311	PJ02 TVT	WHY11	LX11 DVF	WVL231	LX06 DZO	WVL435	LJ61 GWU
E128	LX09 FCE	PVL312	PJ02 TVU	WHY12	LX11 DVG	WVL232	LX06 DZP	WVL436	LJ61 GWV
ELS1	YU02 GHG	PVL313	PJ52 LVP	WHY13	LX11 DVH	WVL233	LX06 DZR	WVL437	LJ61 GWW
ELS2	YU02 GHH	PVL314	PJ52 LVR	WVL72	LF52 ZPB	WVL234	LX06 DZS	WVL438	LJ61 GWX
ELS3	YU02 GHJ	PVL315	PJ52 LVS	WVL73	LF52 ZPC	WVL235	LX06 DZT	WVL439	LJ61 GWY
ELS4	YU02 GHK	PVL316	PJ52 LVT	WVL78	LF52 ZPJ	WVL236	LX06 DZU	WVL440	LJ61 GWZ
ELS5	YU02 GHD	PVL317	PJ52 LVU	WVL84	LF52 ZNS	WVL237	LX06 DZV	WVL441	LJ61 GXA
ELS6	YU02 GHA	PVL318	PJ52 LVV	WVL129	LX53 AZA	WVL238	LX06 DZW	WVL442	LJ61 GXB
ELS7	YU02 GHN	PVL326	PJ52 LWE	WVL130	LX53 AZB	WVL239	LX06 DZY	WVL443	LJ61 GXC
ELS8	YU02 GHO	PVL327	PJ52 LWF	WVL131	LX53 AZC	WVL240	LX06 DZZ	WVL444	LJ61 GXD
ELS9	YR52 VFJ	PVL328	PJ52 LWG	WVL132	LX53 AZD	WVL241	LX06 EAA	WVL445	LJ61 GWD
ELS10	YR52 VFH	SE85	YX11 CPE	WVL133	LX53 AZF	WVL242	LX06 EAC	WVL446	LJ61 GWE
ELS11	YR52 VFK	SE86	YX11 CPF	WVL134	LX53 AZG	WVL243	LX06 EAE	WVL447	LJ61 GWF
ELS12	YR52 VFL	SE87	YX11 CPK	WVL135	LX53 AZJ	WVL244	LX06 EAF	WVL448	LJ61 GWG
ELS13	YR52 VFM	SE88	YX11 CPN	WVL136	LX53 AZL	WVL245	LX06 EAG	WVL449	LJ61 GWK
ELS14	YR52 VFN	SE89	YX11 CPO	WVL137	LX53 AZN	WVL246	LX06 EAJ	WVL450	LJ61 GWL
LDP196	SN51 UAJ	SE90	YX11 CPU	WVL138	LX53 AZO	WVL247	LX06 EAK		
LDP199	SN51 UAW	SE91	YX11 CPV	WVL139	LX53 AYM	WVL248	LX06 EAM		
LDP249	SN53 KKF	SE92	YX11 CPY	WVL140	LX53 AYN	WVL249	LX06 EAO		

Stagecoach London bus 18497 exiting from its home depot, **Catford Bus Garage**, on August 21st, 2014.

CATFORD (TL)

180 Bromley Road, Catford, London SE6 2XA
Operated by: Stagecoach London
Location: TQ37827249 [51.434474, -0.018465]
Nearest Station: Bellingham (0.3 miles)
Nearest Bus Routes: 47/54/136/171/199/208/320/ N47 & N136 - Catford Bus Garage (Stop)
Bus Routes Serviced: 47/54/75/124/136/178/199/ 208/273/354/356/380/621/660/N47/N136 & P4

The garage was originally opened by the London General Omnibus Company in 1914 but was immediately requisitioned for war use. It re-opened in 1920 as a garage for Thomas Tilling and was doubled in size three years later. It has since undergone modifications to accommodate double-decker buses and was last modernized in 1970.

VEHICLE ALLOCATION

10124	LX12 DDY	12278	SN14 TWW	18491	LX06 AGU	34388	LX03 BZW	36320	LX58 CBY
10125	LX12 DDZ	12279	SN14 TWX	18492	LX06 AGV	34389	LX03 BZY	36321	LX58 CCA
10126	LX12 DEU	12280	SN14 TWY	18493	LX06 AGY	34390	LX03 CAA	36322	LX58 CCD
10127	LX12 DFA	12281	SN14 TWZ	18494	LX06 AGZ	34391	LX03 CAE	36323	LX58 CCE
10128	LX12 DFC	12282	SN14 TXA	18495	LX06 AHA	34392	LX03 CAU	36324	LX58 CCF
10129	LX12 DFD	12283	SN14 TXB	18496	LX06 AHC	34393	LX03 CAV	36325	LX58 CCJ
10130	LX12 DFE	12284	SN14 TXC	18497	LX06 AHD	34394	LX03 CBF	36326	LX58 CCK
10131	LX12 DFF	12285	SN14 TXD	18498	LX06 AHE	34395	LX03 CBU	36338	LX09 ACU
10132	LX12 DFG	12286	SN14 TXE	18499	LX06 AHF	34396	LX03 CBV	36339	LX09 ACV
10133	LX12 DFJ	12287	SN14 TXF	19836	LX61 DDF	34397	LX03 CBY	36341	LX09 ACZ
10134	LX12 DFK	12288	SN14 TXG	19837	LX61 DDJ	34551	LX53 LGF	36342	LX09 ADO
10135	LX12 DFL	12289	SN14 TXH	19838	LX61 DDK	34552	LX53 LGG	36343	LX09 ADU
10136	LX12 DFN	12290	SN14 TXJ	19839	LX61 DAA	34553	LX53 LGJ	36528	LX12 DHG
10137	LX12 DFO	12291	SN14 TXK	19840	LX61 DAO	34554	LX53 LGK	36529	LX12 DHJ
10138	LX12 DFP	12292	SN14 TXL	19841	LX61 DAU	34556	LX53 LGN	36530	LX12 DHK
10197	SL14 DDE	17427	LX51 FKA	19842	LX61 DBO	34557	LX53 LGO	36531	LX12 DHL
12261	SN14 TVW	17503	LX51 FNF	19843	LX61 DBU	34558	LX53 LGU	36532	LX12 DHM
12262	SN14 TVX	17505	LX51 FNM	19844	LX61 DBV	34559	LX53 LGV	36533	LX12 DHN
12263	SN14 TVY	17506	LX51 DNJ	19845	LX61 DBY	34560	LX53 LGW	36534	LX12 DHO
12264	SN14 TVZ	17797	LX03 BWL	19846	LX61 DBZ	36301	LX56 DZU	36535	LX12 DHP
12265	SN14 TWA	18455	LX55 EPA	25111	YJ08 PGO	36302	LX56 DZV	36536	LX12 DHU
12266	SN14 TWC	18463	LX55 EPN	25112	WLT 461	36303	LX56 DZW	36537	LX12 DHV
12267	SN14 TWD	18464	LX55 EPO	25113	LX09 BGK	36304	LX56 DZY	36538	LX12 DHY
12268	SN14 TWE	18481	LX55 BDY	25114	LX09 BGU	36305	LX56 DZZ	36539	LX12 DHZ
12269	SN14 TWF	18482	LX55 BDZ	25115	LX09 BGV	36306	LX56 EAA	36540	LX12 DJD
12270	SN14 TWG	18483	LX55 BEO	34353	LV52 HKE	36307	LX56 EAC	36584	YX64 GRX
12271	SN14 TWJ	18484	LX55 BEY	34357	LV52 HKJ	36308	LX56 EAE	36585	YX64 GR-
12272	SN14 TWK	18485	LX55 BFA	34358	LV52 HKK	36314	LX58 CAU	36586	YX64 GR-
12273	SN14 TWL	18486	LX55 BFE	34359	LV52 HKL	36315	LX58 CAV	36587	YX64 G--
12274	SN14 TWM	18487	LX55 BFF	34360	LV52 HKM	36316	LX58 CBF		
12275	SN14 TWP	18488	LX55 BEJ	34370	LV52 HGG	36317	LX58 CBO		
12276	SN14 TWU	18489	LX06 AFZ	34376	LV52 HGO	36318	LX58 CBU		
12277	SN14 TWV	18490	LX06 AGO	34387	LX03 BZV	36319	LX58 CBV		

Clapton Bus Garage viewed on August 5th, 2014.

CLAPTON (CT)
15 Bohemia Place, Mare Street, London E8 1DU
Operated by: Arriva London
Location: TQ35128499 [51.547676, -0.053296]
Nearest Station: Hackney Central (200 yards)
Nearest Bus Routes: 30/38/242/276/394 & N38 -
Hackney Central (Stop T)
Bus Routes Serviced: 38/242/393 & N38

This garage was originally a horse tram depot, opened by the North Metropolitan Tramways in 1883 and taken over by London County Council on July 1st, 1903. It was rebuilt and enlarged in 1909, closed to trams by London Transport on September 10th, 1939 and trolleybuses on April 14th, 1959. It later had a spell of use as a Go-Kart circuit, before re-opening as a bus garage.

VEHICLE ALLOCATION

DW201	LJ09 KRO	DW226	LJ59 AEV	LT173	LTZ 1173	LT203	LTZ 1203	LT228	LTZ 1228
DW202	LJ09 SUO	DW227	LJ59 AEW	LT176	LTZ 1176	LT204	LTZ 1204	LT229	LTZ 1229
DW203	LJ09 SUU	DW228	LJ59 AEX	LT177	LTZ 1177	LT205	LTZ 1205	LT230	LTZ 1230
DW204	LJ09 SUV	DW229	LJ59 AEY	LT178	LTZ 1178	LT206	LTZ 1206	LT231	LTZ 1231
DW205	LJ09 SUX	DW235	LJ59 AEE	LT179	LTZ 1179	LT207	LTZ 1207	LT232	LTZ 1232
DW206	LJ09 SUY	DW237	LJ59 AEG	LT180	LTZ 1180	LT208	LTZ 1208	LT233	LTZ 1233
DW207	LJ09 SVA	DW238	LJ59 AEK	LT181	LTZ 1181	LT209	LTZ 1209	LT234	LTZ 1234
DW208	LJ09 SVC	DW257	LJ59 GVG	LT182	LTZ 1182	LT210	LTZ 1210	PDL115	LJ54 LHR
DW209	LJ09 SVD	ENL18	LJ58 AWF	LT183	LTZ 1183	LT211	LTZ 1211	VLW87	LF52 UPX
DW210	LJ09 SVE	ENL19	LJ58 AWG	LT184	LTZ 1184	LT212	LTZ 1212	VLW88	WLT 888
DW211	LJ09 SVF	ENS1	LJ07 EDK	LT185	LTZ 1185	LT213	LTZ 1213	VLW89	LF52 UPZ
DW212	LJ09 SSO	ENS2	LJ07 EDL	LT186	LTZ 1186	LT214	LTZ 1214	VLW90	LF52URA
DW213	LJ09 SSU	ENS3	LJ07 EDO	LT187	LTZ 1187	LT215	LTZ 1215	VLW91	LF52 UPD
DW214	LJ09 SSV	ENS4	LJ07 EDP	LT191	LTZ 1191	LT216	LTZ 1216	VLW92	WLT 892
DW215	LJ09 SSX	ENS5	LJ07 EDR	LT192	LTZ 1192	LT217	LTZ 1217	VLW93	LF52 UPG
DW216	LJ09 SSZ	ENS6	LJ07 EDU	LT193	LTZ 1193	LT218	LTZ 1218	VLW94	LF52 UPH
DW217	LJ09 STX	ENS7	LJ07 EDV	LT194	LTZ 1194	LT219	LTZ 1219	VLW95	LF52 UPJ
DW218	LJ09 STZ	ENS8	LJ07 EDX	LT195	LTZ 1195	LT220	LTZ 1220	VLW96	LF52 UPK
DW219	LJ09 SUA	ENS9	LJ07 EEA	LT196	LTZ 1196	LT221	LTZ 1221		
DW220	LJ09 SUF	ENS10	LJ07 EEB	LT197	LTZ 1197	LT222	LTZ 1222		
DW221	LJ09 SUH	ENS11	LJ07 ECF	LT198	LTZ 1198	LT223	LTZ 1223		
DW222	LJ59 AEO	ENS12	LJ07 ECN	LT199	LTZ 1199	LT224	LTZ 1224		
DW223	LJ59 AEP	ENS13	LJ07 ECT	LT200	LTZ 1200	LT225	LTZ 1225		
DW224	LJ59 AET	ENS14	LJ07 ECV	LT201	LTZ 1201	LT226	LTZ 1226		
DW225	LJ59 AEU	LT172	LTZ 1172	LT202	LTZ 1202	LT227	LTZ 1227		

The entrance to **Cricklewood Bus Garage** on September 6th, 2014 with the modern maintenance facility visible on the right.

CRICKLEWOOD (W)
329 Edgware Road, Dollis Hill, London NW2 6JP
Operated by: Metroline
Location: TQ23348632 [51.558423, -0.214375]
Nearest Station: Cricklewood (0.6 miles)
Nearest Bus Routes: 32/245/266/332 & N16 - Dollis Hill, Cricklewood Bus Garage (Stop BA)
Bus Routes Serviced: 16/32/112/139/189/210/232/316/326/332/632/643/C11 & N16

The first garage on this site opened for service in May 1905. Originally known as Dollis Hill, it was the first depot to be used by the London General Omnibus Company for motor vehicles. It closed temporarily in 2007 to allow for the complete rebuilding of the depot with its buses parking on a site on the opposite side of Edgware Road. The rebuilt depot opened again in January 2009.

Metroline bus **TEH1453** departing from **Cricklewood Bus Garage** on September 6th, 2014.

Metroline bus **DE1127** leaving **Cricklewood Bus Garage** on November 2nd, 2013 to take up duties on Route 143 to Archway.

VEHICLE ALLOCATION

DE859	LK08 DWO	DE1115	LK10 BYB	DEL2069	LK64 ECX	TE1085	LK60 AFV	TEH1217	LK61 BJO
DE860	LK08 DWP	DE1116	LK10 BYC	DEL2070	LK64 ECY	TE1086	LK60 AFX	TEH1218	LK61 BJU
DE861	LK08 DWU	DE1117	LK10 BYD	DEL2071	LK64 ECZ	TE1087	LK60 AFY	TEH1219	LK61 BJV
DE862	LK08 DWV	DE1118	LK10 BYG	TA638	LK05 GFO	TE1088	LK60 AFZ	TEH1220	LK61 BJX
DE863	LK08 DWW	DE1119	LK10 BYJ	TA639	LK05 GFV	TE1089	LK60 AGO	TEH1221	LK61 BJY
DE864	LK08 DWX	DE1120	LK10 BYL	TA640	LK05 GFX	TE1090	LK60 AGU	TEH1222	LK61 BJZ
DE865	LK08 DWY	DE1121	LK10 BYM	TA641	LK05 GFY	TE1091	LK60 AGV	TEH1223	LK61 BKA
DE866	LK08 DWZ	DE1122	LK10 BYN	TA642	LK05 GFZ	TE1092	LK60 AGY	TEH1224	LK61 BKD
DE867	LK08 DXA	DE1123	LK10 BYO	TA643	LK05 GGA	TE1093	LK60 AGZ	TEH1225	LK61 BKE
DE868	LK08 DXB	DE1124	LK10 BYP	TA644	LK05 GGE	TE1094	LK60 AHA	TEH1226	LK61 BKF
DE869	LK08 DXC	DE1125	LK10 BYR	TA645	LK05 GGF	TE1095	LK60 AHC	TEH1227	LK61 BKG
DE870	LK08 DXD	DE1126	LK10 BYS	TA646	LK05 GGJ	TE1096	LK60 AHD	TEH1228	LK61 BKJ
DE871	LK58 CPX	DE1127	LK10 BYT	TA647	LK05 GGO	TE1097	LK60 AHE	TEH1229	LK61 BKL
DE872	LK58 CPY	DE1128	LK10 BYU	TA648	LK05 GGP	TE1098	LK60 AHG	TEH1230	LK61 BKN
DE873	LK58 CPZ	DE1129	LK10 BYV	TA649	LK05 GGU	TE1099	LK60 AHJ	TEH1231	LK61 BKO
DE874	LK58 CMY	DE1130	LK10 BYW	TA650	LK05 GGV	TE1100	LK60 AHL	TEH1232	LK61 BKU
DE875	LK58 CMZ	DE1131	LK10 BYX	TA651	LK05 GGX	TE1101	LK60 AHN	TEH1233	LK61 BKV
DE876	LK58 CNA	DE1132	LK10 BYY	TA652	LK05 GGY	TE1102	LK60 AHO	TEH1234	LK61 BKY
DE877	LK58 CNC	DE1133	LK10 BYZ	TA653	LK05 GGZ	TE1103	LK60 AHP	TEH1235	LK61 BKZ
DE952	LK58 CSX	DE1134	LK10 BZA	TA654	LK05 GHA	TE1104	LK60 AHU	TEH1236	LK61 BLF
DE953	LK58 CSY	DE1135	LK10 BZB	TA655	LK05 GHB	TE1307	LK12 AVD	TEH1237	LK61 BLJ
DE954	LK58 CSZ	DE1136	LK10 BZC	TA656	LK05 GHD	TE1308	LK12 AVJ	TEH1238	LK61 BLN
DE955	LK58 CTE	DE1137	LK10 BZD	TA657	LK05 GHF	TE1309	LK12 AVN	TEH1239	LK61 BLV
DE956	LK58 CTF	DE1138	LK10 BZE	TA658	LK05 GHG	TE1310	LK12 AVT	TEH1240	LK61 BLX
DE957	LK58 CTO	DE1139	LK10 BZF	TA659	LK05 GHH	TE1311	LK12 AVU	TEH1241	LK61 BLZ
DE958	LK58 CTU	DE1140	LK10 BZG	TE925	LK58KGE	TE1312	LK12 AWA	TEH1242	LK61 BMO
DE959	LK58 CTV	DE1141	LK10 BZH	TE926	LK58KGF	TE1313	LK12 AWC	TEH1449	LK13 BGE
DE960	LK58 CTX	DE1142	LK10 BZJ	TE927	LK58KGG	TE1314	LK12 AWJ	TEH1450	LK13 BGF
DE1015	LK59 AUW	DE1143	LK10 BZL	TE928	LK58KGJ	TE1315	LK12 AWN	TEH1451	LK13 BGO
DE1016	LK59 AUY	DE1144	LK10 BZM	TE929	LK58KGN	TE1316	LK12 AWO	TEH1452	LK13 BGU
DE1017	LK59 AVB	DE1145	LK10 BZN	TE930	LK58KGO	TE1317	LK12 AWP	TEH1453	LK13 BGV
DE1018	LK59 AVC	DE1146	LK10 BZO	TE931	LK09EKO	TE1448	LK13 BFZ	TEH1454	LK13 BGX
DE1019	LK59 AVD	DE1147	LK10 BZP	TE932	LK58KGU	TEH915	SN08 AAO	TEH1455	LK13 BGY
DE1020	LK59 AVF	DE1148	LK10 BZR	TE933	LK58KGV	TEH916	LK58 CPN	TEH1456	LK13 BGZ
DE1021	LK59 AVG	DE1149	LK10 BZS	TE934	LK58KGY	TEH917	LK58 CPO	TEH1457	LK13 BHA
DE1022	LK59 AVJ	DE1150	LK10BZT	TE1073	LK10 BZV	TEH918	LK58 CPU	TEH1458	LK13 BHD
DE1023	LK59 AVL	DE1171	LK11CXD	TE1074	LK10 BZX	TEH919	LK58 CPV	TEH1459	LK13 BHE
DE1024	LK59 AVM	DE1172	LK11CXE	TE1075	LK10 BZY	TEH1105	LK60 AHV	TEH1460	LK13 BHF
DE1025	LK59 AVN	DE1173	LK11 CXF	TE1076	LK60 AEX	TEH1106	LK60 AHX	TEH1461	LK13 BHJ
DE1026	LK59 AVO	DE1174	LK11 CXG	TE1077	LK60 AEY	TEH1107	LK60 AHY	TEH1462	LK13 BHL
DE1027	LK59 AVP	DEL2062	LK64 ECE	TE1078	LK60 AEZ	TEH1108	LK60 AHZ	TEH1463	LK13 BHN
DE1028	LK59 AVR	DEL2063	LK64 ECF	TE1079	LK60 AFA	TEH1109	LK60 AJO	TEH1464	LK13 BHO
DE1029	LK59 AVT	DEL2064	LK64 ECJ	TE1080	LK60 AFE	TEH1110	LK60 AJU	TEH1465	LK13 BHP
DE1030	LK59 AVU	DEL2065	LK64 ECN	TE1081	LK60 AFF	TEH1111	LK60 AJV	TEH1466	LK13 BHU
DE1031	LK59 AVV	DEL2066	LK64 ECT	TE1082	LK60 AFN	TEH1112	LK60 AJX	TEH1467	LK13 BHV
DE1032	LK59 AVW	DEL2067	LK64 ECV	TE1083	LK60 AFO	TEH1113	LK60 AJY		
DE1033	LK59 AVX	DEL2068	LK64 ECW	TE1084	LK60 AFU	TEH1114	LK60 AKF		

Croydon Depot on August 19th, 2014 with Metrobus 926 departing from the yard.

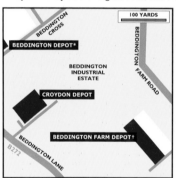

*SEE PAGE 14   †SEE PAGE 108

CROYDON (C)
134 Beddington Lane, Croydon, Surrey CR9 4ND
Operated by: Metrobus
Location: TQ30116625 [51.381692, -0.134208]
Nearest Tram Station: Therapia Lane (0.6 miles)
Nearest Bus Routes: 455 - Beddington, Beddington Cross (Southbound)
Bus Routes Serviced: 64/119/127/130/202/293/359/405/434/N64 & T32

VEHICLE ALLOCATION

189	YY13 VKO	286	SN03 YCK	561	YN08 OAS	721	AJ58 WBK	952	YN07 EXO
190	YY13 VKP	334	W334VGX	562	YN58 BNA	722	AJ58 WBF	955	YR58 SNY
191	YY13 VKR	431	YV03 PZW	563	YN08 OAV	723	AE09 DHV	956	YR58 SNZ
192	YY13 VKS	432	YV03 PZX	564	YN08 OAW	917	YN06 JYB	957	YP58 UFV
210	SN03 WLX	433	YV03 PZY	565	YN08 OAX	918	YN06 JYC	958	YT59 DYA
211	SN03 WLZ	434	YV03 PZZ	566	YN08 OAY	919	YN06 JYD	959	YT59 DYB
212	SN03 WMC	435	YV03 PZE	567	YN08 OAZ	920	YN06 JYE	960	YT59 DYC
213	SN03 WMF	436	YV03 PZF	706	YX58 DXB	921	YN06 JYF	961	YT59 DYD
214	SN03 WMG	437	YV03 PZG	707	YX58 DXC	922	YN06 JYG	962	YT59 DYF
215	SN03 WMK	438	YV03 PZH	708	YX58 DXD	923	YN06 JYH	963	YT59 DYG
216	SN03 WMP	439	YV03 PZJ	709	AE09 DHG	924	YN06 JYJ	964	YT59 DYH
219	SN03 WMY	440	YV03 PZK	710	AE09 DHK	925	YN06 JYK	965	YT59 DYN
257	PN06 UYL	441	YV03 PZL	711	AJ58 WBD	926	YN06 JYL	966	YT59 DYJ
258	PN06 UYM	442	YV03 PZM	712	AE09 DHM	927	YN06 JYO	967	YT59 DYM
259	PN06 UYO	443	YV03 RCY	713	AE09 DHP	928	YN56 FDA	968	YT59 DYO
260	PN06 UYP	444	YV03 RCZ	714	AJ58 WBE	929	YN56 FDC	969	YT59 DYP
261	PN06 UYR	445	YV03 RAU	715	AE09 DHJ	943	YN56 FDY	970	YT59 DYS
262	PN06 UYS	446	YV03 RAX	716	AE09 DHO	947	YN07 EXF	971	YT59 DYU
263	PN06 UYT	447	YV03 RBF	717	AJ58 WBG	948	YN07 EXG	972	YT59 DYV
264	PN06 UYU	451	YU52 XVK	718	AE09 DHU	949	YN07 EXH	973	YT59 DYW
265	PN06 UYV	455	YN03 DFA	719	AE09 DHN	950	YN07 EXK	LDP198	SN51 UAL
266	PN06 UYW	481	YN53 RYR	720	AE09 DHL	951	YN07 EXM		

TC	CROYDON	ZONE 5

Croydon Bus Garage on August 19th, 2014 with Arriva London bus **EN7** leaving on a Route 312 service. The depot was opened by the London General Omnibus Company in 1915 but was totally destroyed by bombing during WWII and reconstructed during the mid-1950s.

CROYDON (TC)
Brighton Road, Croydon, Surrey CR2 6EL
Operated by: Arriva London
Location: TQ32626343 [51.354497, -0.097483]
Nearest Station: South Croydon (0.8 miles)
Nearest Bus Routes: 60/166/312/407/466 & N68 - South Croydon Bus Garage (Stop)
Bus Routes Serviced: 60/166/194/197/264/312/403/405/412/466/612/627/685 & T31

VEHICLE ALLOCATION									
DLA239	X439 FGP	DW29	LJ53 BGU	DW111	LJ05 BHP	ENL3	LJ07 ECY	T54	LJ08 CYG
DLA270	Y452 UGC	DW30	LJ53 NHV	DW112	LJ05 BHU	ENL4	LJ07 ECZ	T55	LJ08 CYH
DLA271	Y471 UGC	DW31	LJ53 NHX	DW113	LJ05 BHV	ENL5	LJ07 EDC	T56	LJ08 CYK
DLA287	Y487 UGC	DW32	LJ53 NHY	DW114	LJ05 BHW	ENL6	LJ07 EDF	T57	LJ08 CYL
DLA327	LG52 DBY	DW33	LJ53 NHZ	DW115	LJ05 BHX	ENL7	LJ07 EBO	T58	LJ08 CYO
DW1	801 DYE	DW34	734 DYE	DW116	LJ05 BHY	ENL8	LJ07 EBP	T59	LJ08 CYP
DW2	LJ03 MWN	DW35	LJ53 NJF	DW117	LJ05 BHZ	ENL9	LJ07 EBU	T60	LJ08 CYS
DW3	LJ03 MWP	DW36	LJ53 NJK	DW252	LJ59 AAY	ENL21	LJ58 AUV	T61	LJ08 CXR
DW4	LJ03 MWU	DW37	LJ53 NJN	DW253	LJ59 AAZ	ENL22	LJ58 AUW	T62	LJ08 CXS
DW5	LJ03 MWV	DW38	LJ53 NHE	DW254	LJ59 GVC	ENL23	LJ58 AUX	T63	LJ08 CXT
DW6	LJ03 MVT	DW39	LJ53 NHF	DW255	LJ59 GVE	ENL24	LJ58 AUY	T64	LJ08 CXU
DW7	WLT 807	DW40	LJ53 NHG	DW256	LJ59 GVF	ENL25	LJ58 AVB	T65	LJ08 CXV
DW8	LJ03 MVV	DW41	LJ53 NHH	DW258	LJ59 GVK	ENL26	LJ58 AVC	T118	LJ10 HVO
DW9	LJ03 MVW	DW42	LJ53 NHK	DW259	LJ59 GTF	ENL27	LJ58 AVD	T119	LJ10 HVP
DW10	LJ03 MVX	DW43	LJ53 NHL	DW260	LJ59 GTU	ENL28	LJ58 AUC	T120	LJ10 HVR
DW11	LJ03 MVY	DW44	LJ53 NHM	DW261	361 CLT	ENL29	LJ58 AUE	T121	LJ10 HVA
DW12	LJ03 MVZ	DW94	LJ54 BFP	DW262	LJ59 GUA	PDL117	LJ05 GOP	T279	LJ13 CHL
DW13	LJ03 MWA	DW95	VLT 295	DW263	LJ59 LXU	PDL118	LJ05 GOU	T280	LJ13 CHN
DW14	LJ03 MWC	DW96	LJ54 BFV	DW264	LJ59 LXV	PDL119	LJ05 GOX	T281	LJ13 CHO
DW15	LJ03 MWD	DW97	LJ54 BFX	DW265	LJ59 LXW	PDL120	LJ05 GPF	T282	LJ13 CHV
DW16	LJ03 MVF	DW98	LJ54 BFY	DW266	LJ59 LXX	PDL123	LJ05 GPU	T283	LJ13 CHX
DW17	LJ03 MVG	DW99	LJ54 BFZ	DW267	LJ59 LXY	T42	LJ08 CSU	T284	LJ13 CHY
DW18	LJ53 NHT	DW100	LJ54 BGE	DW268	LJ59 LXZ	T43	LJ08 CSV	T285	LJ13 CGG
DW19	WLT 719	DW101	LJ54 BGF	DW269	LJ59 LWS	T44	LJ08 CSX	T286	LJ13 CGK
DW20	LJ53 BFP	DW102	LJ54 BGK	DW270	LJ59 LWT	T45	LJ08 CSY	T287	LJ13 CGO
DW21	LJ53 BFU	DW103	LJ05 BJV	DW271	LJ59 LWU	T46	LJ08 CSZ		
DW22	822 DYE	DW104	LJ05 BJX	DW272	LJ59 LWV	T47	LJ08 CTE		
DW23	LJ53 BFX	DW105	LJ05 BJY	DW273	LJ59 LWW	T48	LJ08 CTF		
DW24	LJ53 BFY	DW106	LJ05 BJZ	DW274	LJ59 LWX	T49	LJ08 CTK		
DW25	725 DYE	DW107	LJ05 BKA	DW275	LJ59 LWY	T50	LJ08 CTO		
DW26	LJ53 BGF	DW108	LJ05 BHL	DW276	LJ59 LWZ	T51	LJ08 CYC		
DW27	LJ53 BGK	DW109	LJ05 BHN	ENL1	LJ07 ECW	T52	LJ08 CYE		
DW28	LJ53 BGO	DW110	LJ05 BHO	ENL2	LJ07 ECX	T53	LJ08 CYF		

Dartford Bus Garage on September 7th, 2013 with an interesting ensemble of vans, taxis and a Polish Coach Reg No.854 9435.

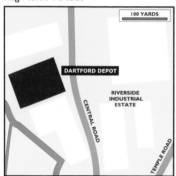

DARTFORD (DT)
Central Road, Dartford, Kent, DA1 5BG
Operated by: Arriva Southern
Location: TQ54427468 [51.450276, 0.221242]
Nearest Station: Dartford (0.3 miles)
Nearest Bus Routes: 96/428 & 492 - Dartford, Home Gardens (Stop D)
Bus Routes Serviced: 160/428/492/B12/B13 & B15

Arriva London single-deckers **3294, 3292, 3293, 3302 & 3295** parked in the yard at **Dartford Bus Garage** on September 7th, 2013.

VEHICLE ALLOCATION

3945	GK53 AOH	3984	GN07 DLJ	4001	GN08 CGU	4029	GN09 AVW	6458	GN61 JPY
3946	GK53 AOJ	3985	GN07 DLK	4002	GN08 CGV	4030	GN09 AVX	6459	GN61 JSV
3947	GK53 AOL	3986	GN07 DLO	4003	GN08 CGX	4031	GN09 AVY	6460	GN61 JRV
3948	GK53 AON	3987	GN07 DLU	4004	GN08 CGY	4032	GN09 AVZ	6461	GN61 JRX
3949	GK53 AOO	3988	GN07 DLV	4005	GN08 CGZ	4033	GN09 AWA	6462	GN61 JRO
3950	GK53 AOP	3989	GN07 DLX	4006	GN08 CHC	4034	GN09 AWC	6463	GN61 JRZ
3951	GK53 AOR	3990	GN07 DLY	4007	GN08 CHD	4035	GN09 AWF	6464	GN61 JSU
3952	GK53 AOT	3991	GN07 DLZ	4008	GN08 CHF	6213	GK53 AOA	6465	GN61 JRU
3953	GK53 AOU	3992	GN07 DME	4023	GN58 BUP	6214	GK53 AOB	6466	KX61 LDL
3954	GK53 AOV	3993	GN07 DMF	4024	GN58 BUU	6215	GK53 AOC	6467	KX61 LDN
3955	GK53 AOW	3994	GN07 DMO	4025	GN58 BUV	6216	GK53 AOD	6468	KX61 LDO
3956	GK53 AOX	3995	GN07 DMU	4026	GN58 LVA	6217	GK53 AOE	6469	KX61 LDU
3957	GK53 AOY	3996	GN07 DMV	4027	GN58 LVB	6218	GK53 AOF	6470	KX61 LDV
3983	GN07 DLF	4000	GN08 CGO	4028	GN09 AVV	6219	GK53 AOG		

Edgware Bus Garage viewed on April 23rd, 2014 with Metroline buses **TE712 & TE721** parked in the yard.

EDGWARE (BT)
Approach Road, Edgware, Middlesex HA8 7AN
Operated by: London Sovereign
Location: TQ19679171 [51.611558, -0.272959]
Nearest Tube Station: Edgware (adjacent)
Nearest Bus Routes: Edgware Bus Station (adjacent)
Bus Routes Serviced: 13/114/183/251/292/324/
605 & N13

A depot has been sited at Edgware since the London General Omnibus Company opened one in 1925. It was approximately located where the bus station is today and this garage was built in 1984.

NB This depot is also used by Metroline and is coded as EW Edgware (See Page 34)

VEHICLE ALLOCATION

DE57	YX11 GBE	SLE24	YN55 NHX	SP83	YT59 RYJ	VH14	BT13 YWN	VLP18	PJ53 OUN
DE58	YX11 GBF	SLE25	YN55 NHY	SP84	YT59 RYK	VH15	BT13 YWJ	VLP19	PJ53 OUO
DE59	YX11 GBO	SLE26	YN55 NHZ	SP85	YT59 RYM	VH16	BT13 YWM	VLP20	PJ53 OUP
DE60	YX11 GBU	SLE29	YN55 NJJ	SP86	YT59 RYN	VH17	BT13 YWP	VLP22	PJ53 OUV
DE61	YX11 GBV	SLE31	YN55 NJU	SP87	YT59 RYO	VH18	BT13 YWO	VLP23	PJ53 OUW
DE62	YX11 GBY	SLE35	YN55 NKD	VE1	PG04 WGN	VH19	BT13 YWR	VLP24	PJ53 OUX
DE63	YX11 GBZ	SLE37	YN55 NKF	VE2	PG04 WGP	VH20	BT13 YWS	VLP25	PJ53 OUY
DE64	YX11 GCF	SLE40	YN55 NKJ	VE4	PG04 WGV	VH21	BT13 YWW	VLP26	PJ53 OVA
DE65	YX11 GCK	SP68	YT59 RXR	VE5	PG04 WGW	VH22	BT13 YWU	VLP27	PJ53 OVB
DE66	YX11 GCO	SP69	YT59 RXS	VE6	PG04 WGX	VH23	BT13 YWV		
DE67	YX11 GCU	SP70	YT59 RXU	VH1	BD13 OHU	VLE27	PA04 CYK		
DE68	YX11 GCV	SP71	YT59 RXV	VH2	BD13 OHV	VLE28	PA04 CYL		
DE69	YX11 GCY	SP72	YT59 RXW	VH3	BD13 OHW	VLE29	PA04 CYP		
DE70	YX11 GCZ	SP73	YT59 RXX	VH4	BD13 OHX	VLE30	PA04 CYS		
SDE18	YX60 BZA	SP74	YT59 RXY	VH5	BD13 OHY	VLE31	PA04 CYT		
SDE19	YX60 BZB	SP75	YT59 RXZ	VH6	BD13 OHZ	VLE32	PO54 ABZ		
SDE20	YX60 BZC	SP76	YT59 RYA	VH7	BD13 OJA	VLE33	PO54 ACF		
SDE21	YX60 BZD	SP77	YT59 RYB	VH8	BD13 OJB	VLE34	PO54 ACJ		
SDE22	YX60 BZE	SP78	YT59 RYC	VH9	BD13 OJC	VLE35	PO54 ACU		
SDE23	YX60 BZF	SP79	YT59 RYD	VH10	BD13 OJE	VLE36	PO54 ACV		
SDE24	YX60 BZG	SP80	YT59 RYF	VH11	BD13 OHJ	VLE37	PO54 ACX		
SLE21	YN55 NHT	SP81	YT59 RYG	VH12	BT13 YWK	VLE38	PO54 ACY		
SLE22	YN55 NHU	SP82	YT59 RYH	VH13	BT13 YWL	VLE39	PO54 ACZ		

Metroline **TE878** in the wash unit at **Edgware Bus Garage** on April 23rd, 2014 with Metroline **TE833** alongside.

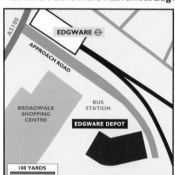

EDGWARE (EW)
Approach Road, Edgware, Middlesex HA8 7AN
Operated by: Metroline
Location: TQ19679171 [51.611558, -0.272959]
Nearest Tube Station: Edgware (Adjacent)
Nearest Bus Routes: Edgware Bus Station adjacent
Bus Routes Serviced: 107/113/186/204/240/606/
N5/N98 & N113

In 1992, as Cricklewood Bus Garage (See Page 28), was due to open with new facilities, Edgware was considered for closure and a year later became a midibus base. In 1999 London Sovereign took over half of the depot and Metroline subsequently moved in to share the facilities in 2000.

NB This depot is also used by London Sovereign and is coded as BT Edgware (See Page 33)

VEHICLE ALLOCATION

TE712	LK56 FHE	TE728	LK07 AZD	TE833	LK57 AXN	TE879	LK08 DXP	TE979	LK59 DZC
TE713	LK56 FHF	TE729	LK07 AZF	TE834	LK57 AXO	TE880	LK08 DXR	TE980	LK59 DZD
TE714	LK56 FHG	TE730	LK07 AZG	TE835	LK57 AXP	TE881	LK08 DXS	TE981	LK59 DZE
TE715	LK56 FHH	TE731	LK07 AZJ	TE836	LK57 AXR	TE882	LK08 DXU	TE982	LK59 DZF
TE716	LK56 FHJ	TE732	LK07 AZL	TE837	LK57 AXS	TE883	LK08 DXV	TE983	LK59 DZG
TE717	LK56 FHM	TE733	LK07 AZN	TE838	LK57 AXT	TE884	LK08 DXW	TE984	LK59 DZH
TE718	LK56 FHN	TE734	LK07 AZO	TE839	LK57 AXU	TE885	LK08 DXX	TE985	LK59 DZJ
TE719	LK56 FHO	TE735	LK07 AZP	TE840	LK57 AXV	TE886	LK08 DXY	TE986	LK59 DZL
TE720	LK56 FHP	TE736	LK07 AZR	TE841	LK57 AXW	TE887	LK08 DXZ	TE987	LK59 DZM
TE721	LK56 FHR	TE737	LK07 AZT	TE842	LK57 AXX	TE888	LK08 DYA	TE988	LK59 DZN
TE722	LK56 FHS	TE738	LK07 AZU	TE843	LK57 AXY	TE889	LK08 NVD	TE989	LK59 DZO
TE723	LK56 FHT	TE828	LK57 AXF	TE844	LK57 AXZ	TE890	LK08 NVE	TE990	LK59 DZP
TE724	LK07 AYZ	TE829	LK57 AXG	TE845	LK57 AYA	TE891	LK08 NVF	TE991	LK59 DZR
TE725	LK07 AZA	TE830	LK57 AXH	TE846	LK57 AYB	TE976	LK59 DYY	TE992	LK59 DZT
TE726	LK07 AZB	TE831	LK57 AXJ	TE847	LK57 AYC	TE977	LK59 DZA		
TE727	LK07 AZC	TE832	LK57 AXM	TE878	LK08 DXO	TE978	LK59 DZB		

Edmonton Bus Garage on July 22nd, 2014. The depot was opened in 1993 by London Suburban Bus to accommodate its buses being used on Route Nos 4 & 271. The company was taken over in 1995 and the depot closed. It was re-opened by Arriva County Bus in 1997 and continued in use with Arriva until formally closed on March 24th, 2012. In 2013 it was in use as a maintenance depot and was then utilized as a running depot from March 1st, 2014 following the closure of the nearby Lee Valley depot the day before.

EDMONTON (EC)
Unit 1E, Towpath Road, Stonehill Business Park, London N18 3QT
Operated by: Arriva London
Location: TQ35759160 [51.606783, -0.041104]
Nearest Station: Northumberland Park (0.8 miles)
Nearest Bus Routes: 34/192 & 444
Bus Routes Serviced: 123/125/184/318/382/397/444/629/657/W6 & W11

Buses parked up on the large concourse at **Edmonton Bus Garage** on July 22nd, 2014.

VEHICLE ALLOCATION

DLA293	Y493 UGC	DWL47	LF52 UNY	ENL40	LJ09 KOX	PDL80	LF52 UOR	PDL121	LJ05 GPK
DLA299	Y499 UGC	DWL48	LF52 UNZ	ENL41	LJ09 KPA	PDL81	LF52 UNV	PDL122	LJ05 GPO
DLA348	LJ03 MKU	DWL49	LF52 UOA	ENL42	LJ09 KPE	PDL82	LF52 URY	VLA79	LJ54 BFF
DLA349	LJ03 MKV	DWL51	LF52 UOC	ENL43	LJ09 KPF	PDL83	LF52 URZ	VLA80	LJ54 BFK
DLA357	LJ03 MKA	DWL52	LF52 UOD	ENL44	LJ09 KPG	PDL84	LF52 USB	VLA81	LJ54 BFL
DLA358	LJ03 MKC	EN16	GN57 BPF	ENL45	LJ09 KPK	PDL86	LF52 USD	VLA82	LJ54 BFM
DLA359	LJ03 MKD	EN17	GN57 BPK	ENL46	LJ09 KPL	PDL88	LF52 USH	VLA83	LJ54 BFN
DLA360	LJ03 MKE	EN18	GN57 BPO	ENL47	LJ09 KPN	PDL89	LF52 USJ	VLA84	LJ54 BFO
DLA361	LJ03 MKF	EN19	GN57 BPU	ENL48	LJ09 KPO	PDL91	LF52 URN	VLA85	LJ54 BCY
DLA362	LJ03 MKG	EN20	GN57 BPV	ENS15	LJ12 BYY	PDL92	LF52 URO		
DLA363	LJ03 MKK	EN21	GN57 BPK	ENS16	LJ12 BYZ	PDL93	LF52 URP		
DLA364	LJ03 MKL	EN22	GN57 BPY	ENS17	LJ12 BZA	PDL94	LF52 URR		
DLA365	LJ03 MWE	ENL20	LJ58 AVE	ENS18	LJ12 BZB	PDL101	LJ54 BBF		
DLA366	LJ03 MWF	ENL30	LJ09 KPR	ENS19	LJ12 BZC	PDL102	LJ54 BBK		
DLA367	LJ03 MWG	ENL31	LJ09 KPT	ENS20	LJ12 BZD	PDL103	LJ54 BBN		
DLA368	LJ03 MWK	ENL32	LJ09 KPU	ENS21	LJ12 BZE	PDL104	LJ54 BBO		
DLA369	LJ03 MWL	ENL33	LJ09 KPV	ENS22	LJ12 BZF	PDL105	LJ54 BBU		
DLA370	LJ03 MUY	ENL34	LJ09 KPX	ENS23	LJ12 BYL	PDL106	LJ54 LHF		
DW236	LJ59 AEF	ENL35	LJ09 KPY	ENS24	LJ12 BYM	PDL107	LJ54 LHG		
DWL42	LF02 POA	ENL36	LJ09 KPZ	ENS25	LJ12 BYN	PDL108	LJ54 LHH		
DWL43	LF02 POH	ENL37	LJ09 KRD	ENS26	LJ12 BYO	PDL109	LJ54 LHK		
DWL45	LF52 UNW	ENL38	LJ09 KRE	ENS27	LJ12 BYP	PDL110	LJ54 LHL		
DWL46	LF52 UNX	ENL39	LJ09 KRF	ENS28	LJ12 BYR	PDL116	LJ54 LGV		

A general view of **Enfield Bus Garage** on August 20th, 2013. It was opened in 1927 by the London General Omnibus Company, subsequently expanded and then modernized and refurbished in the 1980s, re-opening in 1984.

ENFIELD (E)
Southbury Road, Ponders End, Middlesex EN3 4HX
Operated by: Arriva London
Location: TQ34989617 [51.606783, -0.041104]
Nearest Station: Southbury (200 yards)
Nearest Bus Routes: 121/191/307/313/349 & 377
Bus Routes Serviced: 121/192/279/307/313/317/349/377/379 & N279

Buses, including Arriva Trainer 23 in blue, parked along the east side of **Enfield Bus Garage** on July 22nd, 2014.

VEHICLE ALLOCATION

DW411	LJ11 AEB	EN3	LJ57 USU	PDL141	SN06 BPV	T245	LJ61 LKU	VLW108	LJ03 MHY
DW556	LJ13 CEN	EN4	LJ57 USV	PDL142	SN06 BPX	T246	LJ61 LKV	VLW109	LJ03 MHZ
DW557	LJ62 FNF	EN5	LJ57 USW	PDL143	SN06 BPY	T247	LJ61 LKX	VLW110	LJ03 MJE
DW558	LJ62 FNG	EN6	LJ57 USX	PDL144	SN06 BPZ	T248	LJ61 LKY	VLW111	LJ03 MJF
DW559	LJ62 FNR	EN7	LJ57 USY	PDL145	SN06 BRF	T249	LJ61 LKZ	VLW112	LJ03 MJK
DW560	LJ62 FOD	EN8	LJ57 USZ	T224	LJ61 CFP	T250	LJ61 LLA	VLW113	LJ03 MJU
DW561	LJ13 CEO	EN9	LJ57 UTA	T225	LJ61 CFU	T251	LJ61 LJY	VLW117	LF52 UPN
DW562	LJ13 CEU	EN10	LJ57 UTB	T226	LJ61 CFV	T252	LJ61 LJZ	VLW118	LF52 UPO
DW563	LJ13 CKC	EN11	LJ57 UTC	T227	LJ61 CFX	T253	LJ61 LKA	VLW119	LF52 UOS
DW564	LJ13 CKD	EN12	LJ57 UTE	T228	LJ61 CFY	T254	LJ61 LKC	VLW120	LF52 UOT
DW565	LJ13 CKE	EN13	LJ57 UTF	T229	LJ61 CFZ	T255	LJ61 LKD	VLW121	LF52 UOU
DW566	LJ13 CKF	EN14	LJ12 BYW	T230	LJ61 CGE	T256	LJ61 LKE	VLW122	LF52 UOV
DW567	LJ13 CKG	EN15	LJ12 BYX	T231	LJ61 LLC	T257	LJ61 LKF	VLW123	LF52 UOW
DW568	LJ13 CKK	ENX1	LJ61 CKF	T232	LJ61 LLD	T258	LJ61 LKG	VLW124	LF52 UOX
DW569	LJ13 CKL	ENX2	LJ61 CKG	T233	LJ61 LLE	T259	LJ61 LKK	VLW125	LF52 UOY
DW570	LJ13 CKN	ENX3	LJ61 CKK	T234	LJ61 LLF	VLW97	LF52 UPL		
DW571	LJ13 CKO	ENX4	LJ61 CKL	T235	LJ61 LLG	VLW98	LF52 UPM		
DW572	LJ13 CKP	ENX5	LJ61 CKN	T236	LJ61 LLK	VLW99	LG52 DDA		
DW573	LJ13 CHZ	ENX6	LJ61 CKO	T237	LJ61 LLM	VLW100	LG52 DDE		
DW574	LJ13 CJE	ENX7	LJ61 CHY	T238	LJ61 LLN	VLW101	LG52 DDF		
DW575	LJ13 CJF	ENX8	LJ61 CHZ	T239	LJ61 LLO	VLW102	LG52 DDJ		
DW576	LJ13 CJO	PDL90	LF52 USL	T240	LJ61 LLP	VLW103	LG52 DDK		
DW577	LJ13 CJU	PDL13	SN06 BPE	T241	LJ61 LKM	VLW104	LG52 DDL		
DW578	LJ13 CJV	PDL13	SN06 BPF	T242	LJ61 LKN	VLW105	LJ03 MHU		
EN1	LJ57 USS	PDL13	SN06 BPK	T243	LJ61 LKO	VLW106	LJ03 MHV		
EN2	LJ57 UST	PDL14	SN06 BPU	T244	LJ61 LKP	VLW107	LJ03 MHX		

Epsom Bus Garage viewed on October 16th, 2013.

EPSOM (EB)
3 Roy Richmond Way, Epsom, Surrey KT19 9AF
Operated by: Quality Line
Location: TQ21166208 [51.344875, -0.262117]
Nearest Station: Ewell West (0.7 miles)
Nearest Bus Routes: 418/668/868/E5 & E9 - Longmead, opposite Blenheim High School
Bus Routes Serviced: 404/406/411/418/463/465/467/470/641/K5/S1/S3/S4 & X26

VEHICLE ALLOCATION

DD01	SK07 DZA	MCL14	BN12 EOW	OP10	YE52 FHS	OPL04	YJ62 FVT	SD41	PL05 PLV
DD02	SK07 DZB	MCL15	BN12 EOX	OP11	YE52 FGU	OPL05	YJ62 FWB	SD42	PL05 PLX
DD03	SK07 DZC	MCL16	BN12 EOY	OP14	YN53 SUF	OPL06	YJ62 FXA	SD43	PE56 UFH
DD04	SK07 DZD	MCL17	BN12 EOZ	OP15	YN53 SVK	OPL07	YJ62 FXG	SD44	PE56 UFJ
DD05	SK07 DZE	OM1	YJ14 BFA	OP16	YN53 SVL	OPL08	YJ62 FXK	SD45	PE56 UFK
DD06	SK07 DZF	OM2	YJ14 BFE	OP17	YN53 SVO	OV01	YJ60 KGA	SD46	PE56 UFL
DD07	SK07 DZG	OM3	YJ14 BFF	OP18	YN53 SVP	OV02	YJ60 KGE	SD47	PE56 UFM
DD08	SK07 DZH	OM4	YJ14 BFK	OP19	YN53 SVR	OV03	YJ60 KGF	SD48	PE56 UFN
DD09	SK07 DZJ	OM5	YJ14 BFL	OP20	YN53 ZXA	OV04	YJ60 KGG	SD49	PE56 UFP
DD10	SK07 DZL	OM6	YJ14 BFM	OP21	YN53 ZXB	OV05	YJ60 KGK	SD50	PE56 UFR
DD11	SN11 BVG	OM7	YJ14 BFN	OP23	YJ09 MHK	OV06	YJ60 KGN	SD51	PE56 UFS
DD12	SN11 BVH	OM8	YJ14 BFO	OP24	YJ09 MHL	OV07	YJ60 KGO	SD52	PN07 KRZ
DD13	YX61 FYR	OM9	YJ14 BFP	OP25	YJ09 MHM	OV08	YJ60 KGP	SD53	PN07 KSE
DD14	SL14 LND	OM10	YJ14 BFU	OP26	YJ09 MHN	OV09	YJ12 PKV	SD54	LJ08 RJY
DD15	SL14 LNE	OM11	YJ14 BFV	OP27	YJ09 MHO	OV10	YJ12 PKX	SDE1	YX08 MFO
DD16	SL14 LNF	OM12	YJ14 BFX	OP28	YJ09 MHU	OV11	YJ12 PKY	SDE2	YX08 MFV
DD17	SL14 LNG	OP01	YE52 FHH	OP29	YJ09MHV	OV12	YJ12 PKZ	SDE3	YX08 MFY
DD18	SL14 LNH	OP02	YE52 FHJ	OP30	YJ09 MHX	OV13	YJ12 PLF	SDE4	YX08 MDZ
MCL1	BW03 ZMZ	OP03	YE52 FHK	OP31	YJ11 EJA	SD26	W874 VGT	SDE5	YX08 MFN
MCL8	BN12 EOP	OP04	YE52 FHL	OP32	YJ11 EJC	SD27	W875 VGT	SDL01	Y539 XAG
MCL9	BN12 EOR	OP05	YE52 FHM	OP33	YJ11 EJD	SD28	W876 VGT	SDL02	SN51 TDO
MCL10	BN12 EOS	OP06	YE52 FHN	OP34	YJ13 HJN	SD33	SN51 UCO	SDL03	SN51 TCU
MCL11	BN12 EOT	OP07	YE52 FHO	OPL01	YJ62 FUD	SD38	PL05 PLN		
MCL12	BN12 EOU	OP08	YE52 FHP	OPL02	YJ62 FUG	SD39	PL05 PLO		
MCL13	BN12 EOV	OP09	YE52 FHR	OPL03	YJ62 FVN	SD40	PL05 PLU		

A general view of **Fulwell Bus Garage** on August 17th, 2013.

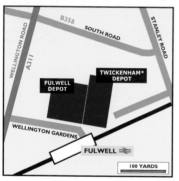

FULWELL (FW)
Wellington Road, Fulwell, Middlesex TW2 5NX
Operated by: London United
Location: TQ14817191 [51.434809, -0.350929]
Nearest Station: Fulwell (Adjacent)
Nearest Bus Routes: 267 & R70 - Fulwell (Stop A)
Bus Routes Serviced: 33/65/71/216/267/281/371/391/671/681 & 691

Fulwell was originally opened as a tramshed by the London United Tramways Company Ltd on April 2nd, 1903. On June 16th, 1931 the ten northernmost roads were taken over for trolleybuses and it was subsequently closed to trams on October 27th, 1935 by London Transport. The depot was then used as a trolleybus garage and works before conversion to an omnibus depot on May 9th, 1962.

NB Both London United and Abellio* utilize this depot with the former occupying the west end and Abellio the east. (*See Page 92)

London United bus **SLE58** exiting from **Fulwell Bus Garage** on September 6th, 2014

London United buses **TA229** & **OV18** standing in the yard at **Fulwell Bus Garage** on September 6th, 2014.

VEHICLE ALLOCATION

DE23	YX09 HJK	DPS591	SN51 TBU	OV18	YJ58 VBY	SP60	YT09 ZCK	SP116	YR59 FYX
DE24	YX09 HJN	DPS672	LG02 FHB	OV19	YJ58 VBZ	SP61	YT09 ZCL	SP117	YR59 FYY
DE25	YX09 HJO	DPS681	SN03 LDY	SLE43	YN55 NKM	SP62	YT09 ZCN	SP118	YR59 FYZ
DE26	YX09 HJU	DPS686	SN03 LFA	SLE44	YN55 NKO	SP63	YT09 ZCO	SP119	YR59 FZA
DE27	YX09 HJV	DPS687	SN03 LFB	SLE45	YN55 NKP	SP64	YT09 ZCU	SP120	YR59 FZB
DE28	YX09 HJY	DPS689	SN03 LFE	SLE46	YN55 NKR	SP65	YT09 BJV	SP121	YR59 FZC
DE29	YX09 HJZ	DPS690	SN03 LFF	SLE47	YN55 NKS	SP66	YT09 BJX	SP123	YR59 FZE
DE30	YX09 HKZ	DPS691	SN03 LFG	SLE48	YN55 NKT	SP67	YT09 BJY	SP125	YR59 FZG
DE31	YX09 HLA	DPS693	SN03 LFJ	SLE50	YN55 NKW	SP88	YT59 SFK	SP126	YT59 PBF
DE68	SK07 DXT	DPS724	SN55 DVT	SLE51	YN55 NKX	SP89	YT59 SFN	SP127	YT59 PBO
DE69	SK07 DXU	DPS725	SN55 DVU	SLE53	YN55 NLA	SP90	YT59 SFO	SP128	YT59 PBV
DE70	SK07 DXV	DPS726	SN55 DVV	SLE54	YN55 NLC	SP91	YT59 SFU	SP129	YT59 PBX
DE71	SK07 DXW	DPS727	SN55 DVW	SLE55	YN55 NLD	SP92	YT59 SFV	SP130	YT59 PBY
DE72	SK07 DXX	HDE1	SN09 CHC	SLE56	YN55 NLE	SP93	YT59 SFX	SP131	YT59 PBZ
DE73	SK07 DXY	HDE2	SN09 CHD	SLE57	YN55 NLG	SP94	YT59 SFY	SP132	YT59 PCF
DE109	YX60 CAA	HDE3	SN09 CHF	SLE58	YN55 NLJ	SP95	YT59 SFZ	SP163	YP59 OEY
DE110	YX60 CAE	HDE4	SN09 CHG	SLE59	YN55 NLK	SP96	YT59 SGO	SP164	YP59 OEZ
DE111	YX60 CAO	HDE5	SN09 CHH	SLE60	YN55 NLL	SP97	YT59 SGU	TA205	SN51 SYC
DE112	YX60 CAU	OV1	YJ58 VBA	SLE61	YN55 NLM	SP98	YT59 SGV	TA213	SN51 SYS
DE113	YX60 CAV	OV2	YJ58 VBB	SLE62	YN55 NLO	SP99	YT59 SGX	TA215	SN51 SYU
DE114	YX60 CBF	OV3	YJ58 VBC	SLE63	YN55 NLP	SP100	YT59 SGY	TA216	SN51 SYV
DE115	YX60 CBO	OV4	YJ58 VBD	SLE64	YN55 NLR	SP101	YT59 SGZ	TA217	SN51 SYW
DE116	YX60 CBU	OV5	YJ58 VBE	SP26	YN08 DHM	SP102	YT59 SHJ	TA218	SN51 SYX
DE117	YX60 CBV	OV6	YJ58 VBF	SP28	YN08 DHP	SP103	YT59 SHV	TA229	LG02 FAA
DE118	YX60 CBY	OV7	YJ58 VBG	SP38	YP58 ACF	SP104	YT59 SFF	TA232	LG02 FAK
DE119	YX60 CCA	OV8	YJ58 VBK	SP39	YP58 ACJ	SP105	YT59 DXY	TA233	LG02 FAM
DE120	YX60 CCD	OV9	YJ58 VBL	SP40	YP58 ACO	SP106	YT59 DXZ	TA237	LG02 FBB
DE121	YX60 CCE	OV10	YJ58 VBM	SP52	YT09 BNK	SP107	YT59 DYX	TA239	LG02 FBD
DE122	YX60 CCF	OV11	YJ58 VBN	SP53	YT09 BNL	SP109	YR59 FYO	TA243	LG02 FBK
DE123	YX60 CCJ	OV12	YJ58 VBO	SP54	YT09 BNN	SP110	YR59 FYP	TA244	LG02 FBL
DE124	YX60 CCK	OV13	YJ58 VBP	SP55	YT09 BJU	SP111	YR59 FYS	TA249	LG02 FBX
DE125	YX60 CCN	OV14	YJ58 VBT	SP56	YT09 ZCA	SP112	YR59 FYT	TA250	LG02 FBY
DE126	YX60 CCO	OV15	YJ58 VBU	SP57	YT09 ZCE	SP113	YR59 FYU	TA282	LG02 FDZ
DE127	YX60 BZH	OV16	YJ58 VBV	SP58	YT09 ZCF	SP114	YR59 FYV	TA283	LG02 FEF
DE128	YX60 BZJ	OV17	YJ58 VBX	SP59	YT09 ZCJ	SP115	YR59 FYW		

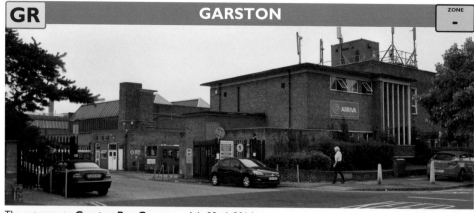

The entrance to **Garston Bus Garage** on July 22nd, 2014.

GARSTON (GR)

Marshwood House, 934 – 974 St Albans Road,
Watford, Hertfordshire WD25 9NN
Operated by: Arriva Shires
Location: TL11760035 [51.690754, -0.384822]
Nearest Station: Garston (0.4 miles)
Nearest Bus Routes: 142/258/268/288/303/305/
340/631/640/642/H2/H3/H18 & H19
Bus Routes Serviced: 142/258/268/288/303/305/
340/631/642/H2/H3/H18 & H19

Arriva bus **6170** passing **Garston Bus Garage** on July 22nd, 2014.

Arriva bus **6024** on the exit road at **Garston Bus Garage** on July 22nd, 2014.

VEHICLE ALLOCATION

2468	YJ06 YRP	3716	YJ06 HRJ	3813	LJ58 AVX	6025	YJ54 CFG	6164	LJ55 BVS
2469	YJ06 YRR	3717	YJ06 HPA	3814	LJ58 AVY	6026	YJ55 WPO	6165	LJ55 BVT
2470	YJ06 YRS	3718	YJ06 HPC	3815	LJ58 AVZ	6027	YJ55 WOA	6166	LJ55 BVU
2471	YJ06 YRT	3719	YJ06 HPF	3816	LJ58 AWA	6028	YJ55 WOB	6167	LJ55 BVV
2472	YJ06 YRU	3720	YJ06 HPJ	3817	LJ58 AWC	6029	YJ55 WOC	6168	LJ55 BVW
3515	LJ03 MUW	3721	YJ06 HPK	5448	SN08 AAE	6030	YJ55 WOD	6169	LJ55 BVX
3704	YJ06 LFE	3722	YJ06 HPL	6014	KL52 CXF	6031	YJ55 WOH	6170	LJ55 BVY
3705	YJ06 LFF	3723	YJ06 HPN	6015	KL52 CXG	6032	YJ55 WOM	6171	LJ55 BVZ
3706	YJ06 LFG	3724	YJ06 HPO	6016	KL52 CXH	6033	YJ55 WOR	6172	LJ55 BVD
3707	YJ06 LFH	3725	YJ06 HPP	6017	KL52 CXJ	6034	YJ55 WOU	6173	LJ55 BVE
3708	YJ06 LFK	3726	YJ06 HPU	6018	KL52 CXK	6035	YJ55 WOV	6174	LJ55 BVF
3709	YJ06 LFL	3727	YJ06 HNT	6019	KL52 CXM	6036	YJ55 WOX	6175	LJ55 BVG
3710	YJ06 LDK	3728	YJ06 HNU	6020	KL52 CXN	6041	LJ05 GLY	6176	LJ55 BVH
3711	YJ06 HRA	3804	SN56 AXG	6021	KL52 CXO	6100	KX59 AEE	6177	LJ55 BVK
3712	YJ06 HRC	3805	SN56 AXH	6022	KL52 CXP	6101	KX59 AEF	6178	LJ55 BVL
3713	YJ06 HRD	3811	LJ58 AVU	6023	KL52 CXR	6109	LJ05 BLV	6179	LJ55 BVM
3714	YJ06 HRF	3812	LJ58 AVV	6024	KL52 CXS	6123	LJ05 BKX		

Grays Bus Garage viewed on September 18th, 2013.

GRAYS (GY)
Unit 7, Europa Park, London Road, Grays,
Essex RM20 4DB
Operated by: Arriva Southern
Location: TQ59567800 [51.478434, 0.296224]
Nearest Station: Grays (1.7 miles)
Nearest Bus Routes: 22/22A/25/44/73/73A/83/100
& 201 - South Stifford, The Shant (Eastbound)
Bus Routes Serviced: 66/346/370/375 & 499

Arriva Southern **DWL13** leaving **Grays Bus Garage** on September 18th, 2013.

The entrance and wash plant at **Grays Bus Garage** on September 18th, 2013, with Arriva Southern **3997** on the left and **3973** on the right.

VEHICLE ALLOCATION

3309	LJ54 BCX	4009	GN08 CHG	4076	YX10 EBP	6116	LJ05 BKG	6204	LJ09 SUV
3310	LJ54 BAA	4010	GN08 CHH	4077	YX10 EBU	6117	LJ05 BKK	6205	LJ09 SUX
3524	LJ51 DDX	4068	GN10 KWE	4078	YX10 EBV	6118	LJ05 BKL	6206	LJ09 SUY
3525	LJ51 DDV	4069	GN10 KWF	4079	YX10 EBZ	6119	LJ05 BKN	6207	LJ09 SVA
3971	YE06 HPX	4070	GN10 KWG	6110	LJ05 BLX	6120	LJ05 BKO	6208	LJ09 SVC
3972	YE06 HPY	4071	GN10 KWH	6111	LJ05 BLZ	6121	LJ05 BKU	6209	LJ09 SVD
3973	YE06 HPZ	4072	GN10 KWJ	6112	LJ05 BMO	6122	LJ05 BKV	6210	LJ09 SVE
3997	GN57 BOU	4073	GN10 KWK	6113	LJ05 BMU	6201	LJ09 KRO	6211	LJ09 SVF
3998	GN57 BOV	4074	YX10 EBN	6114	LJ05 BKD	6202	LJ09 SUO	6212	LJ09 SSO
3999	GN57 BPE	4075	YX10 EBO	6115	LJ05 BKF	6203	LJ09 SUU		

The compound at **Greenford Bus Garage** on September 27th, 2014 with Metroline buses **DE1897, DE1693, DES1703 & DES1697** parked up between duties. This is part of a council depot and, in London Transport days, the space was rented here to replace Hanwell bus garage.

GREENFORD (G)
Council Depot, Greenford Road, Greenford, Middlesex UB6 9AP
Operated by: Metroline
Location: TQ14438187 (Office), TQ14538186 (Compound) [51.524035, -0.350297]
Nearest Station: Greenford (1.6 miles)
Nearest Bus Routes: 92/282 & E5 - Greenford Depot (Stop U)
Bus Routes Serviced: 92/95/282/E5/E7 & E9

The depot consists of an office on the approach road, with a maintenance building behind, and a compound sited to the east of it.

VEHICLE ALLOCATION

DE1675	YX09 FLA	DE1897	YX11 AEU	TE1722	SN09 CEJ	TE1742	SN09 CFX	TE1991	SN12 EHT
DE1676	YX09 FLB	DE1898	YX11 AEV	TE1723	SN09 CEK	TE1743	SN09 CFY	TE1992	SN12 EHU
DE1677	YX09 FLC	DE1899	YX11 AEW	TE1724	SN09 CEO	TE1744	SN09 CFZ	TE1993	SN12 EHV
DE1678	YX09 FLD	DE1900	YX11 AEY	TE1725	SN09 CEU	TE1745	SN09 CGE	TE1994	SN12 EHW
DE1679	YX09 FLE	DE1901	YX11 AEZ	TE1726	SN09 CEV	TE1746	SN09 CGF	TE1995	SN12 AAF
DE1680	YX09 FLF	DE1902	YX11 AFA	TE1727	SN09 CEX	TE1747	SN09 CGG	TE1996	SN12 AAK
DE1681	YX09 FLG	DE1904	YX11 AFF	TE1728	SN09 CEY	TE1748	SN09 CGK	TE1997	SN12 AAO
DE1682	YX09 FLH	DE1905	YX11 AFJ	TE1729	SN09 CFA	TE1749	SN09 CGO	TE1998	SN12 AAV
DE1683	YX09 FLJ	DE1906	YX11 CNK	TE1730	SN09 CFD	TE1750	SN09 CGU	TE1999	SN12 EGY
DE1684	YX09 FLK	DE1907	YX11 CNN	TE1731	SN09 CFE	TE1751	SN09 CGV	TE2000	SN12 EGZ
DE1685	YX09 FLL	DE1908	YX11 CNO	TE1732	SN09 CFF	TE1981	SN12 EHD	TP1508	LK03 NKC
DE1686	YX09 FNJ	DE1909	YX11 CNU	TE1733	SN09 CFG	TE1982	SN12 EHE	TP1510	LK03 NKE
DE1687	YX09 FNK	DE1910	YX11 CNV	TE1734	SN09 CFJ	TE1983	SN12 EHF	TP1514	LK03 NKR
DE1688	YX09 FKS	TE1715	SN09 CDU	TE1735	SN09 CFK	TE1984	SN12 EHG	TP1518	LK03 NKW
DE1689	YX09 FKT	TE1716	SN09 CDV	TE1736	SN09 CFL	TE1985	SN12 EHH	TP1519	LK03 NKX
DE1690	YX09 FKU	TE1717	SN09 CDX	TE1737	SN09 CFM	TE1986	SN12 EHJ	TP1520	LK03 NKZ
DE1691	YX09 FKV	TE1718	SN09 CDY	TE1738	SN09 CFO	TE1987	SN12 EHK		
DE1692	YX09 FKW	TE1719	SN09 CDZ	TE1739	SN09 CFP	TE1988	SN12 EHP		
DE1693	YX09 FKY	TE1720	SN09 CEA	TE1740	SN09 CFU	TE1989	SN12 EHR		
DE1694	YX09 FLM	TE1721	SN09 CEF	TE1741	SN09 CFV	TE1990	SN12 EHS		

Harrow Bus Garage on July 20th, 2013 with London Sovereign bus DPS629 parked on the drive before operating on the H9 service.

HARROW (SO)
331 Pinner Road, Harrow HA1 4HJ
Operated by: London Sovereign
Location: TQ14028843 [51.582973, -0.355871]
Nearest Tube Station: North Harrow (400 yards)
Nearest Bus Routes: 183 & H18/183 & H19 - The Gardens (Stop WK)
Bus Routes Serviced: 398/H9/H10/H11/H13/H14 & H17

London Sovereign DE76 on the exit road at Harrow Bus Garage on May 3rd, 2014. The depot opened in 1994 but due to a low roof beam across the centre of the site it can only accommodate single-deck vehicles.

The entrance to the garage building at Harrow Bus Garage on May 3rd, 2014.

VEHICLE ALLOCATION

DE50	YX59 BYA	DE74	YX11 FZA	DE84	YX11 FZL	DE94	YX11 FZW	DPS633	SK02 XHH
DE51	YX59 BYB	DE75	YX11 FZB	DE85	YX11 FZM	DE95	YX11 FZY	DPS635	SK02 XHL
DE52	YX59 BYC	DE76	YX11 FZC	DE86	YX11 FZN	DE96	YX11 FZZ	DPS636	SK02 XHM
DE53	YX59 BYD	DE77	YX11 FZD	DE87	YX11 FZO	DE97	YX11 COH	DPS637	SK02 XHN
DE54	YX59 BYF	DE78	YX11 FZE	DE88	YX11 FZP	DE98	YX11 COJ	DPS638	SK02 XHO
DE55	SK02 XHJ	DE79	YX11 FZF	DE89	YX11 FZR	DE99	YX11 CNJ	DPS639	SK02 XHP
DE56	YX59 BYH	DE80	YX11 FZG	DE90	YX11 FZS	DPS628	SK02 XGX	DPS640	SK02 XHR
DE71	YX11 GDA	DE81	YX11 FZH	DE91	YX11 FZT	DPS629	SK02 XHD		
DE72	YX11 GDE	DE82	YX11 FZJ	DE92	YX11 FZU	DPS630	SK02 XHE		
DE73	YX11 GDF	DE83	YX11 FZK	DE93	YX11 FZV	DPS632	SK02 XHG		

Harrow Weald Bus Garage on September 6th, 2014 with Metroline buses **VP622** & **VP62** parked in the entrance whilst **VP337** departs on Route No.140. It was opened in 1930 by the London General Omnibus Company and within two years extended over the forecourt to provide extra covered space.

HARROW WEALD (HD)
467 High Road, Harrow Weald, Middlesex HA3 6EJ
Operated by: Metroline
Location: TQ14999104 [51.606461, -0.340454]
Nearest Station: Headstone Lane (0.9 miles)
Nearest Bus Routes: 182/258/340/640/H12 & H18
- Harrow Weald Bus Garage (Stop WT)
Bus Routes Serviced: 140/182/H12 & N16

Metroline bus **VP337** exiting from **Harrow Weald Bus Garage** on September 6th, 2014.

VEHICLE ALLOCATION

VP317	LR52 BLK	VP333	LR52 BNK	VP467	LK03 GKF	VP610	LK04 UWS	VP626	LK54 FWE
VP318	LR52 BLN	VP334	LR52 BNL	VP468	LK03 GKG	VP611	LK04 UWT	VP627	LK54 FWF
VP319	LR52 BLV	VP335	LR52 BNN	VP469	LK03 GKJ	VP612	LK04 UWU	VP628	LK54 FWG
VP320	LR52 BLX	VP336	LR52 BNO	VP470	LK03 GKL	VP613	LK04 UWV	VPL184	Y184 NLK
VP321	LR52 BLZ	VP337	LR52 BNU	VP471	LK03 GKN	VP614	LK04 UWW	VW1243	LK12 AAF
VP322	LR52 BMO	VP338	LR52 BNV	VP472	LK03 GKP	VP615	LK04 UWX	VW1244	LK12 AAJ
VP323	LR52 BMU	VP339	LR52 BNX	VP485	LK03 GMG	VP616	LK04 UWY	VW1245	LK12 AAN
VP324	LR52 BMV	VP340	LR52 BNY	VP486	LK03 GMU	VP617	LK04 UWZ	VW1246	LK12 AAU
VP325	LR52 BMY	VP341	LR52 BNZ	VP487	LK03 GMV	VP618	LK04 UXA	VW1247	LK12 ABF
VP326	LR52 BMZ	VP342	LR52 BOF	VP488	LK03 GMX	VP619	LK04 UXB	VW1248	LK12 ABO
VP327	LR52 BNA	VP343	LR52 BOH	VP604	LK04 UWJ	VP620	LK04 UXC		
VP328	LR52 BNB	VP344	LR52 BOJ	VP605	LK04 UWL	VP621	LK04 UXD		
VP329	LR52 BND	VP345	LR52 BOU	VP606	LK04 UWM	VP622	LK04 UXE		
VP330	LR52 BNE	VP346	LR52 BOV	VP607	LK04 UWN	VP623	LK04 UXF		
VP331	LR52 BNF	VP347	LR52 BPE	VP608	LK04 UWP	VP624	LK04 UXG		
VP332	LR52 BNJ	VP466	LK03 GKE	VP609	LK04 UWR	VP625	LK04 UXH		

Looking east towards **Hayes Bus Garage** on October 29th, 2014 with Metroline bus **DE1789** standing in the yard.

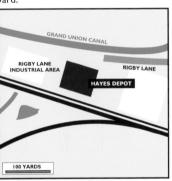

HAYES (HZ)
12 Rigby Lane, Hayes, Middlesex UB3 1ET
Operated by: Metroline
Location: TQ08037980 [51.506779, -0.444692]
Nearest Station: Hayes & Harlington (1.4 miles)
Nearest Bus Routes: 350 – Hayes Town, Swallowfield Way (Northbound)
Bus Routes Serviced: 195/207/427 & N207

Metroline buses **SN1955, SN1919, SN1957, SN1931 & SN1946** parked in the yard at **Hayes Bus Garage** on October 29th, 2014.

VEHICLE ALLOCATION

DE1783	YX10 BCU	DE1911	YX11 CNY	SN1934	YR61 RSY	SN1950	YR61 RVA	VW1825	BK10 MFE
DE1784	YX10 BCV	SN1919	YR61 RPU	SN1935	YR61 RSZ	SN1951	YR61 RVC	VW1826	BK10 MFN
DE1785	YX10 BCY	SN1920	YR61 RPV	SN1936	YR61 RTO	SN1952	YR61 RVE	VW1827	BK10 MFF
DE1786	YX10 BCZ	SN1921	YR61 RPX	SN1937	YR61 RTU	SN1953	YR61 RVF	VW1828	BK10 MFJ
DE1787	YX10 BDE	SN1922	YR61 RPY	SN1938	YR61 RTV	SN1954	YR61 RVJ	VW1829	BK10 LSO
DE1788	YX10 BDF	SN1923	YR61 RPZ	SN1939	YR61 RTX	SN1955	YR61 RVK	VW1830	BK10 LSU
DE1789	YX10 BDO	SN1924	YR61 RRO	SN1940	YR61 RTZ	SN1956	YR61 RVL	VW1831	BK10 LSV
DE1790	YX10 BDU	SN1925	YR61 RRU	SN1941	YR61 RUA	SN1957	YR61 RVM	VW1832	BK10 LSX
DE1791	YX10 BDV	SN1926	YR61 RRV	SN1942	YR61 RUC	VW1817	BF10 LSZ	VW1833	BK10 LSY
DE1792	YX10 BDY	SN1927	YR61 RRX	SN1943	YR61 RUH	VW1818	BF10 LTA	VW1834	BK10 LTE
DE1793	YX10 BDZ	SN1928	YR61 RRY	SN1944	YR61 RUJ	VW1819	BV10 WVP	VW1835	BK10 LTJ
DE1794	YX10 BEJ	SN1929	YR61 RRZ	SN1945	YR61 RUO	VW1820	BV10 WVR	VW1836	BV10 WVN
DE1795	YX10 BEO	SN1930	YR61 RSO	SN1946	YR61 RUU	VW1821	BV10 WVS	VW1837	BV10 WVO
DE1796	YX10 BEU	SN1931	YR61 RSU	SN1947	YR61 RUV	VW1822	BV10 WVT	VW1838	BV10 WVU
DE1797	YX10 BEY	SN1932	YR61 RSV	SN1948	YR61 RUW	VW1823	BK10 MEV	VW1839	BV10 WVW
DE1903	YX11 AFE	SN1933	YR61 RSX	SN1949	YR61 RUY	VW1824	BK10 MFA	VW1840	BV10 WVX

Hayes Depot on October 29th, 2014 with Abellio London buses **2444**, **2448**, **9764** & **8113** parked in the yard.

HAYES (WS)
West London Coach Centre, North Hyde Gardens, Hayes, Middlesex UB3 4QT
Operated by: Abellio
Location: TQ10627916 [51.501164, -0.410775]
Nearest Station: Hayes & Harlington (1 mile)
Nearest Bus Routes: 195 – Hayes Town, The Crane (Eastbound)
Bus Routes Serviced: 350/E1/H28/U7 & U9

The depot is built on the site of Hayes Creosoting Works which were opened by the Great Western Railway in 1935 for the production of railway sleepers.

VEHICLE ALLOCATION

2444	SK14 CTZ	8113	KX06 LYS	8489	KX03 HZR	8588	YX62 DFO	9767	YN51 KWB
2445	SK14 CUA	8114	KX06 LYT	8490	KX03 HZS	8589	YX62 DVA	9768	YN51 KWC
2446	SK14 CUC	8115	KX56 HCZ	8499	KX05 KFW	8590	YX62 DVC	9769	YN51 KWD
2447	SK14 CUG	8438	RX51 FGN	8583	YX62 DAU	8591	YX62 DVG	9770	YN51 KWE
2448	SK14 CUH	8439	RX51 FGO	8584	YX62 DBU	9763	YN51 KVW	9771	YN51 KWF
2449	SK14 SYY	8440	RX51 FGP	8585	YX62 DDE	9764	YN51 KVX	9772	YN51 KWG
2450	SK14 SYZ	8465	RL02 ZTC	8586	YX62 DDO	9765	YN51 KVZ		
2451	SK14 SZC	8466	GM03 TGM	8587	YX62 DFE	9766	YN51 KWA		

Heathrow Bus Garage viewed on October 29th, 2014, with TGM (Arriva) bus **3948** parked in the yard.

HEATHROW (HE)
TGM (Arriva), Bedfont Road, Staines TW19 7LZ
Operated by: Tellings Golden Miller
Location: TQ07247398 [51.454659, -0.45797172]
Nearest Tube Station: Hatton Cross (1.9 miles)
Nearest Bus Routes: 203 & 555
Bus Routes Serviced: E10

TGM
BUILDING 16300 MT2
ELECTRA AVENUE
LONDON HEATHROW AIRPORT
HOUNSLOW, MIDDLESEX, TW6 2DN

TGM (Arriva) bus **3430** at the Ealing Broadway terminus of Route E10 on September 27th, 2014.

VEHICLE ALLOCATION

3425	YX14 RYO	3427	YX14 RYR	3429	YX14 RYU	3431	YX14 RYW	3433	YX14 RYZ
3426	YX14 RYP	3428	YX14 RYT	3430	YX14 RYV	3432	YX14 RYY	3948	GK53 AON

47

The entrance to **Holloway Bus Garage**, off Pemberton Gardens, on August 5th, 2014 with Metroline bus **LT103** waiting to enter.

HOLLOWAY (HT)
37A Pemberton Gardens, London N19 5RR
Operated by: Metroline
Location: TQ29458639 [51.561868, -0.133199]
Nearest Station: Upper Holloway (0.3 miles)
Nearest Bus Routes: 17/43/263/271 & N41 – Upper Holloway, Upper Holloway (Stop T)
Bus Routes Serviced: 4/17/24/43/91/134/143/271/ 390/603/N5/N20/N91/N113 & W7

It was opened between 1907 and 1909 by London County Council as a tram depot and closed to trams by London Transport on April 6th, 1952. Trolleybuses were run until April 25th, 1961 and it was subsequently utilized as an omnibus garage. Although the garage was re-named as Highgate in 1950, the original name was reapplied in 1971.

The exit from **Holloway Bus Garage** on August 5th, 2014 with Metroline bus **LT103** departing.

VEHICLE ALLOCATION

LT8	LTZ 1008	LT116	LTZ 1116	TP458	LK03 GJU	VW1253	LK12 ADU	VW1378	LK62 DPE
LT9	LTZ 1009	LT117	LTZ 1117	TPL263	LN51 KYX	VW1254	LK12 ADV	VW1379	LK62 DPU
LT10	LTZ 1010	LT190	LTZ 1190	TPL265	LN51 KYZ	VW1255	LK12 ADX	VW1380	LK62 DPY
LT11	LTZ 1011	TE665	LK55 KJV	TPL267	LN51 KZB	VW1256	LK12 AEA	VW1381	LK62 DRV
LT12	LTZ 1012	TE666	LK55 KJX	TPL268	LN51 KZC	VW1257	LK12 AEB	VW1382	LK62 DRZ
LT13	LTZ 1013	TE667	LK55 KJY	TPL270	LR02 BAA	VW1258	LK12 AEF	VW1383	LK62 DSE
LT14	LTZ 1014	TE668	LK55 KJZ	VPL581	LK04 NLZ	VW1259	LK12 AEG	VW1384	LK62 DSU
LT15	LTZ 1015	TE669	LK55 KKA	VPL582	LK04 NMA	VW1260	LK12 AET	VW1385	LK62 DSV
LT16	LTZ 1016	TE670	LK55 KKB	VPL583	LK04 NME	VW1261	LK12 AEU	VW1386	LK62 DTN
LT17	LTZ 1017	TE671	LK55 KKC	VPL584	LK04 NMF	VW1262	LK12 AFO	VW1387	LK62 DTU
LT18	LTZ 1018	TE672	LK55 KKD	VPL585	LK04 NMJ	VW1263	LK12 AEW	VW1388	LK62 DTV
LT19	LTZ 1019	TE673	LK55 KKE	VPL586	LK04 NMM	VW1264	LK12 AEZ	VW1468	LK13 BJE
LT20	LTZ 1020	TE674	LK55 KKF	VPL587	LK04 NMU	VW1265	LK12 AFA		
LT21	LTZ 1021	TE675	LK55 KKG	VPL588	LK04 NMV	VW1266	LK12 AFE		
LT22	LTZ 1022	TE676	LK55 KKH	VPL589	LK04 NMX	VW1267	LK12 AFU		
LT23	LTZ 1023	TE677	LK55 KKJ	VPL590	LK04 NMY	VW1268	LK12 AFV		
LT24	LTZ 1024	TE678	LK55 KKL	VPL591	LK04 NMZ	VW1269	LK12 AFX		
LT25	LTZ 1025	TE679	LK55 KKM	VPL592	LK04 NNA	VW1270	LK12 AHA		
LT26	LTZ 1026	TE680	LK55 KKO	VPL593	LK04 NNB	VW1271	LK12 AHC		
LT27	LTZ 1027	TE681	LK55 KKP	VPL594	LK04 NNC	VW1272	LK12 AHD		
LT28	LTZ 1028	TE682	LK55 KKR	VPL595	LK04 NND	VW1273	LK12 AHO		
LT29	LTZ 1029	TE683	LK55 KKS	VPL596	LK04 NNE	VW1274	LK12 AHU		
LT30	LTZ 1030	TE684	LK55 KKT	VPL597	LK04 NNF	VW1275	LK12 AHZ		
LT31	LTZ 1031	TE685	LK55 KKU	VPL598	LK04 NNG	VW1276	LK12 AJX		
LT32	LTZ 1032	TE686	LK55 KKV	VPL599	LK04 NNH	VW1277	LK12 AKN		
LT33	LTZ 1033	TE687	LK06 FLA	VPL600	LK04 NNJ	VW1278	LK12 AKO		
LT34	LTZ 1034	TE688	LK55 KKY	VPL601	LK04 NNL	VW1279	LK12 ALO		
LT35	LTZ 1035	TE689	LK55 KKZ	VPL602	LK04 NNM	VW1280	LK12 AMO		
LT36	LTZ 1036	TE690	LK55 KLA	VPL603	LK04 NNP	VW1281	LK12 AMV		
LT37	LTZ 1037	TE691	LK55 KLB	VPL629	LK54 FWH	VW1282	LK12 ANF		
LT38	LTZ 1038	TE692	LK55 KLC	VPL630	LK54 FWJ	VW1283	LK12 AOA		
LT39	LTZ 1039	TE914	LK58 CPF	VPL631	LK54 FWL	VW1284	LK12 AOL		
LT40	LTZ 1040	TE920	LK58 KFW	VPL632	LK54 FWM	VW1285	LK12 AOO		
LT95	LTZ 1095	TE921	LK58 KFX	VPL633	LK54 FWN	VW1286	LK12 AOT		
LT96	LTZ 1096	TE922	LK58 KFY	VPL634	LK54 FWO	VW1287	LK12 AOX		
LT97	LTZ 1097	TE923	LK58 KFZ	VPL635	LK54 FWP	VW1288	LK12 AOY		
LT98	LTZ 1098	TP403	LK03 CEJ	VPL636	LK54 FWR	VW1289	LK12 APF		
LT99	LTZ 1099	TP404	LK03 CEN	VPL637	LK54 FWT	VW1290	LK12 APV		
LT100	LTZ 1100	TP405	LK03 CEU	VW1196	LK11 CYO	VW1291	LK12 APZ		
LT101	LTZ 1101	TP407	LK03 CEX	VW1198	LK11 CYS	VW1292	LK12 ARO		
LT102	LTZ 1102	TP408	LK03 CEY	VW1201	LK11 CYV	VW1293	LK12 ARU		
LT103	LTZ 1103	TP409	LK03 CFA	VW1205	LK61 BMU	VW1294	LK12 ARX		
LT104	LTZ 1104	TP410	LK03 CFD	VW1207	LK61 BMY	VW1295	LK12 ARZ		
LT105	LTZ 1105	TP414	LK03 CFJ	VW1208	LK61 BMZ	VW1296	LK12 ASZ		
LT106	LTZ 1106	TP418	LK03 CFP	VW1209	LK61 BNA	VW1297	LK12 ATU		
LT107	LTZ 1107	TP419	LK03 CFU	VW1210	LK61 BNB	VW1298	LK12 ATV		
LT108	LTZ 1108	TP421	LK03 CFX	VW1211	LK61 BNE	VW1299	LK12 AUE		
LT109	LTZ 1109	TP422	LK03 CFY	VW1212	LK61 BNF	VW1300	LK12 AUF		
LT110	LTZ 1110	TP423	LK03 CFZ	VW1213	LK61 BNJ	VW1301	LK12 AUM		
LT111	LTZ 1111	TP432	LK03 GFY	VW1214	LK61 BNL	VW1302	LK12 AUN		
LT112	LTZ 1112	TP434	LK03 GGA	VW1215	LK61 BNN	VW1303	LK12 AUU		
LT113	LTZ 1113	TP444	LK03 GHB	VW1216	LK61 BNO	VW1304	LK12 AUV		
LT114	LTZ 1114	TP449	LK03 GHJ	VW1250	LK12 ACF	VW1305	LK12 AUW		
LT115	LTZ 1115	TP451	LK03 GHU	VW1252	LK12 ACZ	VW1306	LK12 AUY		

London United bus **SP15** leaving **Hounslow Bus Garage** on September 27th, 2014.

HOUNSLOW (AV)
Kingsley Road, Hounslow, London TW3 1PA
Operated by: London United
Location: TQ14347607 [51.471623, -0.354852]
Nearest Tube Station: Hounslow East (200 yards)
Nearest Bus Routes: 81/120/222/281/423/681/
H32 & H98 - Hounslow Bus Station
Bus Routes Serviced: 81/110/111/120/203/222/
696/697/H32/H37/H98 & N9

The site of the garage and bus station was originally occupied by Hounslow Town District Line station which closed on May 2nd, 1909. The garage was opened by the London General Omnibus Company in 1913 and re-roofed in the 1930s. It was substantially rebuilt in the 1950s with the bus station also being constructed alongside at the same time.

London United buses queuing to enter **Hounslow Bus Garage** on September 27th, 2014 with **ADE37** at the rear.

The side entrance to **Hounslow Bus Garage** off Kingsley Road, viewed on September 27th, 2014 when it was in use as additional parking space for London United buses **TA235** and **OC1**.

VEHICLE ALLOCATION

ADE1	YX12 FNG	ADE32	YX12 GHU	DLE22	SN60 ECF	SP8	YN56 FBA	SP171	YT10 XBU
ADE2	YX12 FNH	ADE24	YX62 AEW	DLE23	SN60 ECJ	SP9	YN56 FBB	SP172	YT10 XBV
ADE3	YX12 FNJ	ADE25	YX62 AGU	DLE24	SN60 ECT	SP11	YN56 FBU	SP173	YT10 XBW
ADE4	YX12 FNK	ADE33	YX62 AHE	DLE25	SN60 ECV	SP12	YN56 FBV	SP174	YT10 XBX
ADE5	YX12 FNL	ADE34	YX62 AOE	MCL1	BD11 LWN	SP13	YN56 FBX	SP175	YT10 XBY
ADE6	YX12 FNM	ADE35	YX62 ARZ	MCL2	BD11 LWO	SP14	YN56 FBY	SP176	YT10 XBZ
ADE7	YX12 FNN	ADE36	YX62 BXF	MCL3	BD11 LWP	SP15	YN56 FBZ	SP177	YT10 XCA
ADE8	YX12 FNO	ADE37	YX62 BXR	MCL4	BD11 LWR	SP23	YN08 DHJ	SP178	YT10 XCB
ADE9	YX12 FNP	ADE38	YX62 BXU	MCL5	BD11 LWS	SP24	YN08 DHK	SP179	YT10 XCC
ADE10	YX12 FNR	ADE39	YX62 BXY	MCL6	BD11 LWT	SP25	YN08 DHL	SP180	YT10 XCD
ADE11	YX12 FNS	ADE40	YX62 BXZ	MCL7	BD11 LWU	SP27	YN08 DHO	SP181	YT10 XCE
ADE12	YX12 FNT	ADE41	YX62 BYG	OT1	YJ11 EHG	SP41	YT09 BKA	SP182	YT10 XCF
ADE13	YX12 FNU	ADE42	YX62 BYJ	OT2	YJ11 EHH	SP42	YT09 BMO	SP183	YT10 XCG
ADE14	YX12 FNV	ADE43	YX62 BYK	OT3	YJ11 EHK	SP43	YT09 BMU	SP184	YT10 XCH
ADE15	YX12 FNW	ADE44	YX62 BZE	OT4	YJ11 EHL	SP44	YT09 BMY	SP185	YT10 XCJ
ADE16	YX12 FNY	ADE45	YX62 BZS	OT5	YJ11 EHM	SP45	YT09 BMZ	SP186	YT10 XCK
ADE17	YX12 FNZ	DLE1	SN60 EAX	OT6	YJ11 EHN	SP46	YT09 BNA	SP187	YT10 XCL
ADE18	YX12 FOA	DLE2	SN60 EAY	OT7	YJ11 EHO	SP47	YT09 BNB	SP188	YT10 XCM
ADE19	YX12 FOC	DLE3	SN60 EBA	OT8	YJ11 EHP	SP48	YT09 BND	SP189	YT10 XCN
ADE20	YX12 FOD	DLE4	SN60 EBC	OT9	YJ11 EHR	SP49	YT09 BNE	SP190	YT10 XCO
ADE21	YX12 FOF	DLE5	SN60 EBD	OT10	YJ11 EHS	SP50	YT09 BNF	SP108	YT59 DYY
ADE22	YX12 FOH	DLE6	SN60 EBF	OT11	YJ11 EHT	SP51	YT09 BNJ	TA230	LG02 FAF
ADE23	YX12 FOJ	DLE7	SN60 EBG	OT12	YJ11 EHU	SP136	YP59 ODS	TA234	LG02 FAO
ADE26	YX12 FON	DLE8	SN60 EBJ	OT13	YJ11 EHV	SP165	YT10 UWA	TA235	LG02 FAU
ADE27	YX12 FOP	DLE9	SN60 EBK	OT14	YJ11 EHW	SP166	YT10 UWB	TA242	LG02 FBJ
ADE28	YX12 GHJ	DLE11	SN60 EBM	OT15	YJ11 EHX	SP167	YT10 UWD	TA246	LG02 FBO
ADE29	YX12 GHK	DLE19	SN60 ECC	OT16	YJ11 EHZ	SP168	YT10 UWF	TA281	LG02 FDY
ADE30	YX12 GHN	DLE20	SN60 ECD	SP6	YN56 FCG	SP169	YT10 UWG		
ADE31	YX12 GHO	DLE21	SN60 ECE	SP7	YN56 FCJ	SP170	YT10 UWH		

A view of the north entrance to **Hounslow Heath Bus Garage** on September 27th, 2014.

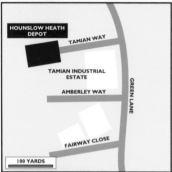

HOUNSLOW HEATH (HH)
Tamian Way, Hounslow, Middlesex TW4 6BL
Operated by: London United
Location: TQ11317505 [51.463274, -0.398773]
Nearest Tube Station: Hounslow West (1.5 miles)
Nearest Bus Routes: 117 & 635 - Green Lane (Stop R)
Bus Routes Serviced: 116/216/285/423/482/635/698/H22 & H91

London United bus **DPS680** in the yard at **Hounslow Heath Bus Garage** on September 27th, 2014

London United buses, including **TLA7, DE3, SP205 & TLA1**, lined up in the yard at **Hounslow Heath Bus Garage** on September 27th, 2014

VEHICLE ALLOCATION

DE1	YX58 DVA	DE18	YX58 DVW	DPS674	LG02 FHD	DPS716	SN55 HKX	SP193	YR10 FFY
DE2	YX58 DVB	DE19	YX58 DUV	DPS675	LG02 FHE	DPS717	SN55 HKY	SP194	YR10 FFZ
DE3	YX58 DVC	DE20	YX58 DUY	DPS677	LG02 FHH	DPS718	SN55 HSD	SP195	YR10 FGA
DE4	YX58 DVF	DE21	YX58 DWK	DPS678	LG02 FHJ	SP1	YN56 FCA	SP196	YR10 FGC
DE5	YX58 DVG	DE22	YX09 HJJ	DPS679	LG02 FHK	SP2	YN56 FCC	SP197	YR10 FGD
DE6	YX58 DVH	DLE10	SN60 EBL	DPS680	LG02 FHL	SP3	YN56 FCD	SP198	YR10 FGE
DE7	YX58 DVJ	DLE12	SN60 EBO	DPS682	SN03 LDZ	SP4	YN56 FCE	SP199	YR10 FGF
DE8	YX58 DVK	DLE13	SN60 EBP	DPS694	SN03 LFK	SP5	YN56 FCF	SP200	YR10 FGG
DE9	YX58 DVL	DLE14	SN60 EBU	DPS707	SN55 HKK	SP16	YN08 DEU	SP201	YR10 FGJ
DE10	YX58 DVM	DLE15	SN60 EBV	DPS708	SN55 HKL	SP17	YN08 DHA	SP202	YR10 FGK
DE11	YX58 DVN	DLE16	SN60 EBX	DPS709	SN55 HKM	SP18	YN08 DHC	SP203	YR10 FGM
DE12	YX58 DVO	DLE17	SN60 EBZ	DPS710	SN55 HKO	SP19	YN08 DHD	SP204	YR10 FGN
DE13	YX58 DVP	DLE18	SN60 ECA	DPS711	SN55 HKP	SP20	YN08 DHE	SP205	YR10 FGO
DE14	YX58 DVR	DPS587	SN51 TBO	DPS712	SN55 HKT	SP21	YN08 DHF	SP206	YR10 FGP
DE15	YX58 DVT	DPS588	SN51 TCJ	DPS713	SN55 HKU	SP22	YN08 DHG		
DE16	YX58 DVU	DPS590	SN51 TDZ	DPS714	SN55 HKV	SP191	YR10 FFW		
DE17	YX58 DVV	DPS673	LG02 FHC	DPS715	SN55 HKW	SP192	YR10 FFX		

A general view of **Kings Cross Bus Garage** on September 17th, 2013. The depot opened on July 10th, 2010 and the office and entrance can be seen at the far end of the road.

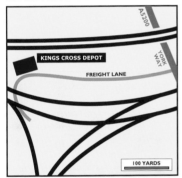

KINGS CROSS (KC)
1 Freight Lane, London N1 0FF
Operated by: Metroline
Location: TQ29928409 [51.540767, -0.127971]
Nearest Station: King's Cross (0.8 miles)
Nearest Bus Routes: 390 - York Way Railway Bridge (Stop A)
Bus Routes Serviced: 46/214 & 274

The entrance and office at **Kings Cross Bus Garage**, viewed on September 6th, 2014.

A closer view of the wash plant at **Kings Cross Bus Garage** on September 6th, 2014 with Metroline bus **DE1163** alongside.

VEHICLE ALLOCATION

DE999	LK09 EOA	DE1162	LK11 CWU	DE1321	LK12 AWZ	DE1333	LK12 AYN	DLD700	LK55 KLS
DE1151	LK10 BZU	DE1163	LK11 CWV	DE1322	LK12 AXA	DE1334	LK12 AYP	DLD701	LK55 KLU
DE1152	LK11 CWF	DE1164	LK11 CWW	DE1323	LK12 AXG	DE1335	LK12 AYZ	DLD702	LK55 KLV
DE1153	LK11 CWG	DE1165	LK11 CWX	DE1324	LK12 AXH	DE1366	LK12 AZA	DLD703	LK55 KLX
DE1154	LK11 CWJ	DE1166	LK11 CWY	DE1325	LK12 AXP	DLD207	LN51 KXO	DLD704	LK55 KLZ
DE1155	LK11 CWL	DE1167	LK11 CWZ	DE1326	LK12 AXR	DLD693	LK55 KLE	DLD705	LK55 KMA
DE1156	LK11 CWM	DE1168	LK11 CXA	DE1327	LK12 AXS	DLD694	LK55 KLF	DLD706	LK55 KME
DE1157	LK11 CWN	DE1169	LK11 CXB	DE1328	LK12 AXV	DLD695	LK55 KLJ	DLD707	LK55 KMF
DE1158	LK11 CWO	DE1170	LK11 CXC	DE1329	LK12 AXW	DLD696	LK55 KLL	DLD708	LK55 KMG
DE1159	LK11 CWP	DE1318	LK12 AWU	DE1330	LK12 AXZ	DLD697	LK55 KLM	DLD709	LK55 KMJ
DE1160	LK11 CWR	DE1319	LK12 AWX	DE1331	LK12 AYF	DLD698	LK55 KLO	DLD710	LK55 KMM
DE1161	LK11 CWT	DE1320	LK12 AWY	DE1332	LK12 AYG	DLD699	LK55 KLP	DLD711	LK55 KMO

Lee Interchange Bus Garage on September 20th, 2014 with Tower Transit buses **VN37851, VN36142, VN37862 & VN36145** in view. The garage was opened in 2007 to replace Stratford, Waterden Road which was removed to make way for the development of the Olympic Park.

LEE INTERCHANGE (LI)
151 Ruckholt Road, Leyton, London E10 5PB
Operated by: Tower Transit
Location: TQ37718596 [51.555692, -0.014951]
Nearest Tube Station: Leyton (0.6 miles)
Nearest Bus Routes: 308/N26 & W15
Bus Routes Serviced: 25/26/30/58/236/308/339/425/N26/N550/N551/RV1/W14 & W15

A general view of **Lee Interchange Bus Garage**, looking south from the railway bridge on Ruckholt Road on September 17th, 2013.

Tower Transit bus **DMV44253** at **Lee Interchange Bus Garage** viewed from the entrance in Temple Mills Lane on September 20th, 2014.

VEHICLE ALLOCATION

DM41444 LN51 DUA	DML44292 YX61 FYP	DN33630 SN11 BOF	VN36104 BJ11 DTF	VN36149 BJ11 EAO		
DM41445 LN51 DUH	DMV44221 YX12 AYZ	DN33631 SN11 BOH	VN36105 BJ11 DSV	VN36150 BJ11 EBD		
DM44167 YX60 DXL	DMV44222 YX12 AZA	DN33632 SN11 BOJ	VN36106 BJ11 DTV	VN36151 BJ11 EBC		
DM44168 YX60 DXM	DMV44223 YX12 AKK	DN33633 SN11 BOU	VN36107 BJ11 DTY	VN36152 BJ11 EAE		
DM44169 YX60 DXO	DMV44224 YX12 AKN	DN33634 SN11 BOV	VN36108 BJ11 DTO	VN36153 BJ11 DVX		
DM44170 YX60 DXP	DMV44225 YX12 AEW	DN33635 SN11 BPE	VN36109 BJ11 DUV	VN36154 BJ11 EAA		
DM44260 YX61 FZC	DMV44226 YX12 AEY	DN33636 SN11 BPF	VN36110 BJ11 DUA	VN36155 BJ11 DZZ		
DM44261 YX61 FZD	DMV44227 YX12 AEO	DN33637 SN11 BPK	VN36111 BJ11 DVH	VN36156 BJ11 DZY		
DM44262 YX61 FZE	DMV44228 YX12 AEP	DN33638 SN11 BPO	VN36112 BJ11 DVF	VN36157 BJ11 EAC		
DM44263 YX61 FZF	DMV44229 YX12 AUA	DN33639 SN11 BPU	VN36113 BJ11 DVP	VN36158 BJ11 EAG		
DM44264 YX61 FZG	DMV44230 YX12 AGY	DN33640 SN11 BPV	VN36114 BJ11 DVM	VN36159 BJ11 EAP		
DM44265 YX61 FZH	DMV44231 YX12 AXV	DN33641 SN11 BPX	VN36115 BJ11 DVL	VN36160 BJ11 EAY		
DM44266 YX61 FZJ	DMV44232 YX12 AFZ	DN33642 SN11 BPY	VN36116 BJ11 DUU	VN36161 BJ11 EBA		
DM44267 YX61 FZK	DMV44233 YX12 AZN	DN33643 SN11 BPZ	VN36117 BJ11 DVK	VN36162 BJ11 EBK		
DM44268 YX61 FZL	DMV44234 YX12 AJY	DN33644 SN11 BRF	VN36118 BJ11 DVC	VN36163 BJ11 EBM		
DM44269 YX61 FZM	DMV44235 YX12 AGZ	DN33645 SN11 BRV	VN36119 BJ11 DSY	VN36164 BJ11 EBO		
DM44270 YX61 FZN	DMV44236 YX12 AON	DN33646 SN11 BRZ	VN36120 BJ11 DRZ	VN36165 BJ11 EBN		
DMC42516 LK03 NKJ	DMV44237 YX12 AKP	DN33647 SN11 BSO	VN36121 BJ11 DSO	VN37842 BV10 WVM		
DMC42517 LK03 NKL	DMV44251 YX12 AKU	DN33648 SN11 BSU	VN36122 BJ11 DTK	VN37844 BV10 WWT		
DMC42518 LK03 NKM	DMV44252 YX12 AKV	DN33649 SN11 BSV	VN36123 BJ11 DTX	VN37847 BV10 WWE		
DML44074 YX58 HVD	DMV44253 YX12 AKY	DN33650 SN11 BSX	VN36124 BJ11 DTU	VN37849 BV10 WWG		
DML44075 YX58 HVE	DMV44254 YX12 AKZ	DN33651 SN11 BSY	VN36125 BJ11 DVG	VN37850 BV10 WWH		
DML44163 YX10 BGV	DMV44255 YX12 AHJ	DN33652 SN11 BSZ	VN36126 BJ11 DUY	VN37851 BV10 WWJ		
DML44164 YX10 BGY	DMV44256 YX12 AHK	DN33653 SN11 BTE	VN36127 BJ11 DVA	VN37852 BV10 WWK		
DML44171 YX11 AFK	DMV44257 YX12 ABF	DN33654 SN11 BTO	VN36128 BJ11 DVB	VN37853 BV10 WWL		
DML44172 YX11 AFN	DMV44258 YX12 ABK	DN33655 SN11 BTU	VN36129 BJ11 DVO	VN37854 BV10 WWM		
DML44173 YX11 AFO	DMV44259 YX12 AWU	DN33789 SN13 CGY	VN36130 BJ11 DVN	VN37855 BV10 WWN		
DML44174 YX11 AFU	DN33612 SN11 BMU	DN33790 SN13 CGZ	VN36131 BJ11 DVR	VN37859 BV10 WWS		
DML44175 YX11 AFV	DN33613 SN11 BMV	DN33791 SN13 CHC	VN36132 BJ11 DSX	VN37860 BV10 WWB		
DML44176 YX11 AFY	DN33614 SN11 BMY	DN33792 SN13 CHD	VN36133 BJ11 DTN	VN37861 BV10 WWU		
DML44177 YX11 AFZ	DN33615 SN11 BMZ	DN33793 SN13 CHF	VN36134 BJ11 DTZ	VN37862 BV10 WWX		
DML44178 YX11 AGO	DN33616 SN11 BNA	DN33794 SN13 CHG	VN36135 BJ11 DUH	VN37863 BV10 WVY		
DML44279 YX61 FYB	DN33617 SN11 BNB	DN33795 SN13 CHH	VN36136 BJ11 DVV	VN37864 BV10 WVZ		
DML44280 YX61 FYC	DN33618 SN11 BND	DN33796 SN13 CHJ	VN36137 BJ11 DVW	VN37943 BK10 MFZ		
DML44281 YX61 FYD	DN33619 SN11 BNE	DN33797 SN13 CHK	VN36138 BJ11 DVT	WSH62991 LK60 HPE		
DML44282 YX61 FYE	DN33620 SN11 BNF	DN33798 SN13 CHL	VN36139 BJ11 DVU	WSH62992 LK60 HPF		
DML44283 YX61 FYF	DN33621 SN11 BNJ	DP42600 LG02 FFP	VN36140 BJ11 DZX	WSH62993 LK60 HPJ		
DML44284 YX61 FYG	DN33622 SN11 BNK	DP42601 LG02 FFR	VN36141 BJ11 EBP	WSH62994 LK60 HPL		
DML44285 YX61 FYH	DN33623 SN11 BNL	DP42602 LG02 FGO	VN36142 BJ11 EAM	WSH62995 LK60 HPN		
DML44286 YX61 FYJ	DN33624 SN11 BNO	DP42603 KP02 PUF	VN36143 BJ11 EAF	WSH62996 LJ13 JWP		
DML44287 YX61 FYK	DN33625 SN11 BNU	DP42604 KP02 PVO	VN36144 BJ11 EAX	WSH62997 LF63 XZU		
DML44288 YX61 FYL	DN33626 SN11 BNV	TNL33036 LK51 UYE	VN36145 BJ11 EBG	WSH62998 LJ13 JZO		
DML44289 YX61 FYM	DN33627 SN11 BNX	VN36101 BJ11 DSE	VN36146 BJ11 EBL			
DML44290 YX61 FYN	DN33628 SN11 BNY	VN36102 BJ11 DSZ	VN36147 BJ11 EAK			
DML44291 YX61 FYO	DN33629 SN11 BNZ	VN36103 BJ11 DSU	VN36148 BJ11 EAW			

Stagecoach London buses 15153 & 15159 parked in the entrance to **Leyton Bus Garage** on September 20th, 2014.

LEYTON (T)
High Road Leyton, London E10 6AD
Operated by: Stagecoach London
Location: TQ38128797 [51.573806, -0.008546]
Nearest Station: Leyton Midland Road (0.3 miles)
Nearest Bus Routes: 20/48/55/56/69/97/230/257/357/W15/W16 & W19
Bus Routes Serviced: 48/55/56/69 (Night Service only)/97/179/215/275 & N55

The depot was opened by the London General Omnibus Company in 1912 to replace one that had been acquired from the London Metropolitan. It was badly damaged by bombing during WWII and not substantially rebuilt until 1955.

VEHICLE ALLOCATION

10113	LX12 DCZ	15128	LX59 CLZ	15154	LX59 CPF	17753	LX03 BTV	17855	LX03 NEU
10114	LX12 DDA	15129	LX59 CME	15155	LX59 CPK	17754	LX03 BTY	17871	LX03 NFT
10115	LX12 DDE	15130	LX59 CMF	15156	LX59 CPN	17781	LX03 BVT	17873	LX03 NFV
10116	LX12 DDF	15131	LX59 CMK	15157	LX59 CPO	17782	LX03 BVU	17875	LX03 NFZ
10117	LX12 DDJ	15132	LX59 CMO	15158	LX59 CPU	17783	LX03 BVV	17876	LX03 NGE
10118	LX12 DDK	15133	LX59 CMU	15159	LX59 CPV	17784	LX03 BVW	17877	LX03 NGF
10119	LX12 DDL	15134	LX59 CMV	15160	LX59 CPY	17801	LX03 BWU	17879	LX03 NGJ
10120	LX12 DDN	15135	LX59 CMY	15161	LX59 CPZ	17803	LX03 BWW	17892	LX03 ORC
10121	LX12 DDO	15136	LX59 CMZ	15162	LX59 CRF	17804	LX03 BWY	17905	LX03 ORY
10122	LX12 DDU	15137	LX59 CNA	15163	LX59 CRJ	17805	LX03 BWZ	17906	LX03 ORZ
10123	LX12 DDV	15138	LX59 CNC	15164	LX59 CRK	17806	LX03 BXA	17907	LX03 OSA
10172	SN63 JVX	15139	LX59 CNE	15165	LX59 CRU	17807	LX03 BXB	17908	LX03 OSB
10173	SN63 JVY	15140	LX59 CNF	15166	LX59 CRV	17808	LX03 BXC	18207	LX04 FWT
10174	SN63 JVZ	15141	LX59 CNJ	15167	LX59 CRZ	17809	LX03 BXD	18208	LX04 FWU
10175	SN63 JWA	15142	LX59 CNK	15168	LX59 CSF	17810	LX03 BXE	18209	LX04 FWV
10176	SN63 JWC	15143	LX59 CNN	15169	LX59 CSO	17811	LX03 BXF	18210	LX04 FWW
10177	SN63 JWD	15144	LX59 CNO	15170	LX10 AUC	17812	LX03 BXG	18211	LX04 FWY
10178	SN63 JWE	15145	LX59 CNU	15171	LX10 AUE	17813	LX03 BXH	18212	LX04 FWZ
10179	SN63 JWF	15146	LX59 CNV	15172	LX10 AUF	17814	LX03 BXJ	18218	LX04 FXF
10180	SN63 JWG	15147	LX59 CNY	15173	LX10 AUH	17819	LX03 BXP	18219	LX04 FXG
10181	SN63 JWJ	15148	LX59 CNZ	15174	LX10 AUJ	17826	LX03 BXZ	19000	LX55 HGC
10182	SN63 JWK	15149	LX59 COA	17745	LY52 ZFD	17827	LX03 BYA		
10183	SN63 JWL	15150	LX59 COH	17746	LY52 ZFE	17828	LX03 BYB		
15125	LX59 CLU	15151	LX59 COJ	17750	LX03 BTE	17851	LX03 BZE		
15126	LX59 CLV	15152	LX59 COU	17751	LX03 BTF	17852	LX03 BZF		
15127	LX59 CLY	15153	LX59 CPE	17752	LX03 BTU	17853	LX03 BZG		

Mandela Way Bus Garage on September 12th, 2014.

MANDELA WAY (MW)
Unit 2, 5 Mandela Way, London SE1 5SS
Operated by: Go-Ahead London
Location: TQ33587871 [51.491317, -0.077672]
Nearest Station: Elephant & Castle (1.3 miles)
Nearest Bus Routes: 21/53/168/172/453 & N21 -
Dunton Road (Stop EC)
Bus Routes Serviced: 1/100/453/507/521 & N1

East Thames Buses vacated Ash Grove (See Page 7) on October 13th, 2005 and moved to a brand new facility here. In 2009 the company was sold to London General (Go-Ahead London).

VEHICLE ALLOCATION

8301	BX54 DKA	E167	SN61 BGV	E191	SN61 BJO	LT286	LTZ 1286	LT310	LTZ 1310
8302	BX54 DKD	E168	SN61 BGX	E192	SN61 BJU	LT287	LTZ 1287	LT311	LTZ 1311
8303	BX54 DKE	E169	SN61 BGY	E193	SN61 BJV	LT288	LTZ 1288	PVL233	Y733 TGH
8304	BX54 DKF	E170	SN61 BGZ	E194	SN61 BJX	LT289	LTZ 1289	VWL27	LF52 THV
8305	BX54 DKJ	E171	SN61 BHA	E195	SN61 BJY	LT290	LTZ 1290	VWL28	LF52 THX
8306	BX54 DKK	E172	SN61 BHD	E196	SN61 BJZ	LT291	LTZ 1291	VWL29	LF52 THZ
8307	BX54 DKL	E173	SN61 BGE	E197	SN61 BKA	LT292	LTZ 1292	VWL30	LF52 TJO
8308	BX54 DKO	E174	SN61 BHE	E198	SN61 BKD	LT293	LTZ 1293	VWL31	LF52 TJU
8309	BX54 DKU	E175	SN61 BHF	E199	SN61 BKE	LT294	LTZ 1294	VWL32	BX04 AZW
8310	BX54 DKV	E176	SN61 BHJ	E200	SN61 BKF	LT295	LTZ 1295	VWL33	BX04 AZV
8318	BX54 DLU	E177	SN61 BHK	E201	SN61 BKG	LT296	LTZ 1296	VWL34	BX04 AZU
8321	YX10 EBA	E178	SN61 BHL	LT273	LTZ 1273	LT297	LTZ 1297	VWL35	BX04 AZZ
8322	YX10 EBC	E179	SN61 BHO	LT274	LTZ 1274	LT298	LTZ 1298	VWL36	BX04 BAA
8323	YX10 EBD	E180	SN61 BHP	LT275	LTZ 1275	LT299	LTZ 1299	VWL37	BX04 BAU
8324	YX10 EBF	E181	SN61 BHU	LT276	LTZ 1276	LT300	LTZ 1300	VWL38	BX04 BAV
8325	YX10 EBG	E182	SN61 BHV	LT277	LTZ 1277	LT301	LTZ 1301	VWL39	BX04 BBE
8326	YX10 EBJ	E183	SN61 BHW	LT278	LTZ 1278	LT302	LTZ 1302	VWL40	BX04 BBF
8327	YX10 EBK	E184	SN61 BHX	LT279	LTZ 1279	LT303	LTZ 1303	VWL41	BX04 BBJ
8328	YX10 EBL	E185	SN61 BHY	LT280	LTZ 1280	LT304	LTZ 1304	VWL42	BX04 BKL
8329	YX10 EBM	E186	SN61 BHZ	LT281	LTZ 1281	LT305	LTZ 1305	VWL43	BX04 BKK
E163	SN61 BGF	E187	SN61 BJE	LT282	LTZ 1282	LT306	LTZ 1306	VWL44	BX04 BKJ
E164	SN61 BGK	E188	SN61 BJF	LT283	LTZ 1283	LT307	LTZ 1307		
E165	SN61 BGO	E189	SN61 BJJ	LT284	LTZ 1284	LT308	LTZ 1308		
E166	SN61 BGU	E190	SN61 BJK	LT285	LTZ 1285	LT309	LTZ 1309		

Go-Ahead London bus **PVL400** exiting from **Merton Bus Garage** on September 6th, 2014.

MERTON (AL)
High Street, London SW19 1DN
Operated by: Go-Ahead London
Location: TQ26547030 [51.417402, -0.181738]
Nearest Tube Station: Colliers Wood (0.3 miles)
Nearest Bus Routes: 57/131/152/200/219 & N155 -
Merton Abbey Savacentre (Stop E)
Bus Routes Serviced: 22/44/77/118/155/163/164/
200/219/270/280/655 & N155

Merton Garage opened in 1913 and was the largest depot operated by the London General Omnibus Company. It was modernized in 1960 and further modernization in 1991 included the installation of a new roof and a repositioning of some of the ancillary buildings within the depot to improve the parking areas.

Go-Ahead London bus **DW2** parked inside **Merton Bus Garage** on September 19th, 2013.

London United bus **VLE111** passing **Merton Bus Garage** on September 6th, 2014 with a service to Tooting Broadway.

VEHICLE ALLOCATION

E57	LX07 BYH	E143	SN60 BZR	PVL390	LX54 HAA	SE3	LX07 BXK	SOE19	LX09 AZB
E68	LX57 CJO	E144	SN60 BZS	PVL391	LX54 HAE	SE4	LX07 BXL	SOE20	LX09 AZC
E69	LX57 CJU	E145	SN60 BZT	PVL392	LX54 HAO	SE5	LX07 BXM	SOE21	LX09 AZD
E70	LX57 CJV	E146	SN60 BZU	PVL393	LX54 HAU	SE6	LX07 BXN	SOE22	LX09 AZF
E71	LX57 CJY	E147	SN60 BZV	PVL394	LX54 HBA	SE7	LX07 BXO	SOE23	LX09 AZG
E72	LX57 CJZ	E148	SN60 BZW	PVL395	LX54 HBB	SE8	LX07 BXP	SOE24	LX09 AZJ
E73	LX57 CKA	E149	SN60 BZX	PVL396	LX54 GZG	SE9	LX07 BXR	SOE25	LX09 AZL
E74	LX57 CKC	E150	SN60 BZY	PVL397	LX54 GZH	SE10	LX07 BXS	SOE26	LX09 AZN
E75	LX57 CKD	E277	SN13 CJF	PVL398	LX54 GZK	SE11	LX07 BXU	SOE27	LX09 AZO
E76	LX57 CKE	E278	SN13 CJJ	PVL399	LX54 GZL	SE12	LX07 BXV	SOE28	LX09 AZP
E77	LX57 CKF	E279	SN13 CJO	PVL400	LX54 GZM	SE13	LX07 BXW	WDL1	LX58 CWG
E78	LX57 CKG	E280	SN13 CJU	PVL401	LX54 GZN	SE14	LX07 BXY	WS10	LJ13 GJU
E79	LX57 CKJ	PVL152	X552 EGK	PVL402	LX54 GZO	SE15	LX07 BXZ	WS11	LJ13 GJV
E80	LX57 CKK	PVL371	PJ53 NKG	PVL403	LX54 GZP	SE16	LX07 BYA	WS12	LJ13 GJX
E81	LX57 CKL	PVL372	PJ53 NKH	PVL404	LX54 GZR	SOE1	LX09 AYF	WS13	LJ13 GJY
E82	LX57 CKN	PVL373	PJ53 NKK	PVL405	LX54 GZT	SOE2	LX09 AYG	WS14	LJ13 GJZ
E83	LX57 CKO	PVL374	PJ53 NKL	PVL406	LX54 GYV	SOE3	LX09 AYH	WS15	LJ13 GKA
E84	LX57 CKP	PVL375	PJ53 NKM	PVL407	LX54 GYW	SOE4	LX09 AYJ	WS16	LJ13 GKC
E85	LX57 CKU	PVL376	PJ53 NKN	PVL408	LX54 GYY	SOE5	LX09 AYK	WS17	LJ13 GKD
E86	LX57 CKV	PVL377	PJ53 NKO	PVL409	LX54 GYZ	SOE6	LX09 AYL	WS18	LJ13 GKE
E87	LX57 CKY	PVL378	PJ53 NKP	PVL410	LX54 GZB	SOE7	LX09 AYM	WS19	LJ13 GKF
E88	LX57 CLF	PVL379	PJ53 NKR	PVL411	LX54 GZC	SOE8	LX09 AYN	WS20	LJ13 GKG
E89	LX57 CLJ	PVL380	PJ53 NKT	PVL412	LX54 GZD	SOE9	LX09 AYO	WVL86	LF52 ZNU
E90	LX57 CLN	PVL381	PJ53 NKU	PVL413	LX54 GZE	SOE10	LX09 AYP	WVL101	LF52 ZNO
E91	LX57 CLO	PVL382	PJ53 NKW	PVL414	LX54 GZF	SOE11	LX09 AYS	WVL102	LF52 ZLZ
E92	LX57 CLV	PVL383	PJ53 NKX	PVL415	LX54 GZU	SOE12	LX09 AYT	WVL152	LX53 BEY
E93	LX57 CLY	PVL384	PJ53 NKZ	PVL416	LX54 GZV	SOE13	LX09 AYU	WVL206	LX05 EZC
E138	SN60 BZK	PVL385	PJ53 NLA	PVL417	LX54 GZW	SOE14	LX09 AYV	WVL207	LX05 EZD
E139	SN60 BZL	PVL386	PJ53 NLC	PVL418	LX54 GZY	SOE15	LX09 AYW	WVL208	LX05 EZE
E140	SN60 BZM	PVL387	PJ53 NLD	PVL419	LX54 GZZ	SOE16	LX09 AYY	WVL209	LX05 EZF
E141	SN60 BZO	PVL388	PJ53 NLE	SE1	LX07 BXH	SOE17	LX09 AYZ	WVL210	LX05 EZG
E142	SN60 BZP	PVL389	PJ53 NLF	SE2	LX07 BXJ	SOE18	LX09 AZA	WVL211	LX05 EZH

Go-Ahead London buses **E250**, **WVL276** & **SE200** parked outside of the exit from the main building at **New Cross Bus Garage** on August 19th, 2014.

NEW CROSS (NX)
208 New Cross Road, London SE14 5PL
Operated by: Go-Ahead London
Location: TQ35977671 [51.473044, -0.044027]
Nearest Station: New Cross Gate (300 yards)
Nearest Bus Routes: 36/136/171/177/343/436/ N89/N136,N171/N343 & P13 - New Cross Bus Garage (Stop K)
Bus Routes Serviced: 21/36/108/129/171/225/ 286/321/436/N21 & N171

New Cross was opened as a tram depot by London County Council on May 15th, 1905; closed to trams by London Transport on July 6th, 1952 and subsequently utilized as an omnibus depot.

Go-Ahead London buses including **SE207**, **PVL248**, **WVL410** and Metrobus **752** line up inside **New Cross Bus Garage** on August 19th, 2014.

Go-Ahead London bus **WVL290** climbing up the slope from New Cross Road into **New Cross Bus Garage** on August 19th, 2014.

VEHICLE ALLOCATION

DP192	EJ52 WXF	E249	YX12 FPE	EH11	SN61 DAU	PVL355	PL03 AGZ	WVL294	LX59 CZM
DWL21	FJ54 ZDV	E250	YX12 FPE	EH12	SN61 DBO	SE198	YY14 WDT	WVL295	LX59 CZN
DWL22	FJ54 ZDW	E251	YX12 FPG	EH13	SN61 DBU	SE199	YY14 WDU	WVL296	LX59 CZO
DWL26	FJ54 ZFA	E252	YX12 FPJ	EH14	SN61 DBV	SE200	YY14 WDV	WVL297	LX59 CZP
DWL27	FJ54 ZTV	E253	YX12 FPK	EH15	SN61 DBX	SE201	YY14 WDW	WVL298	LX59 CZR
DWL31	FJ54 ZTZ	E254	YX12 FPL	EH16	SN61 DBY	SE202	YY14 WDX	WVL299	LX59 CZS
DWL32	FJ54 ZUA	E255	YX12 FPN	EH17	SN61 DBZ	SE203	YY14 WDZ	WVL300	LX59 CZT
DWL34	FJ54 ZUD	E256	YX12 FPO	EH18	SN61 DCE	SE204	YY14 WEA	WVL301	LX59 CZU
DWL35	FJ54 ZVA	E257	YX12 FPP	EH19	SN61 DCO	SE205	YY14 WEC	WVL302	LX59 CZV
DWL36	FJ54 ZVB	E258	YX12 FPT	EH20	SN61 DCU	SE206	YY14 WEF	WVL386	LX11 CVL
E94	LX08 EBP	E259	YX12 FPU	LDP210	SN51 UAZ	SE207	YY14 WEH	WVL387	LX11 CVM
E95	LX08 EBU	E260	YX12 FPV	LDP273	LX06 EYT	SE208	YY14 WEJ	WVL388	LX11 CVN
E96	LX08 EBV	E261	SN62 DDE	LDP274	LX06 EYU	SE209	YY14 WEK	WVL389	LX11 CVO
E97	LX08 EBZ	E262	SN62 DDO	LDP275	LX06 EYV	SE210	YY14 WEO	WVL390	LX11 CVP
E98	LX08 ECA	E263	SN62 DDX	LDP276	LX06 EYW	SE211	YY14 WEP	WVL391	LX11 CVR
E99	LX08 ECC	E264	SN62 DFL	LDP277	LX06 FBD	SE212	YY14 WEU	WVL392	LX11 CVS
E208	SN61 DCZ	E265	SN62 DFX	LDP278	LX06 FBE	WVL75	LF52 ZPE	WVL393	LX11 CVT
E209	SN61 DDA	E266	SN62 DGF	LDP279	LX06 FAA	WVL77	LF52 ZPH	WVL394	LX11 CVU
E210	SN61 DDE	E267	SN62 DGU	LDP280	LX06 FAF	WVL97	LF52 ZNK	WVL395	LX11 CVV
E211	SN61 DDF	E268	SN62 DHA	PVL159	X559 EGK	WVL98	LF52 ZNL	WVL396	LX11 CVW
E212	SN61 DDJ	E269	SN62 DHX	PVL170	X707 EGK	WVL274	LX59 CYL	WVL397	LX11 CVY
E213	SN61 DDK	E270	SN62 DHZ	PVL319	PJ52 LVW	WVL275	LX59 CYO	WVL398	LX11 CVZ
E214	SN61 DDL	E271	SN62 DJO	PVL320	PJ52 LVX	WVL276	LX59 CYP	WVL399	LX11 CWA
E215	SN61 DDO	E272	SN62 DKJ	PVL321	PJ52 LVY	WVL277	LX59 CYS	WVL400	LX11 CWC
E216	SN61 DDU	E273	SN62 DLY	PVL322	PJ52 LVZ	WVL278	LX59 CYT	WVL401	LX11 CWD
E217	SN61 DDV	E274	SN62 DLZ	PVL323	PJ52 LWA	WVL279	LX59 CYU	WVL402	LX11 CWE
E218	SN61 DDX	E275	SN62 DMV	PVL324	PJ52 LWC	WVL280	LX59 CYV	WVL403	LX11 CWG
E219	SN61 DDY	ED1	AE06 HCA	PVL325	PJ52 LWD	WVL281	LX59 CYW	WVL404	LX11 CWJ
E220	SN61DDZ	ED2	AE06 HCC	PVL343	PF52 WPT	WVL282	LX59 CYY	WVL405	LX11 CWK
E221	SN61 DEU	ED3	AE06 HCD	PVL344	PF52 WPU	WVL283	LX59 CYZ	WVL406	LX11 CWL
E222	SN61 DFA	ED4	AE06 HCF	PVL345	PF52 WPV	WVL284	LX59 CZA	WVL407	LX11 CWM
E223	SN61 DFC	ED5	AE06 HCG	PVL346	PF52 WPW	WVL285	LX59 CZB	WVL408	LX11 CWN
E224	SN61 DFD	ED6	AE06 HCH	PVL347	PF52 WPX	WVL286	LX59 CZC	WVL409	LX11 CWO
E225	SN61 DFE	ED7	AE06 HCJ	PVL348	PF52 WPY	WVL287	LX59 CZD	WVL410	LX11 CWP
E226	SN61 DFF	ED8	AE06 HCK	PVL349	PF52 WPZ	WVL288	LX59 CZF	WVL411	LX11 CWR
E227	SN61 DFG	EH6	SN61 BLJ	PVL350	PF52 WRA	WVL289	LX59 CZG	WVL412	LX11 CWT
E228	SN61 DFJ	EH7	SN61 BLK	PVL351	PF52 WRC	WVL290	LX59 CZH		
E246	YX12 FPA	EH8	SN61 BLV	PVL352	PF52 WRD	WVL291	LX59 CZJ		
E247	YX12 FPC	EH9	SN61 DAA	PVL353	PF52 WRE	WVL292	LX59 CZK		
E248	YX12 FPC	EH10	SN61 DAO	PVL354	PF52 WRG	WVL293	LX59 CZL		

Go-Ahead London buses **SEN11, SEN29** & **WVN53** parked outside of the maintenance building at **Northumberland Park Bus Garage** on September 20th, 2014.

NORTHUMBERLAND PARK (NP)
Marsh Lane, Tottenham, London N17 0XB
Operated by: Go-Ahead London
Location: TQ35089080 [51.600213, -0.050748]
Nearest Station: Northumberland Park (400 yards)
Nearest Bus Routes: 192
Bus Routes Serviced: 20/191/231/257/259/299/327/357/389/399/476/491/616/692/699/W4/W10 & W16

The garage was opened in 1991 to accommodate vehicles used on the Walthamstow Citybus operation. Through a subsequent management buyout and then purchase by First Group it operated buses under the First Capital branding until the depot was sold to the Go-Ahead group on March 28th, 2012.

Go-Ahead London buses parked at **Northumberland Park Bus Garage** on September 20th, 2014.

Go-Ahead bus **WVN42** parked in the yard at **Northumberland Park Bus Garage** on September 20th, 2014.

VEHICLE ALLOCATION

142	LT02 ZDR	PVN5	LK03 NHV	WS22	LJ13 GKL	WVL461	LJ61 NUV	WVN26	BG59 FXC
DMN1	LT02 NUK	PVN6	LK03 NHX	WS23	LJ13 GKN	WVL462	LJ61 NUW	WVN27	BG59 FXD
E276	SN13 CJE	SEN1	YX60 FUA	WS24	LJ13 GKO	WVL463	LJ61 NUX	WVN28	BG59 FXE
EN1	SN58 CDY	SEN2	YX60 FUB	WS25	LJ13 GKP	WVL464	LJ61 NUY	WVN29	BG59 FXF
EN2	SN58 CDZ	SEN3	YX60 FUD	WS26	LJ13 GKU	WVL465	LJ61 NVA	WVN30	BG59 FXH
EN3	SN58 CEA	SEN4	YX60 FUE	WS27	LJ13 GKV	WVL466	LJ61 NVB	WVN31	BV10 WVD
EN4	SN58 CEF	SEN5	YX60 FUF	WS28	LJ13 GKX	WVL467	LJ61 NWW	WVN32	BV10 WVE
EN5	SN58 CEJ	SEN6	YX60 FUG	WS29	LJ13 GKY	WVN1	LK59 FEP	WVN33	BV10 WVF
EN6	SN58 CEK	SEN7	YX60 FUH	WS30	LJ13 GKZ	WVN2	LK59 FET	WVN34	BV10 WVG
EN7	SN58 CEO	SEN8	YX60 FUJ	WS31	LJ13 GLF	WVN3	LK59 FEU	WVN35	BV10 WVH
EN8	SN58 CEU	SEN9	YX60 FUM	WS32	LJ13 GLK	WVN4	LK59 FDV	WVN36	BV10 WVJ
EN9	SN58 CEV	SEN10	YX60 FUO	WVL189	LX05 FBC	WVN5	LK59 FDX	WVN37	BV10 WVK
EN10	SN58 CEX	SEN11	YX60 FUP	WVL190	LX05 EZV	WVN6	LK59 FDY	WVN38	BV10 WVL
EN11	SN58 CEY	SEN12	YX60 FUT	WVL191	LX05 EZW	WVN7	LK59 FDZ	WVN39	BV10 WWA
EN12	SN58 CFA	SEN13	YX11 FYS	WVL192	LX05 EZZ	WVN8	LK59 FEF	WVN40	BV10 WWC
EN13	SN58 CFD	SEN14	YX11 FYT	WVL193	LX05 EZK	WVN9	LK59 FEG	WVN41	BV10 WWD
EN14	SN58 CFE	SEN15	YX11 FYU	WVL194	LX05 EZL	WVN10	LK59 FEH	WVN42	BV10 WWF
EN15	SN58 CFF	SEN16	YX11 FYV	WVL195	LX05 EZM	WVN11	LK59 FEO	WVN43	BV10 WWO
EN16	SN58 CFG	SEN17	YX11 FYW	WVL196	LX05 EZN	WVN12	LK59 FDG	WVN44	BV10 WWP
EN17	SN58 CFJ	SEN18	YX11 FYY	WVL197	LX05 EZO	WVN13	LK59 FEJ	WVN45	BV10 WWR
EN18	LK08 FLH	SEN19	YX11 FYZ	WVL198	LX05 EZP	WVN14	LK59 FEM	WVN46	BL61 ACY
EN19	LK08 FLJ	SEN20	YX11 AGU	WVL199	LX05 EZR	WVN15	LK59 FDE	WVN47	BL61 ACX
EN20	LK08 FLL	SEN21	YX61 FYT	WVL200	LX05 EZS	WVN16	LK59 FDF	WVN48	BL61 ADU
EN21	LK08 FLM	SEN22	YX61 FYU	WVL201	LX05 EZT	WVN17	LK59 FDJ	WVN49	BL61 ACZ
EN22	LK08 FLN	SEN23	YX61 FYV	WVL202	LX05 EZU	WVN18	LK59 FDL	WVN50	BL61 ADV
EN23	LK08 FLP	SEN24	YX61 FYW	WVL203	LX05 EYZ	WVN19	LK59 FDM	WVN51	BL61 ADO
EN24	LK08 FLR	SEN25	YX61 FYY	WVL204	LX05 EZA	WVN20	LK59 FDN	WVN52	BL61 ADX
LDP207	SN51 UAW	SEN26	YX61 FYZ	WVL205	LX05 EZB	WVN21	LK59 FDO	WVN53	BL61 ADZ
PVN1	LK03 NHF	SEN27	YX61 FZA	WVL457	LJ61 NUM	WVN22	LK59 FDP		
PVN2	LK03 NHG	SEN28	YX61 FZB	WVL458	LJ61 NUO	WVN23	LK59 FDU		
PVN3	LK03 NHP	SEN29	YX61 FZZ	WVL459	LJ61 NUP	WVN24	BG59 FXA		
PVN4	LK03 NHT	WS21	LJ13 GKK	WVL460	LJ61 NUU	WVN25	BG59 FXB		

Go-Ahead London bus **WVL270** passing **Norwood Bus Garage** on August 19th, 2014.

NORWOOD (N)
Ernest Avenue, West Norwood, London SE27 0HN
Operated by: Arriva London
Location: TQ31957174 [51.429335, -0.103346]
Nearest Station: West Norwood (0.2 miles)
Nearest Bus Routes: 2/196/315/432/468/690/N2/
N68 & X68 - West Norwood, West Norwood Bus
Garage (Stop U)
Bus Routes Serviced: 2/59/133/176/415/417/432/
690/N2/N133 & N137

The garage was originally opened in 1909 by the London General Omnibus Company and totally rebuilt between 1981 and 1984.

VEHICLE ALLOCATION

DLA173	W373 VGJ	T95	LJ59 LYU	VLA5	LJ03 MXV	VLA32	LJ53 BDX	VLA59	LJ04 LFP
DLA186	W386 VGJ	T96	LJ59 LYV	VLA6	LJ03 MXW	VLA33	LJ53 BDY	VLA60	LJ04 LFR
DLA207	W407 VGJ	T97	LJ59 LYW	VLA7	LJ03 MXX	VLA34	LJ53 BDZ	VLA61	LJ04 LFS
DLA210	W438 WGJ	T98	398 CLT	VLA8	LJ03 MXY	VLA35	LJ53 BEO	VLA62	LJ04 LFT
DLA227	X427 FGP	T99	LJ59 LYY	VLA9	LJ03 MXZ	VLA36	LJ53 BBV	VLA63	LJ04 YWS
DLA233	X433 FGP	T100	LJ59 LYZ	VLA10	LJ03 MYA	VLA37	LJ53 BBX	VLA64	LJ04 YWT
DLA235	X435 FGP	T101	LJ59 LZA	VLA11	LJ03 MYB	VLA38	LJ53 BBZ	VLA65	LJ04 YWU
DLA243	X443 FGP	T102	LJ59 LZB	VLA12	LJ03 MYC	VLA39	LJ53 BCF	VLA66	LJ04 YWV
DLA253	X453 FGP	T103	LJ59 LZC	VLA13	LJ03 MYD	VLA40	LJ53 BCK	VLA67	LJ04 YWW
DLA254	X454 FGP	T104	LJ59 LYA	VLA14	LJ03 MYF	VLA41	LJ53 BCO	VLA68	LJ04 YWX
DLA255	X507 GGO	T105	LJ59 LYC	VLA15	LJ03 MXH	VLA42	LJ53 BCU	VLA69	LJ04 YWY
DLA273	Y473 UGC	T106	LJ59 LYD	VLA16	LJ03 MXK	VLA43	LJ53 BCV	VLA70	LJ04 YWZ
DLA275	Y475 UGC	T107	LJ59 LYF	VLA17	LJ03 MXL	VLA44	LJ53 BCX	VLA71	LJ04 YXA
DLA311	Y511 UGC	T108	LJ59 LYG	VLA18	LJ03 MXM	VLA45	LJ53 BCY	VLA72	LJ04 YXB
DLA315	Y529 UGC	T109	LJ59 LYH	VLA19	LJ03 MXN	VLA46	LJ53 BAA	VLA73	LJ04 YWE
DLA316	Y516 UGC	T110	LJ59 LYK	VLA20	LJ03 MXP	VLA47	LJ53 BAO	VLA74	LJ54 BGO
T84	LJ59 LZD	T111	LJ59 LYO	VLA21	LJ53 BFK	VLA48	LJ53 BAU	VLA75	LJ54 BEO
T85	185 CLT	T112	LJ59 LYP	VLA22	LJ53 BFL	VLA49	LJ53 BAV	VLA76	LJ54 BEU
T86	LJ59 LZF	T113	LJ59 LYS	VLA23	LJ53 BFM	VLA50	LJ53 BBE	VLA77	LJ54 BFA
T87	LJ59 LZG	T114	LJ59 LXP	VLA24	LJ53 BFN	VLA51	LJ53 BBF	VLA78	LJ54 BFE
T88	LJ59 LZH	T115	LJ59 LXR	VLA25	LJ53 BFO	VLA52	LJ53 BBK	VLA101	LJ54 BCO
T89	LJ59 LZK	T116	LJ59 LXS	VLA26	LJ53 BCZ	VLA53	LJ53 BBN	VLA104	LJ05 BKY
T90	LJ59 LZL	T117	LJ59 LXT	VLA27	LJ53 BDE	VLA54	LJ53 BBO	VLA105	LJ05 BKZ
T91	LJ59 LZM	VLA1	LJ03 MYP	VLA28	LJ53 BDF	VLA55	LJ53 BBU	VLA106	LJ05 BLF
T92	LJ59 LZN	VLA2	LJ03 MYR	VLA29	LJ53 BDO	VLA56	LJ04 LFL	VLA107	LJ05 BLK
T93	593 CLT	VLA3	LJ03 MYS	VLA30	LJ53 BDU	VLA57	LJ04 LFM	VLA108	LJ05 BLN
T94	LJ59 LYT	VLA4	LJ03 MYT	VLA31	LJ53 BDV	VLA58	LJ04 LFN		

The entrance to **Norwood Bus Garage** on August 19th, 2014 with Arriva London bus **VLA75** waiting to pass through the wash plant.

Arriva London buses **T97 & VLA45** in the yard at the east end of **Norwood Bus Garage** on August 19th, 2014. The front end of Arriva Routemaster **RML901** can just be observed inside the exit door.

The entrance to **Orpington Bus Garage** on September 21st, 2013 on the occasion of an open day to celebrate thirty years of Metrobus. The depot was enlarged and modernized in 2005.

ORPINGTON (MB)
Farnborough Hill, Green Street Green, Orpington, Kent BR6 6DA
Operated by: Metrobus
Location: TQ45486394 [51.356492, 0.087531]
Nearest Station: Chelsfield (1.1 miles)
Nearest Bus Routes: 358/402/R8 & R11 - Farnborough Hill Bus Garage (K)
Bus Routes Serviced: 119 (Night Services only)/ 126/138/146/161/162/181/233/284/320/336/352/ 353/358/464/654/B14/R1/R2/R3/R4/R6/R8/R9& R11

Orpington Garage was originally the sole depot operated by Metrobus until Croydon (C) (See Page 30) opened in December 2005.

The maintenance building at **Orpington Bus Garage** viewed from the entrance gate on August 21st, 2014.

Buses parked at the south end of the depot at **Orpington Bus Garage** on August 21st, 2014.

VEHICLE ALLOCATION

101	YJ56 WVF	183	YX62 DZN	285	SN03 YCF	607	YM55 SXA	761	YX13 AHK
102	YJ56 WVG	184	YX62 DZU	456	YN03 DFC	608	YM55 SXB	762	YX13 AHL
148	YX60 FTO	185	YX13 AJO	457	YU52 XVR	609	YM55 SXC	897	PO59 KFZ
149	YX60 FTP	186	YX13 AJU	458	YN03 DFD	610	YM55 SXD	898	PO59 KGA
150	YX60 FTT	187	YX13 AJV	459	YN03 DFE	611	YM55 SXE	899	PO59 KGE
151	YX60 FTU	188	YX13 AJY	460	YN03 DFG	612	YM55 SXF	901	YN55 PZC
152	YX60 FTV	228	PO56 JEU	461	YN03 DFJ	613	YN06 JXT	902	YN55 PZD
153	YX60 FTY	229	PO56 JFA	462	YN03 DFK	614	YM55 SXH	903	YN55 PZE
154	YX60 FTZ	230	PO56 JFE	465	YN03 DFU	701	PN07 KRK	904	YN55 PZF
155	YX60 FUV	231	PO56 JFF	466	YN03 DFV	702	PN07 KRO	905	YN55 PZG
156	YX60 FUW	232	PO56 JFG	467	YN03 DFX	703	PN07 KRU	906	YN55 PZH
157	YX60 FUY	233	PO56 JFJ	468	YN03 DFY	704	PN07 KRV	907	YN55 PZJ
158	YX60 FVA	234	PO56 JFK	479	YN53 RYM	705	PN07 KRX	908	YN55 PZL
159	YX60 FVB	235	PO56 JFN	480	YN53 RYP	731	YX11 CTE	909	YN55 PZM
160	YX60 FVC	236	PO56 JFU	514	YN53 RXF	732	YX11 CTF	910	YN55 PZO
161	YX60 FVD	251	SN54 GPV	515	YN53 RXG	733	YX11 CTK	911	YN55 PZP
162	YX60 FVE	252	SN54 GPX	516	YN53 RXH	740	YX13 AFF	912	YN55 PZR
163	YX61 ENC	253	SN54 GPY	517	YN53 RXJ	741	YX13 AFJ	913	YN55 PZU
164	YX61 ENE	254	SN54 GPZ	518	YN53 RXK	742	YX13 AFK	914	YN55 PZV
165	YX61 ENF	255	SN54 GRF	519	YN53 RXL	743	YX13 AFN	915	YN55 PZW
166	YX61 ENH	256	SN54 GRK	520	YN53 RXM	744	YX13 AFO	916	YN55 PZX
167	YX61 ENJ	267	PN06 UYX	521	YN53 RXO	745	YX13 AFU	930	YN56 FDD
168	YX61 ENK	268	PN06 UYY	522	YN53 RXP	746	YX13 AFV	931	YN56 FDE
169	YX61 ENL	271	SN03 YBA	523	YN53 RXR	747	YX13 AFY	932	YN56 FDF
170	YX61 ENM	272	SN03 YBB	524	YN53 RXT	748	YX13 AFZ	933	YN56 FDG
171	YX61 ENN	273	SN03 YBC	525	YN53 RXU	749	YX13 AGO	934	YN56 FDJ
172	YX61 ENO	274	SN03 YBG	526	YN53 RXV	750	YX13 AGU	940	YN56 FDU
173	YX61 ENP	275	SN03 YBH	527	YN53 RXW	751	YX13 AGV	941	YN56 FDV
174	YX61 ENR	276	SN03 YBK	528	YN53 RXX	752	YX13 AGY	942	YN56 FDX
175	YX61 ENT	277	SN03 YBR	529	YN53 RXY	753	YX13 AGZ	974	YR10 BCE
176	YX61 ENU	278	SN03 YBS	530	YN53 RXZ	754	YX13 AHA	975	YR10 BCF
177	YX61 ENV	279	SN03 YBT	601	YM55 SWU	755	YX13 AHC	976	YR10 BCK
178	YX61 ENW	280	SN03 YBX	602	YM55 SWV	756	YX13 AHD	977	YR10 BCO
179	YX62 DYH	281	SN03 YBY	603	YN06 JXR	757	YX13 AHE	978	YR10 BCU
180	YX62 DYN	282	SN03 YBZ	604	YM55 SWX	758	YX13 AHF	LDP192	SN51 UAE
181	YX62 DYS	283	SN03 YCD	605	YM55 SWY	759	YX13 AHG	LDP200	SN51 UAO
182	YX62 DZE	284	SN03 YCE	606	YN06 JXS	760	YX13 AHJ	LDP205	SN51 UAU

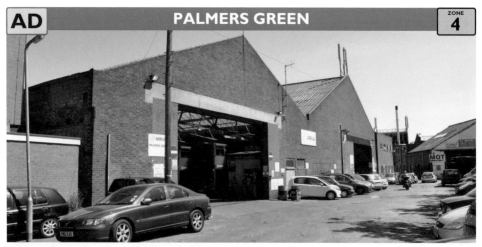

AD | **PALMERS GREEN** | **ZONE 4**

Palmers Green Bus Garage on July 22nd, 2014. The depot was opened in July 1912 by the London General Omnibus Company and modernized in 1952 and 1974.

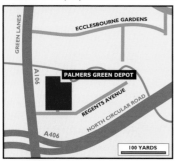

PALMERS GREEN (AD)
Regents Avenue, Palmers Green, London N13 5UR
Operated by: Arriva London
Location: TQ31029218 [51.613207, -0.019065]
Nearest Station: Palmers Green (0.5 miles)
Nearest Bus Routes: 34/102/121/329/629 (North Circular Road/Palmers Green)
Bus Routes Serviced: 34/102/125/141 & 329

Arriva bus DW488 on Route 141 about to enter **Palmers Green Bus Garage** on July 22nd, 2014 to effect a turn around. The route terminates inside the garage during the day as it is the most convenient place to do so but buses have to run to Edmonton Cambridge roundabout in the evenings when the depot fills up with parked buses.

A general view of the inside of the building at **Palmers Green Bus Garage** on July 22nd, 2014.

VEHICLE ALLOCATION

DLA317	Y517 UGC	DLP89	LF02 PKE	T4	LJ08 CVV	T34	LJ08 CTZ	T268	LJ61 LJU
DLA318	Y518 UGC	DLP92	LF52 URT	T5	205 CLT	T35	LJ08CUA	T269	LJ61 LJV
DLA319	Y519 UGC	DLP94	LF52 URV	T6	LJ08 CVX	T36	LJ08 CUC	T270	LJ61 LJX
DLA351	LJ03 MKZ	DLP95	LF52 URW	T7	LJ08 CVY	T37	LJ08 CUG	T271	LJ61 LHP
DLA352	LJ03 MLE	DLP100	LF52 URE	T8	LJ08 CVZ	T38	LJ08 CUH	T272	LJ61 LHR
DLA353	LJ03 MLF	DLP102	LF52 URH	T9	LJ08 CWA	T39	LJ08 CUK	T273	LJ61 LHT
DLA354	LJ03 MLK	DLP103	LF52 URJ	T10	LJ08 CWC	T40	LJ08 CUO	T274	LJ61 LHU
DLA355	LJ03 MJX	DLP104	LF52 URK	T11	LJ08 CVF	T41	LJ08 CSO	T275	LJ61 LHV
DLA356	LJ03 MJY	DLP105	LF52 URL	T27	LJ08 CVB	T261	LJ61 LJC	T276	LJ61 LHW
DLA373	LJ03 MVE	DLP106	LF52 URM	T28	LJ08 CVC	T262	LJ61 LJE	T277	LJ61 LHX
DLA375	LJ03 MTE	DLP107	LF52 UPP	T29	LJ08 CVD	T263	LJ61 LJF	T278	LJ61 LHY
DLP80	LJ51 ORC	DLP110	LF52 UPT	T30	330 CLT	T264	LJ61 LJK		
DLP81	LJ51 ORF	T1	LJ08 CVS	T31	LJ08 CTV	T265	LJ61 LJL		
DLP84	LJ51 ORK	T2	LJ08 CVT	T32	LJ08 CTX	T266	LJ61 LJN		
DLP85	LJ51 ORL	T3	3 CLT	T33	LJ08 CTY	T267	LJ61 LJO		

Park Royal Bus Garage on May 3rd, 2014 with the wash plant in view. The depot was opened on May 26th, 2007 by NCP-Challenger and occupies the site of a former Metroline garage that had been closed in 2005.

Allison Smith

PARK ROYAL (PK)
Atlas Road, Harlesden, London NW10 6DN
Operated by: London United
Location: TQ21438259 [51.529245, -0.251003]
Nearest Station: Willesden Junction (0.5 miles)
Nearest Bus Routes: 228 & 266 - Old Oak Common, Old Oak Common Lane (Stop J)
Bus Routes Serviced: 72/220/283/440 & E11

London United **DPS663** parked in the yard at **Park Royal Bus Garage** on May 10th, 2014.
Allison Smith

*SEE PAGE 8

VEHICLE ALLOCATION

ADE46	YX62 BBO	ADE60	YX62 BKO	DE75	SK07 DYC	OV50	YJ58 PHY	OV64	YJ09 EZB
ADE47	YX62 BBZ	ADE61	YX62 BLZ	DE76	SK07 DYD	OV51	YJ58 PHZ	OV65	YJ09 EZC
ADE48	YX62 BCK	ADE62	YX62 BMV	DE77	SK07 DYF	OV52	YJ58 PJO	OV66	YJ09 EZD
ADE49	YX62 BCV	ADE63	YX62 BMY	DE78	SK07 DYG	OV53	YJ58 PJU	SDE1	YX08 MFO
ADE50	YX62 BFL	ADE64	YX62 BNO	DE79	SK07 DYH	OV54	YJ09 EZE	SDE2	YX08 MDV
ADE51	YX62 BFU	ADE65	YX62 BNV	DE80	SK07 DYJ	OV55	YJ09 EZF	SDE3	YX08 MDY
ADE52	YX62 BGE	ADE66	YX62 BPF	DE81	SK07 DYM	OV56	YJ09 EYT	SDE4	YX08 MDZ
ADE53	YX62 BGF	ADE67	YX62 BPO	DE82	SK07 DYN	OV57	YJ09 EYU	SDE5	YX08 MFN
ADE54	YX62 BHD	ADE68	YX62 BPU	DE83	SK07 DYO	OV58	YJ09 EYV	SDE11	SK07 HLM
ADE55	YX62 BHW	ADE69	YX62 BPZ	DE84	SK07 DYP	OV59	YJ09 EYW	SDE14	SK07 HLP
ADE56	YX62 BJF	ADE70	YX62 BUA	DPS586	SN51 TDX	OV60	YJ09 EYX		
ADE57	YX62 BJU	ADE71	YX62 BUE	DPS659	LG02 FGE	OV61	YJ09 EYY		
ADE58	YX62 BJZ	ADE72	YX62 BVN	DPS661	LG02 FGJ	OV62	YJ09 EYZ		
ADE59	YX62 BKF	ADE73	YX62 BWO	DPS663	LG02 FGM	OV63	YJ09 EZA		

Peckham Bus Garage on May 10th, 2014. It was opened in 1994 to replace one that had been sited in the town and its origins, as a former council yard, were still apparent.   *Allison Smith*

PECKHAM (PM)
Blackpool Road, London SE15 3SU
Operated by: Go-Ahead London
Location: TQ34587629 [51.469371, -0.064478]
Nearest Station: Peckham Rye (0.3 miles)
Nearest Bus Routes: 12/37/63/78/197/343/363/
N63/N343 & P12 - Heaton Road (Stop X)
Bus Routes Serviced: 36/37/63/363/N63/P12 & X68

London Central-branded Go-Ahead London **E20** parked up in the yard at **Peckham Bus Garage** on August 31st, 2013.

VEHICLE ALLOCATION

E16	LX06 EZL	E34	LX06 ECT	PVL341	PJ52 LWW	WVL103	LF52 ZMO	WVL320	LX59 DBY
E17	LX06 EZM	E35	LX06 ECV	PVL342	PJ52 LWX	WVL303	LX59 CYA	WVL321	LX59 DBZ
E18	LX06 EZN	E36	LX06 FKL	SE153	YX61 DVA	WVL304	LX59 CYC	WVL322	LX59 DCE
E19	LX06 EZO	E37	LX06 FKM	SE154	YX61 DVB	WVL305	LX59 CYE	WVL323	LX59 DCF
E20	LX06 EZP	E61	LX07 BYG	SE155	YX61 DVC	WVL306	LX59 CYF	WVL324	LX59 DCO
E21	LX06 EZR	LDP206	SN51 UAV	SE156	YX61 DVF	WVL307	LX59 CYG	WVL325	LX59 DCU
E22	LX06 EZS	PVL329	PJ52 LWH	SE157	YX61 DVG	WVL308	LX59 CYH	WVL326	LX59 DCV
E23	LX06 EZT	PVL330	PJ52 LWK	SE158	YX61 DVH	WVL309	LX59 CYJ	WVL327	LX59 DCY
E24	LX06 EYY	PVL331	PJ52 LWL	SE159	YX61 DVJ	WVL310	LX59 CYK	WVL328	LX59 DCZ
E25	LX06 EYZ	PVL332	PJ52 LWM	SE160	YX61 DVK	WVL311	LX59 CZW	WVL329	LX59 DDA
E26	LX06 EZA	PVL333	PJ52 LWN	SE161	YX61 DVL	WVL312	LX59 CZY	WVL330	LX59 DDE
E27	LX06 EZB	PVL334	PJ52 LWO	SE162	YX61 DVM	WVL313	LX59 CZZ	WVL331	LX59 DDF
E28	LX06 EZC	PVL335	PJ52 LWP	SE163	YX61 DVN	WVL314	LX59 DAA	WVL332	LX59 DDJ
E29	LX06 EZD	PVL336	PJ52 LWR	SE164	YX61 DVO	WVL315	LX59 DAO	WVL333	LX59 DDK
E30	LX06 EZE	PVL337	PJ52 LWS	SE165	YX61 DVP	WVL316	LX59 DAU		
E31	LX06 EZF	PVL338	PJ52 LWT	SE166	YX61 DVR	WVL317	LX59 DBO		
E32	LX06 EZG	PVL339	PJ52 LWU	WVL85	LF52 ZNT	WVL318	LX59 DBU		
E33	LX06 EZH	PVL340	PJ52 LWV	WVL100	LF52 ZNN	WVL319	LX59 DBV		

Perivale (West) Bus Garage on September 13th, 2014 with Metroline Buses **TEH1223**, **SEL762** & **DEL2062** to the fore.

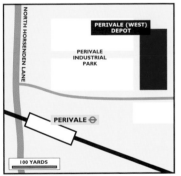

PERIVALE (WEST) (PA)
Unit 12, Perivale Industrial Park, Horsenden Lane, South Greenford UB6 7RL
Operated by: Metroline
Location: TQ16608343 [51.537651, -0.320144]
Nearest Tube Station: Perivale (300 yards)
Nearest Bus Routes: 297 - Perivale (Stop PF)
Bus Routes Serviced: 7/79/90/105/297/395/611/E6 & N7

VEHICLE ALLOCATION

DE1598	YX58 DUA	MM812	LK57 AYF	SEL755	LK07 BCE	VW1181	LK11 CXR	VWH2001	LK14 FAA
DE1599	YX58 DUH	MM815	LK57 AYJ	SEL756	LK07 BCF	VW1182	LK11 CXS	VWH2002	LK14 FAF
DE1600	YX58 DUJ	MM817	LK57 AYM	SEL757	LK07 BCO	VW1183	LK11 CXT	VWH2003	LK14 FAJ
DE1601	YX58 DUU	MM818	LK57 AYN	SEL758	LK07 BCU	VW1184	LK11 CXU	VWH2004	LK14 FAM
DE1602	YX58 DVY	MM822	LK57 AYT	SEL759	LK07 BCZ	VW1185	LK11 CXV	VWH2005	LK14 FAO
DE1603	YX58 DVZ	MM825	LK57 AYW	SEL760	LK07 BCX	VW1186	LK11 CXW	VWH2006	LK14 FAU
DE1604	YX58 DWA	MM827	LK57 AYY	SEL761	LK07 BCY	VW1187	LK11 CXX	VWH2007	LK14 FBA
DE1605	YX58 DWC	SEL739	LK07 AZV	SEL762	LK07 BCZ	VW1188	LK11 CXY	VWH2008	LK14 FBB
DE1606	YX58 DWD	SEL740	LK07 AZW	SEL763	LK07 BDE	VW1189	LK11 CXZ	VWH2009	LK14 FBC
DE1607	YX58 DWE	SEL741	LK07 AZY	SEL764	LK57 KAU	VW1190	LK11 CYA	VWH2010	LK14 FBD
DE1608	YX58 DWF	SEL742	LK07 AZZ	SEL803	LK57 KAX	VW1191	LK11 CYE	VWH2011	LK14 FBE
DE1609	YX58 DWG	SEL743	LK07 BAA	SEL804	LK57 KBE	VW1192	LK11 CYF	VWH2012	LK14 FBF
DE1610	YX58 DWJ	SEL744	LK07 BAO	SEL805	LK57 KBF	VW1193	LK11 CYH	VWH2013	LK14 FBG
DE1611	YX58 DWL	SEL745	LK07 BAU	SEL806	LK57 KBJ	VW1194	LK11 CYJ	VWH2014	LK14 FBJ
DP1011	RL51 DOJ	SEL746	LK07 BBE	SEL807	LK57 KBN	VW1195	LK11 CYL	VWH2015	LK14 FBL
DP1016	RL51 DNU	SEL747	LK07 BBF	SEL808	LK57 KBO	VW1197	LK11 CYP	VWH2016	LK14 FBN
MM779	LK07 AYL	SEL748	LK07 BBJ	SEL809	LK08 DVY	VW1199	LK11 CYT	VWH2017	LK14 FBO
MM782	LK57 EHS	SEL749	LK07 BBN	VW1175	LK11 CXJ	VW1200	LK11 CYU	VWH2018	LK14 FBU
MM783	LK57 EHT	SEL750	LK07 BBO	VW1176	LK11 CXL	VW1202	LK61 BJE	VWH2019	LK14 FBV
MM784	LK57 EHU	SEL751	LK07 BBU	VW1177	LK11 CXM	VW1203	LK61 BJF	VWH2020	LK14 FBX
MM785	LK57 EHV	SEL752	LK07 BBV	VW1178	LK11 CXN	VW1204	LK61 BJJ	VWH2021	LK14 FBY
MM789	LK57 EHZ	SEL753	LK07 BBX	VW1179	LK11 CXO	VW1206	LK61 BMV	VWH2022	LK14 FBZ
MM790	LK57 EJA	SEL754	LK07 BBZ	VW1180	LK11 CXP	VW1469	BF63 HDG	VWH2023	LK14 FCA

Plumstead Bus Garage viewed from the higher level of the A206 Plumstead Road on September 7th, 2013. One of the entrances to the depot is the one on the left, with Stagecoach London bus 17963 in the centre of the picture and nearest the camera.

PLUMSTEAD (PD)
Pettman Crescent, Plumstead, London SE28 0BJ
Operated by: Stagecoach London
Location: TQ44737901 [51.491297, 0.083571]
Nearest Station: Plumstead (0.2 miles)
Nearest Bus Routes: 122/177/180/422/472 & N1 -
Plumstead, Plumstead Road, Plumstead Station
(Stop WM)
Bus Routes Serviced: 51/53/96/99/122/177/291/
386/469/472/601/602 & 672

Plumstead Depot was opened in 1981 and replaced Plumstead (AM) and Abbey Wood (AW) garages.

Stagecoach London bus 34384 parked at the "Plumstead Garage" bus stop adjacent to the exit from **Plumstead Bus Garage** on August 20th, 2014.

The entrance to **Plumstead Bus Garage**, on the north side of the building, viewed on August 20th, 2014.

VEHICLE ALLOCATION

10196	SN63 NCA	13004	BU14 EFZ	15052	LX09 ACF	17945	LX53 JYH	19817	LX11 BKK
12293	SN14 TXM	13005	BN14 VZH	15053	LX09 ACJ	17946	LX53 JYJ	19818	LX11 BKL
12294	SN14 TXO	13006	BN14 VZJ	15054	LX09 ACO	17947	LX53 JYK	19819	LX11 BKN
12295	SN14 TXP	13007	BN14 VZK	15055	LX09 ADZ	17948	LX53 JYL	19820	LX11 BKO
12296	SN14 TXR	13008	BN14 VZL	15056	LX09 AEA	17949	LX53 JYN	19821	LX11 BKU
12297	SN14 TXS	13009	BN14 VZM	15057	LX09 AEB	17950	LX53 JYO	19822	LX11 BKV
12298	SN14 TXT	13010	BN14 VZO	15058	LX09 AEC	17951	LX53 JYP	19823	LX11 BKY
12299	SN14 TXU	13011	BN14 VZP	15059	LX09 AED	17952	LX53 JYR	19824	LX11 BKZ
12300	SN14 TXV	13012	BN14 VZR	15060	LX09 AEE	17953	LX53 JYT	19825	LX11 BLF
12301	SN14 TXW	13013	BN14 WAA	15061	LX09 AEF	17954	LX53 JYU	19826	LX11 BLJ
12302	SN14 TXX	13014	BN14 WAE	15062	LX09 AEG	17955	LX53 JYV	19827	LX11 BLK
12303	SN14 TXY	13015	BN14 WAJ	15063	LX09 AEJ	17956	LX53 JYW	34372	LV52 HGK
12334	SN64 OGG	13016	BN14 WAO	15064	LX09 AEK	17957	LX53 JYY	34377	LX03 BZJ
12335	SN64 OGH	13017	BJ14 KSU	15065	LX09 AEL	17958	LX53 JYZ	34378	LX03 BZK
12336	SN64 OGJ	13018	BJ14 KSV	15066	LX09 AEM	17959	LX53 JZA	34379	LX03 BZL
12337	SN64 OGK	13019	BJ14 KSX	15067	LX09 AEN	17960	LX53 JZC	34380	LX03 BZM
12338	SN64 OGL	13020	BJ14 KSY	15068	LX09 AEO	17961	LX53 JZD	34381	LX03 BZN
12339	SN64 OGM	13021	BG14 ONR	15069	LX09 AEP	17962	LX53 JZE	34382	LX03 BZP
12340	SN64 OGO	13022	BG14 ONT	15070	LX09 AET	17963	LX53 JZF	34383	LX03 BZR
12341	SN64 OGP	13023	BG14 ONS	15071	LX09 AEU	17964	LX53 JZG	34384	LX03 BZS
12342	SN64 OGR	13024	BG14 ONV	15072	LX09 AEV	19742	LX11 BBK	34385	LX03 BZT
12343	SN64 OGS	13025	BG14 ONU	15075	LX09 AEZ	19743	LX11 BBN	34386	LX03 BZU
12344	SN64 OGT	13026	BG14 ONX	15077	LX09 AFE	19744	LX11 BBO	36268	LX11 AVZ
12345	SN64 OGU	13027	BG14 ONW	15082	LX09 AFO	19745	LX11 BBV	36269	LX11 AWC
12346	SN64 OGV	13028	BG14 OOA	15085	LX09 AFY	19746	LX11 BBZ	36270	LX11 AWF
12347	SN64 OGW	13029	BG14 OOD	15093	LX09 AHC	19747	LX11 BCE	36271	LX11 AWG
12348	SN64 OGX	13030	BG14 ONZ	15094	LX09 AHD	19748	LX11 BCF	36272	LX11 AWH
12349	SN64 OGY	13031	BG14 OOB	15096	LX09 AHF	19749	LX11 BCK	36273	LX11 AWJ
12350	SN64 OGZ	13032	BG14 OOC	15124	LX09 FZW	19750	LX11 BCO	36274	LX11 AWM
12351	SN64 OHA	13036	LX58 CGY	17538	LY02 OAD	19751	LX11 BCU	36275	LX11 AWN
12352	SN64 OHB	15037	LX58 CGZ	17540	LY02 OAG	19752	LX11 BCV	36327	LX58 CCN
12353	SN64 OHC	15038	LX58 CHC	17560	LY02 OBM	19753	LX11 BCY	36328	LX58 CCO
12354	SN64 OHD	15039	LX58 CHD	17572	LV52 HFD	19754	LX11 BCZ	36329	LX58 CCU
12355	SN64 OHE	15040	LX09 AAO	17573	LV52 HFE	19755	LX11 BDE	36330	LX58 CCV
12356	SN64 OHF	15041	LX09 AAU	17590	LV52 HFZ	19806	LX11 BJO	36331	LX58 CCY
12357	SN64 OHG	15042	LX09 AAV	17789	LX03 BWC	19807	LX11 BJU	36332	LX58 CDE
12358	SN64 OHH	15043	LX09 AAY	17790	LX03 BWD	19808	LX11 BJV	36333	LX58 CDF
12359	SN64 OHJ	15044	LX09 AAZ	17794	LX03 BWH	19809	LX11 BJY	36334	LX58 CDK
12360	SN64 OHK	15045	LX09 ABF	17800	LX03 BWO	19810	LX11 BJZ	36335	LX58 CDO
12361	SN64 OHL	15046	LX09 ABK	17823	LX03 BXV	19811	LX11 BKA	36336	LX58 CDO
12362	SN64 OHO	15047	LX09 ABN	17836	LX03 BYM	19812	LX11 BKD	36337	LX58 CDU
12363	SN64 OHP	15048	LX09 ABO	17837	LX03 BYN	19813	LX11 BKE	36555	LX13 CYW
13001	BU14 EFW	15049	LX09 ABU	17838	LX03 BYP	19814	LX11 BKF		
13002	BU14 EFX	15050	LX09 ABV	17839	LX03 BYR	19815	LX11 BKG		
13003	BU14 EFY	15051	LX09 ABZ	17840	LX03 BYS	19816	LX11 BKJ		

Potters Bar Bus Garage on July 22nd, 2014 with Metroline bus **DEM1353** parked on the exit road.

POTTERS BAR (PB)

High Street, Potters Bar, Hertfordshire EN6 5BE
Operated by: Metroline
Location: TL26130146 [51.697737, -0.176436]
Nearest Station: Potters Bar (0.5 miles)
Nearest Bus Routes: 84/242/312/398 & PB1 -
Potters Bar, Bus Garage
Bus Routes Serviced: 82/217/234/263/383/384/
634/N20/N91/W8 & W9

The depot was opened in 1930 by "Overground", a subsidiary of the London General Omnibus Company, and during WWII and the early 1950s was also utilized as a bus storage facility. Its location, on the northern fringe of London bus operations, made it vulnerable to closure but it survived and was eventually taken over by Metroline.

VEHICLE ALLOCATION

DEM1337	LK62 DAA	DES800	LK07 BEY	TE938	LK58 KHC	TE1438	LK13 BFJ	VWH2030
DEM1338	LK62 DAO	DES801	LK07 ELJ	TE939	LK58 KHD	TE1439	LK13 BFL	VWH2031
DEM1339	LK62 DBZ	DES802	LK07 ELO	TE940	LK58 KHE	TE1440	LK13 BFM	VWH2032
DEM1340	LK62 DCE	DP1009	RL51 DOA	TE941	LK58 KHF	TE1441	LK13 BFN	VWH2033
DEM1341	LK62 DCF	DP1010	RL51 DNX	TE942	LK58 KHG	TE1442	LK13 BFO	VWH2034
DEM1342	LK62 DCY	DP1012	RL51 DOH	TE943	LK58 KHH	TE1443	LK13 BFP	VWH2035
DEM1343	LK62 DDU	DP1013	RL51 DNY	TE944	LK09 EKU	TE1444	LK13 BFU	VWH2036
DEM1344	LK62 DDY	DSD212	LR02 BEJ	TE945	LK58 KHL	TE1445	LK13 BFV	VWH2037
DEM1345	LK62 DDZ	DSD214	LR02 BEU	TE946	LK58 KHM	TE1446	LK13 BFX	VWH2038
DEM1346	LK62 DEU	DSD215	LR02 BEY	TE947	LK58 KHO	TE1447	LK13 BFY	VWH2039
DEM1347	LK62 DFF	TE892	LK08 NVG	TE948	LK58 KHP	TP417	LK03 CFN	VWH2040
DEM1348	LK62 DFJ	TE893	LK08 NVH	TE949	LK58 KHR	TP435	LK03 GGF	VWH2041
DEM1349	LK62 DFP	TE894	LK08 NVJ	TE950	LK58 KHT	TP437	LK03 GGP	VWH2042
DEM1350	LK62 DFY	TE895	LK08 NVL	TE951	LK58 KHU	TP441	LK03 GGY	VWH2043
DEM1351	LK62 DGF	TE896	LK08 NVM	TE1420	LK62 DXM	TP445	LK03 GHD	VWH2044
DEM1352	LK62 DGO	TE897	LK08 NVN	TE1421	LK62 DXP	TP450	LK03 GHN	VWH2045
DEM1353	LK62 DHC	TE898	LK08 NVO	TE1422	LK62 DXS	TP452	LK03 GHV	VWH2046
DEM1354	LK62 DHD	TE899	LK08 NVP	TE1423	LK62 DXT	TP454	LK03 GHY	VWH2047
DEM1355	LK62 DHE	TE900	LK58 CNE	TE1424	LK62 DXX	TP455	LK03 GHZ	VWH2048
DEM1356	LK62 DHG	TE901	LK58 CNF	TE1425	LK62 DXY	TP456	LK03 GJF	VWH2049
DEM1357	LK62 DHP	TE902	LK58 CNN	TE1426	LK62 DYA	TP457	LK03 GJG	VWH2050
DEM1358	LK62 DHU	TE903	LK58 CNO	TE1427	LK62 DYC	TP459	LK03 GJX	VWH2051
DEM1359	LK62 DHV	TE904	LK58 CNU	TE1428	LK62 DYD	TP460	LK03 GJX	VWH2052
DES791	LK07 BDO	TE905	LK58 CNV	TE1429	LK62 DYF	TP461	LK03 GJY	VWH2053
DES792	LK07 BDU	TE906	LK58 CNX	TE1430	LK62 DYG	TP462	LK03 GJZ	VWH2054
DES793	LK07 BDV	TE907	LK58 CNY	TE1431	LK62 DYH	TP465	LK03 GKD	VWH2055
DES794	LK07 BDX	TE908	LK58 CNZ	TE1432	LK62 DYN			VWH2056
DES795	LK07 BDY	TE909	LK58 COA	TE1433	LK62 DYO	VWH2024		VWH2057
DES796	LK07 BDZ	TE911	LK58 COJ	TE1434	LK13 BEU	VWH2025		VWH2058
DES797	LK07 BEJ	TE935	LK09 EKP	TE1435	LK13 BEY	VWH2026		VWH2059
DES798	LK07 BEO	TE936	LK09 EKR	TE1436	LK13 BFA	VWH2027		VWH2060
DES799	LK07 BEU	TE937	LK09 EKT	TE1437	LK13 BFF	VWH2028		VWH2061
						VWH2029		

Go-Ahead London bus **WVL66** squeezing past Reg No.**P735 TYL**, a Go-Ahead London Dennis Dart SLF Paxton Pointer Crew Rest Unit, as it departs from **Putney Bus Garage** on September 6th, 2014.

PUTNEY (AF)
Chelverton Road, London SW15 1RN
Operated by: Go-Ahead London
Location: TQ23937528 [51.462632, -0.217141]
Nearest Station: Putney (0.2 miles)
Nearest Bus Routes: 14/39/74/85/93/424 & 430 - (Putney Exchange) Putney
Bus Routes Serviced: 14/22/74/85/424/430/670/ N22 & N74

Originally known as Chelverton Road, it can trace its origins back to the 1880s when it was a horse bus depot, becoming a motorized omnibus garage in 1912. It was modernized in 1935 and re-named as Putney in 1963 following the closure of Putney Bridge. The depot was again modernized and refurbished in 1986.

VEHICLE ALLOCATION

LDP281	LX06 FAJ	WVL21	LG02 KHW	WVL47	LF52 ZRG	WVL154	LX53 BFK	WVL180	LX05 FAA
LDP282	LX06 FAK	WVL22	LG02 KHX	WVL48	LF52 ZRJ	WVL155	LX53 BDY	WVL181	LX05 FAF
LDP283	LX06 FAM	WVL23	LG02 KHY	WVL49	LF52 ZRK	WVL156	LX53 BBZ	WVL182	LX05 FAJ
LDP284	LX06 FAO	WVL24	LG02 KHZ	WVL50	LF52 ZRL	WVL157	LX53 BAA	WVL183	LX05 FAK
LDP285	LX06 FAU	WVL25	LG02 KJA	WVL51	LF52 ZRN	WVL158	LX53 BDO	WVL184	LX05 FAM
LDP286	LX06 FBA	WVL26	LG02 KJE	WVL52	LF52 ZPN	WVL159	LX53 BAO	WVL185	LX05 FAO
VE1	LX58 CWK	WVL27	LG02 KJF	WVL53	LF52 ZPO	WVL160	LX05 FBY	WVL186	LX05 FAU
VE2	LX58 CWL	WVL28	LF52 ZSO	WVL54	LF52 ZPP	WVL161	LX05 FBZ	WVL187	LX05 FBA
VE3	LX58 CWM	WVL29	LF52 ZSP	WVL55	LF52 ZPR	WVL162	LX05 FCA	WVL188	LX05 FBB
WHV32	LJ62 KFD	WVL30	LF52 ZSR	WVL56	LF52 ZPS	WVL163	LX05 FCC	WVL496	LJ62 KXX
WHV33	LJ62 KFF	WVL31	LF52 ZST	WVL57	LF52 ZPU	WVL164	LX05 FCD	WVL497	LJ62 KXZ
WHV34	LJ62 KFU	WVL32	LF52 ZRO	WVL58	LF52 ZPV	WVL165	LX05 FCE	WVL498	LJ62 KYA
WHV35	LJ62 KGF	WVL33	LF52 ZRP	WVL59	LF52 ZPW	WVL166	LX05 FCF	WVL499	LJ62 KYG
WHV36	LJ62 KGG	WVL34	LF52 ZRR	WVL60	LF52 ZPX	WVL167	LX05 FBD	WVL500	LJ62 KOX
WHV37	LJ62 KGN	WVL35	LF52 ZRT	WVL61	LF52 ZPY	WVL168	LX05 FBE	WVL501	LJ62 KZD
WHV38	LJ62 KGY	WVL36	LF52 ZRU	WVL62	LF52 ZTG	WVL169	LX05 FBF	WVL502	LJ62 KZP
WHV39	LJ62 KHF	WVL37	LF52 ZRV	WVL63	LF52 ZTH	WVL170	LX05 FBJ	WVL503	LJ62 KBY
WHV40	LJ62 KHV	WVL38	LF52 ZRX	WVL64	LF52 ZTJ	WVL171	LX05 FBK	WVL504	LJ62 KCU
WHV41	LJ62 KKP	WVL39	LF52 ZRY	WVL65	LF52 ZTK	WVL172	LX05 FBL	WVL505	LJ62 KDV
WVL14	LG02 KHM	WVL40	LF52 ZRZ	WVL66	LF52 ZTL	WVL173	LX05 FBN	WVL506	LJ62 KDZ
WVL15	LG02 KHO	WVL41	LF52 ZSD	WVL67	LF52 ZTM	WVL174	LX05 FBO	WVL507	LJ62 KLC
WVL16	LG02 KHP	WVL42	LF52 ZPZ	WVL68	LF52 ZTN	WVL175	LX05 FBU	WVL508	LJ62 KLS
WVL17	LG02 KHR	WVL43	LF52 ZRA	WVL69	LF52 ZTO	WVL176	LX05 EZJ		
WVL18	LG02 KHT	WVL44	LF52 ZRC	WVL70	LF52 ZTP	WVL177	LX05 EYM		
WVL19	LG02 KHU	WVL45	LF52 ZRD	WVL71	LF52 ZTR	WVL178	LX05 EYO		
WVL20	LG02 KHV	WVL46	LF52 ZRE	WVL153	LX53 BGE	WVL179	LX05 FBV		

Go-Ahead London's **Rainham Bus Garage** on August 20th, 2014. The legend on the side of the building indicates that it used to be occupied by a shotblasting concern!

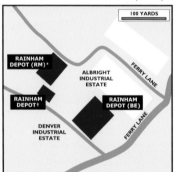

RAINHAM (BE)
Unit 4, Denver Industrial Estate, Ferry Lane, Rainham, Essex RM13 9DD
Operated by: Go-Ahead London
Location: TQ51778172 [51.514064, 0.185806]
Nearest Station: Rainham (0.4 miles)
Nearest Bus Routes: 372 - Rainham, Rainham (London) (Stop B)
Bus Routes Serviced: 167/193/300/347/362/364/368/376/462/498/608/646/648/649/650/651/652/656/667/674/679/686/EL1/EL2 & W19

*SEE PAGE 77 †SEE PAGE 109

VEHICLE ALLOCATION

872	PN09 EKU	DMN6	LN51 DWU	ED23	LX07 BYO	SE35	SN57 DXB	WS1	LJ12 CGF
873	PN09 EKV	DMN7	LT02 NUM	ED24	LX07 BYP	SE36	YN08 DMY	WS2	LJ12 CGG
874	PN09 EKW	DMN8	LT02 NUO	ED25	LX07 BYR	SE38	LX10 AUR	WS3	LJ12 CGK
875	PN09 EKX	DMN9	LT02 NUP	ED26	LX07 BYS	SE39	LX10 AUT	WS4	LJ12 CGO
876	PN09 EKY	DMN10	LT02 NUU	ED27	LX07 BYT	SE40	LX10 AUU	WS5	LJ12 CGU
877	PN09 ELO	DMN11	LT02 NUV	EN25	LK57 EJN	SE41	LX10 AUV	WS6	LJ12 CGV
878	PN09 ELU	DMN12	LT02 NVE	EN26	LK57 EJO	SE42	LX10 AUW	WS7	LJ12 CGX
879	PN09 ELV	DMN13	LT52 WUP	EN27	LK08 FKX	SE43	LX10 AUY	WS8	LJ12 CGY
880	PN09 ELW	DMN14	LT52 WUO	LDP194	SN51 UAG	SE44	LX10 AVB	WS9	LJ12 CGZ
881	PN09 ELX	DMN15	LT02 NVH	LDP195	SN51 UAH	SE45	LX10 AVC	WVL334	LX59 DDL
882	PN09 EMF	DMN16	LT02 NVJ	LDP208	SN51 UAX	SE46	LX10 AVD	WVL335	LX59 DDN
883	PN09 EMK	DMN17	LT52 WUM	PVL115	W415 WGH	SE94	SN11 FFZ	WVL336	LX59 DDO
884	PN09 EMV	DMN18	LT52 WUR	SE18	SK07 DZM	SE95	SN11 FGA	WVL337	LX59 DDU
885	PN09 EMX	DP208	SN56 AYC	SE19	SK07 DZN	SE96	SN11 FGC	WVL338	LX59 DDV
886	PN09 ENC	DW12	LF52 TKA	SE20	SK07 DZO	SE97	SN11 FGD	WVL339	LX59 DDY
887	PN09 ENE	ED9	AE56 OUH	SE21	SN57 DWG	SE98	SN61 BKO	WVL340	LX59 DDZ
888	PN09 ENF	ED10	AE56 OUJ	SE22	SN57 DWJ	SE99	SN61 BKU	WVL341	LX59 DEU
889	PN09 ENH	ED11	AE56 OUK	SE23	SN57 DWK	SE100	SN61 BKV	WVL342	LX59 DFA
890	PN09 ENK	ED12	AE56 OUL	SE24	SN57 DWL	SE101	SN61 BKX	WVL343	LX59 DFC
891	PN09 ENL	ED13	AE56 OUM	SE25	SN57 DWM	SE102	SN61 BKY	WVL344	LX59 DFD
892	PN09 ENM	ED14	AE56 OUN	SE26	SN57 DWO	SE103	SN61 BKZ	WVL345	LX59 DFE
893	PN09 ENO	ED15	AE56 OUO	SE27	SN57 DWP	SEN30	YX61 FZO	WVL346	LX59 DFF
894	PO59 KFW	ED16	AE56 OUP	SE28	SN57 DWU	SEN31	YX61 FZP	WVL347	LX59 DFG
895	PO59 KFX	ED17	AE56 OUS	SE29	SN57 DWV	SEN32	YX61 FZR	WVL348	LX59 DFJ
896	PO59 KFY	ED18	LX07 BYJ	SE30	SN57 DWW	SEN33	YX61 FZS	WVL349	LX59 DFK
DMN2	LN51 DWL	ED19	LX07 BYK	SE31	SN57 DWX	SEN34	YX61 FZT	WVL451	LJ61 GWM
DMN3	LN51 DWM	ED20	LX07 BYL	SE32	SN57 DWY	SEN35	YX61 FZU	WVL452	LJ61 GWN
DMN4	LN51 DWO	ED21	LX07 BYM	SE33	SN57 DWZ	SEN36	YX61 FZV	WVL453	LJ61 GWO
DMN5	LN51 DWP	ED22	LX07 BYN	SE34	SN57 DXA	SEN37	YX61 FZW	WVL454	LJ61 GWP

The main depot building at Stagecoach London's **Rainham Bus Garage** viewed on August 20th, 2014.

100 YARDS

RAINHAM DEPOT (RM)

ALBRIGHT INDUSTRIAL ESTATE

FERRY LANE

RAINHAM DEPOT†

RAINHAM DEPOT (BE)*

DENVER INDUSTRIAL ESTATE

FERRY LANE

*SEE PAGE 76 †SEE PAGE 109

RAINHAM (RM)
Unit 2, Albright Industrial Estate, Ferry Lane, Rainham, Essex RM13 9BU
Operated by: Stagecoach London
Location: TQ51648186 [51.515326, 0.183993]
Nearest Station: Rainham (0.5 mile)
Nearest Bus Routes: 372 - Rainham, Rainham (London) (Stop B)
Bus Routes Serviced: 165/174/248/252/256/287/ 365 & 372

Stagecoach London bus 19788 parked in the yard at **Rainham Bus Garage** on August 20th, 2014.

Looking south towards the administration block and wash plant at **Rainham Bus Garage** on August 20th, 2014.

VEHICLE ALLOCATION

10165	SN63 JVO	15019	LX58 CFK	17397	Y397 NHK	19727	LX11 AZO	36558	LX13 CZA
10166	SN63 JVP	15020	LX58 CFL	17398	Y398 NHK	19728	LX11 AZP	36559	LX13 CZB
10167	SN63 JVR	15021	LX58 CFM	17399	LX51 FHP	19729	LX11 AZR	36560	LX13 CZC
10168	SN63 JVT	15022	LX58 CFN	17404	Y404 NHK	19730	LX11 AZT	36561	LX13 CZD
10169	SN63 JVU	15023	LX58 CFO	17409	Y409 NHK	19731	LX11 AZU	36562	LX13 CZE
10170	SN63 JVV	15024	LX58 CFP	17419	LX51 FJJ	19732	LX11 AZV	36563	LX13 CZF
10171	SN63 JVW	15025	LX58 CFU	17426	LX51 FJY	19786	LX11 BGZ	36564	LX13 CZG
15001	LX58 CDV	15026	LX58 CFV	17434	Y434 NHK	19787	LX11 BHA	36565	LX13 CZH
15002	LX58 CDY	15027	LX58 CFY	19711	LX11 AYS	19788	LX11 BHD	36566	LX13 CZJ
15003	LX58 CDZ	15028	LX58 CFZ	19712	LX11 AYT	19789	LX11 BHE	36567	LX13 CZK
15004	LX58 CEA	15029	LX58 CGE	19713	LX11 AYU	19790	LX11 BHF	36568	LX13 CZL
15005	LX58 CEF	15030	LX58 CGF	19714	LX11 AYV	19791	LX11 BHJ	36569	LX13 CZM
15006	LX58 CEJ	15031	LX58 CGG	19715	LX11 AYW	19792	LX11 BHK	36570	LX13 CZN
15007	LX58 CEK	15032	LX58 CGK	19716	LX11 AYY	19793	LX11 BHL	36571	LX13 CZO
15008	LX58 CEN	15033	LX58 CGO	19717	LX11 AYZ	19828	LX11 BLN	36572	LX13 CZP
15009	LX58 CEO	15034	LX58 CGU	19718	LX11 AZA	19829	LX11 BLV	36573	LX13 CZR
15010	LX58 CEU	15035	LX58 CGV	19719	LX11 AZB	19830	LX11 BLZ	36574	LX13 CZS
15011	LX58 CEV	15073	LX09 AEW	19720	LX11 AZC	19831	LX11 BMO	36575	LX13 CZT
15012	LX58 CEY	17362	Y362 NHK	19721	LX11 AZD	19832	LX11 BMU	36576	LX13 CZU
15014	LX58 CFD	17363	Y363 HNK	19722	LX11 AZF	19833	LX11 BMV	36577	LX13 CZV
15015	LX58 CFE	17364	Y364 NHK	19723	LX11 AZG	19834	LX11 BMY	36578	LX63 CZW
15016	LX58 CFF	17368	Y368 NHK	19724	LX11 AZJ	34362	LV52 HKO	36579	LX13 CZY
15017	LX58 CFG	17395	Y395 NHK	19725	LX11 AZL	36556	LX13 CYY	36580	LX13 CZZ
15018	LX58 CFJ	17396	LX51 FHO	19726	LX11 AZN	36557	LX13 CYZ		

Looking north towards **Romford Bus Garage** on August 20th, 2014, with Arriva Southern bus **4072** paused at the "Romford Bus Garage" bus stop on a No.66 Service to Romford Station.

ROMFORD (NS)
North Street, Romford, Essex RM1 1DS
Operated by: Stagecoach London
Location: TQ50788948 [51.583947, 0.175049]
Nearest Station: Romford (1.3 miles)
Nearest Bus Routes: 66/103/175/247/294/296/365 /375/575/649 & 650 - Romford Bus Garage (Stop NS)
Bus Routes Serviced: 86/103/175/247/294/296/ 496 & N86

Romford Garage was opened in 1953 to supplement a garage at Hornchurch. It was originally known as North Street to differentiate it from another Romford garage located in London Road.

VEHICLE ALLOCATION

10155	EU62 AXT	17767	LX03 BVC	17869	LX03 NFP	17995	LX53 KCE	18477	LX55 ESF
10156	EU62 AXV	17768	LX03 BVD	17870	LX03 NFR	17996	LX53 KCF	18478	LX55 ESG
10157	EU62 AYB	17769	LX03 BVE	17874	LX03 NFY	17997	LX53 KCG	18479	LX55 ESN
10158	EU62 AYE	17770	LX03 BVF	17976	LX53 JZV	17998	LX53 KCJ	18480	LX55 ESO
10159	EU62 AZA	17771	LX03 BVG	17977	LX53 JZW	17999	LX04 GCU	19734	LX11 AZZ
10160	EU62 AZO	17772	LX03 BVH	17978	LX53 KAE	18201	LX04 FWL	19735	LX11 BAA
10161	EU62 AAE	17773	LX03 BVJ	17979	LX53 KAJ	18202	LX04 FWM	19736	LX11 BAO
10162	EU62 AAO	17774	LX03 BVK	17980	LX53 KAK	18203	LX04 FWN	19737	LX11 BAU
10163	EU62 ADZ	17775	LX03 BVL	17981	LX53 KAO	18451	LX05 LLM	19738	LX11 BAV
17559	LY02 OBL	17776	LX03 BVM	17982	LX53 KAU	18452	LX05 LLN	19739	LX11 BBE
17564	LV52 HDX	17777	LX03 BVN	17983	LX53 KBE	18465	LX55 EPP	19740	LX11 BBF
17574	LV52 HFF	17778	LX03 BVP	17984	LX53 KBF	18466	LX55 EPU	19741	LX11 BBJ
17748	LY52 ZFG	17791	LX03 BWE	17985	LX53 KBJ	18467	LX55 EPV	36261	LX11 AVP
17756	LX03 BUA	17792	LX03 BWF	17986	LX53 KBK	18468	LX55 EPY	36262	LX11 AVR
17759	LX03 BUH	17793	LX03 BWG	17987	LX53 KBN	18469	LX55 EPZ	36263	LX11 AVT
17760	LX03 BUJ	17796	LX03 BWK	17988	LX53 KBO	18470	LX55 ERJ	36264	LX11 AVU
17761	LX03 BUP	17829	LX03 BYC	17989	LX53 KBP	18471	LX55 ERK	36265	LX11 AVV
17762	LX03 BUU	17830	LX03 BYD	17990	LX53 KBV	18472	LX05 LNC	36266	LX11 AVW
17763	LX03 BUV	17835	LX03 BYL	17991	LX53 KBY	18473	LX55 ERU	36267	LX11 AVY
17764	LX03 BUW	17854	LX03 BZH	17992	LX53 KBZ	18474	LX55 ERV		
17765	LX03 BVA	17867	LX03 NFM	17993	LX53 KCA	18475	LX55 ERY		
17766	LX03 BVB	17868	LX03 NFN	17994	LX53 KCC	18476	LX55 ERZ		

The Seymer Road entrance to **Romford Bus Garage** viewed on August 20th, 2014

Stagecoach London bus 19739 parked on the exit road into Park Drive at **Romford Bus Garage** on August 20th, 2014.

Shepherds Bush Bus Garage on August 17th, 2013 with London United bus **DE36** in view.

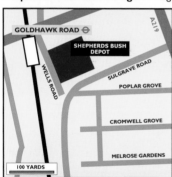

SHEPHERDS BUSH (S)
Wells Road, London W12 8DA
Operated by: London United
Location: TQ23237957 [51.501662, -0.226015]
Nearest Tube Station: Goldhawk Road (adjacent)
Nearest Bus Routes: 94 & 237 - Goldhawk Road (Stop K)
Bus Routes Serviced: 72/94/148/220 (Night Service only)/272/419/C1 & N97

The signboard on the offices at **Shepherds Bush** (or should that be Shepherd's Bush?) **Bus Garage** on February 22nd, 2014.

London United bus **LT136** parked at the rear of **Shepherds Bush Bus Garage** on February 22nd, 2014.

A general view of the interior of **Shepherds Bush Bus Garage** on February 22nd, 2014 with London United buses **LT129 & LT141** parked in the depot.

VEHICLE ALLOCATION

ADH3	SN60 BXX	DE36	YX09 HKE	DE94	SN10 CAX	LT126	LTZ 1126	SP31	YN08 DHX
ADH4	SN60 BXY	DE37	YX09 HKF	DE95	SN10 CBF	LT127	LTZ 1127	SP32	YN08 DHY
ADH5	SN60 BXZ	DE38	YX09 HKG	DE96	SN10 CBO	LT128	LTZ 1128	SP33	YN08 DHZ
ADH6	SN60 BYA	DE39	YX09 HKH	DE97	SN10 CBU	LT129	LTZ 1129	SP35	YN08 MRV
ADH7	SN60 BYB	DE40	YX09 HKJ	DE98	SN10 CBV	LT130	LTZ 1130	SP36	YN08 MRX
ADH8	SN60 BYC	DE41	YX09 HKK	DE99	SN10 CBX	LT131	LTZ 1131	SP37	YN08 MRY
ADH9	SN60 BYD	DE42	YX09 HKL	DE100	SN10 CBY	LT132	LTZ 1132	SP34	YN08 MTU
ADH10	SN60 BYF	DE43	YX09 HKM	DE101	SN10 CCA	LT133	LTZ 1133	SP122	YR59 FZD
ADH11	SN60 BYG	DE44	YX09 HKN	DE102	SN10 CCD	LT134	LTZ 1134	SP135	YT59 PBU
ADH12	SN60 BYH	DE45	YX09 HKO	DE103	SN10 CCE	LT135	LTZ 1135	TA231	LG02 FAJ
ADH13	SN60 BYJ	DE46	YX09 HKP	DE104	SN10 CCF	LT136	LTZ 1136	TA238	LG02 FBC
ADH14	SN60 BYK	DE47	YX09 HKT	DE105	SN10 CCJ	LT137	LTZ 1137	TA240	LG02 FBE
ADH15	SN60 BYL	DE48	YX09 HKU	DE106	SN10 CCK	LT138	LTZ 1138	TA245	LG02 FBN
ADH16	SN60 BYM	DE49	YX09 HKV	DE107	SN10 CCO	LT139	LTZ 1139	TA247	LG02 FBU
ADH17	SN60 BYO	DE74	SK07 DXZ	DE108	SN10 CCU	LT140	LTZ 1140	TA248	LG02 FBV
ADH18	SN60 BYP	DE85	SK07 DYS	DPS668	LG02 FGV	LT141	LTZ 1141	VE1	PG04 WGN
ADH19	SN60 BYR	DE86	SK07 DYT	DPS669	LG02 FGX	LT142	LTZ 1142	VE3	PG04 WGU
ADH20	SN60 BYS	DE87	SK07 DYU	DPS692	SN03 LFH	LT143	LTZ 1143	VE7	PG04 WGY
ADH21	SN60 BYT	DE88	SK07 DYV	LT120	LTZ 1120	LT144	LTZ 1144	VE8	PG04 WGZ
ADH22	SN60 BYU	DE89	SK07 DYW	LT121	LTZ 1121	LT145	LTZ 1145	VE9	PG04 WHA
DE32	YX09 HKA	DE90	SK07 DYX	LT122	LTZ 1122	LT146	LTZ 1146	VE10	PG04 WHB
DE33	YX09 HKB	DE91	SK07 DYY	LT123	LTZ 1123	LT147	LTZ 1147		
DE34	YX09 HKC	DE92	YX58 DXA	LT124	LTZ 1124	SP29	YN08 DHU		
DE35	YX09 HKD	DE93	SN10 CAV	LT125	LTZ 1125	SP30	YN08 DHV		

The entrance to **Silvertown Bus Garage** on September 7th, 2013 with Go-Ahead London bus **SE143** parked in front of the wash plant.

SILVERTOWN (SI)
Factory Road, Silvertown, London E16 2EL
Operated by: Go-Ahead London
Location: TQ42727987 [51.499516, 0.054142]
Nearest DLR Station: King George V (0.4 miles)
Nearest Bus Routes: 474 & 573 - Fernhill Street (Stop C)
Bus Routes Serviced: 150/276/474/541/549/673/ D6/D7 & D8

Go-Ahead London buses **DP195, WVL451 & SE117** standing in the yard at **Silvertown Bus Garage** on September 7th, 2013.

VEHICLE ALLOCATION

870	PN09 EKR	SE115	YX61 BXV	SE134	YX61 BWK	SO1	BV55 UCT	WVL420	LX11 CXC
871	PN09 EKT	SE116	YX61 BXW	SE135	YX61 BWL	SO2	BV55 UCU	WVL421	LX11 CXD
944	YN56 FDZ	SE117	YX61 BXY	SE136	YX61 BWM	SO3	BV55 UCW	WVL422	LX11 FHV
945	YN56 FEF	SE118	YX61 BXZ	SE137	YX61 BWN	SO4	BV55 UCX	WVL423	LX11 FHW
946	YN56 FEG	SE119	YX61 BYA	SE138	YX61 BWO	SO5	BV55 UCY	WVL424	LX11 FHY
ED28	LX07 BYU	SE120	YX61 BWU	SE139	YX61 BWP	WVL79	LF52 ZPK	WVL425	LX11 FHZ
PVL169	X569 EGK	SE121	YX61 BWV	SE140	YX61 BVY	WVL81	LF52 ZPM	WVL426	LX11 FJA
SE17	LX07 BYB	SE122	YX61 BWW	SE141	YX61 BVZ	WVL82	LF52 ZNP	WVL427	LX11 FJC
SE104	YX61 BWA	SE123	YX61 BWY	SE142	YX61 BXK	WVL90	LF52 ZNY	WVL428	LX11 FJD
SE105	YX61 BWB	SE124	YX61 BWZ	SE143	YX61 BXL	WVL92	LF52 ZND	WVL429	LX11 FJE
SE106	YX61 BWC	SE125	YX61 BXA	SE144	YX61 BXM	WVL94	LF52 ZNG	WVL430	LX11 FJF
SE107	YX61 BWD	SE126	YX61 BXB	SE145	YX61 BXN	WVL95	LF52 ZNH	WVL431	LX11 FJJ
SE108	YX61 BWE	SE127	YX61 BXC	SE146	YX61 BXO	WVL413	LX11 CWU	WVL432	LX11 FJK
SE109	YX61 BYD	SE128	YX61 BXD	SE147	YX61 BXP	WVL414	LX11 CWV	WVL433	LX11 FJN
SE110	YX61 BYF	SE129	YX61 BXE	SE148	YX61 DTO	WVL415	LX11 CWW	WVL434	LX11 FJO
SE111	YX61 BYG	SE130	YX61 BWF	SE149	YX61 DTU	WVL416	LX11 CWY		
SE112	YX61 BXR	SE131	YX61 BWG	SE150	YX61 DTV	WVL417	LX11 CWZ		
SE113	YX61 BXS	SE132	YX61 BWH	SE151	YX61 DTY	WVL418	LX11 CXA		
SE114	YX61 BXU	SE133	YX61 BWJ	SE152	YX61 DTZ	WVL419	LX11 CXB		

South Mimms Bus Garage viewed on August 20th, 2013.

SOUTH MIMMS (SM)
South Mimms Service Area, Potters Bar,
Hertfordshire EN6 3NE
Operated by: Sullivan Buses
Location: TL22960048 [51.689652, -0.222587]
Nearest Station: Potters Bar (2.6 miles)
Nearest Bus Routes: 398 & 615 - South Mimms,
Motorway Service Station (Southbound)
Bus Routes Serviced: 298/626/628/653/683 & 688
(Plus Rail Replacement Bus Services for TfL)

Sullivan buses **TAL123, DEL1, TPL927, ALX2, VPL1704 & WVL1** parked inside **South Mimms Bus Garage** on August 20th, 2013.

VEHICLE ALLOCATION

AE1	MS10 SUL	ALX1	V116 MEV	DP82	V782 FKH	ELV4	PN02 XBY	TN2	PO51 UML
AE2	SN57 DXH	ALX2	V117 MEV	DP92	V792 FKH	ELV5	PA04 CYH	TN3	PO51 UMR
AE3	SN57 DXK	ALX3	V119 MEV	DP96	V796 FKH	ELV6	PL51 LGG	TPL926	EY03 FNK
AE4	NH11 SUL	ALX4	V139 MEV	DPS574	SN51 SZK	ELV7	PO04 ADU	TPL927	EY03 FNL
AE5	AH11 SUL	ALX5	V142 MEV	DPS575	SN51 SZL	ELV8	PO04 OOE	VP113	W459 BCW
AE11	CJ61 SUL	ALX6	LY02 OAX	DPS576	SN51 SZO	ELV9	PO04 OOF	VP119	W466 BCW
AE12	DS61 SUL	DEL1	PJ52 BYP	DPS577	SN51 SZP	ELV10	PO04 OOG	VPL174	X157 JOP
AE13	KR61 SUL	DN1	X2 SUL	DT4	G504 VYE	PDL26	PJ02 PZZ	WVL1	GD52 SYC
AE14	KS61 SUL	DN2	DN02 SUL	ELV1	EL04 SUL	TAL123	X343 HLL	WVL2	FJ57 CYZ
AE15	TW6 1SUL	DN3	SC02 SUL	ELV2	PN02 XCR	TAL132	X332 HLL	WVL3	FJ57 CZD
AE16	SB61 SUL	DN4	CN02 SUL	ELV3	PL51 LGD	TN1	PO51 UMH	WVL4	FJ57 CZE

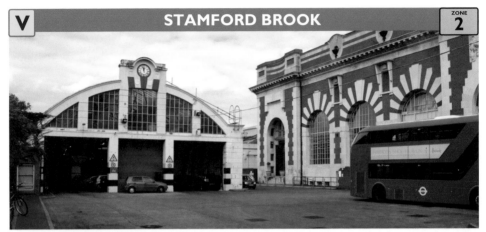

Stamford Brook Bus Garage viewed on September 27th, 2014. Following closure to trams it became a trolleybus depot in 1935 and, later, an omnibus works and store. It was leased out in 1963 but, in 1966, was used as a garage for British Airways bus services. It became a bus garage in 1980, was closed in 1996 and used as a bus store and re-opened in 1999.

STAMFORD BROOK (V)
72-74 Chiswick High Road, London W4 1SY
Operated by: London United
Location: TQ21587867 [51.493877, -0.250044]
Nearest Tube Station: Stamford Brook (0.4 miles)
Nearest Bus Routes: 27/190/237/267/ 391/H91/N9& N11 - Turnham Green, Stamford Brook Bus Garage (Stop PP)
Bus Routes Serviced: 9/10/27 & 419

It was opened as a horse tram depot by the West Metropolitan Tramways in 1883/4 and electrified in 1901. At this point it was converted to a works with a further tram shed added on the western side. The depot closed to trams on May 5th, 1932.

VEHICLE ALLOCATION

ADH1	SN58 EOR	ADH46	YX62 FTD	LT78	LTZ 1078	LT156	LTZ 1156	SP140	YP59 ODW
ADH2	SN58 EOS	ADH47	YX62 FTF	LT79	LTZ 1079	LT157	LTZ 1157	SP141	YP59 ODX
ADH23	YX62 FAU	ADH48	YX62 FTP	LT80	LTZ 1080	LT158	LTZ 1158	SP142	YP59 OEA
ADH24	YX62 FCM	ADH49	YX62 FTZ	LT81	LTZ 1081	LT159	LTZ 1159	SP143	YP59 OEB
ADH25	YX62 FDD	ADH50	YX62 FUT	LT82	LTZ 1082	LT160	LTZ 1160	SP144	YP59 OEC
ADH26	YX62 FDY	ADH51	YX62 FTU	LT83	LTZ 1083	LT161	LTZ 1161	SP145	YP59 OED
ADH27	YX62 FFB	DPS664	LG02 FGN	LT84	LTZ 1084	LT162	LTZ 1162	SP146	YP59 OEE
ADH28	YX62 FFG	DPS671	LG02 FHA	LT85	LTZ 1085	LT163	LTZ 1163	SP147	YP59 OEF
ADH29	YX62 FHA	DPS701	SN55 HKD	LT86	LTZ 1086	LT164	LTZ 1164	SP148	YP59 OEG
ADH30	YX62 FHO	DPS702	SN55 HKE	LT87	LTZ 1087	LT165	LTZ 1165	SP149	YP59 OEH
ADH31	YX62 FJD	DPS703	SN55 HKF	LT88	LTZ 1088	LT166	LTZ 1166	SP150	YP59 OEJ
ADH32	YX62 FJV	DPS704	SN55 HKG	LT89	LTZ 1089	LT167	LTZ 1167	SP151	YP59 OEK
ADH33	YX62 FKE	DPS705	SN55 HKH	LT90	LTZ 1090	LT168	LTZ 1168	SP152	YP59 OEL
ADH34	YX62 FKK	DPS706	SN55 HKJ	LT91	LTZ 1091	LT169	LTZ 1169	SP153	YP59 OEM
ADH35	YX62 FLH	DPS719	SN55 HSE	LT92	LTZ 1092	LT170	LTZ 1170	SP154	YP59 OEN
ADH36	YX62 FME	DPS720	SN55 HKZ	LT93	LTZ 1093	LT171	LTZ 1171	SP155	YP59 OEO
ADH37	YX62 FMG	LT69	LTZ 1069	LT94	LTZ 1094	LT174	LTZ 1174	SP156	YP59 OER
ADH38	YX62 FMV	LT70	LTZ 1070	LT148	LTZ 1148	LT175	LTZ 1175	SP157	YP59 OES
ADH39	YX62 FNZ	LT71	LTZ 1071	LT149	LTZ 1149	SP10	YN56 FBO	SP158	YP59 OET
ADH40	YX62 FOA	LT72	LTZ 1072	LT150	LTZ 1150	SP124	YR59 FZF	SP159	YP59 OEU
ADH41	YX62 FPC	LT73	LTZ 1073	LT151	LTZ 1151	SP133	YT59 PCO	SP160	YP59 OEV
ADH42	YX62 FPF	LT74	LTZ 1074	LT152	LTZ 1152	SP134	YT59 PCU	SP161	YP59 OEW
ADH43	YX62 FPK	LT75	LTZ 1075	LT153	LTZ 1153	SP137	YP59 ODT	SP162	YP59 OEX
ADH44	YX62 FSE	LT76	LTZ 1076	LT154	LTZ 1154	SP138	YP59 ODU		
ADH45	YX62 FSS	LT77	LTZ 1077	LT155	LTZ 1155	SP139	YP59 ODV		

The entrance to **Stamford Hill Bus Garage** on August 5th, 2014 with Arriva London bus **PDL82** parked outside on Rookwood Road.

STAMFORD HILL (SF)

Rookwood Road, London N16 6SS
Operated by: Arriva London
Location: TQ34078790 [51.574106, -0.066831]
Nearest Station: Stamford Hill (0.4 miles)
Nearest Bus Routes: 67/76/149/243/253/254/318/ 349 & 476
Bus Routes Serviced: 67/73/253/N73 & N253

It was opened as an electric tram depot by London County Council on February 9th, 1907 and closed by London Transport on February 5th, 1939. It was then utilized as a trolleybus depot until July 18th, 1961 and subsequently as an omnibus garage. Stamford Hill Garage closed in 1995, reopened in 1996, closed once more in 2000 and finally reopened again in July 2002.

VEHICLE ALLOCATION

DW428	LJ11 ADO	DW455	LJ61 CFD	HV42	LJ11 EFN	HV69	LJ62 BSO	VLW182	LJ03 MLZ		
DW429	LJ11 ADU	DW456	LJ61 CFE	HV43	LJ11 EFO	HV70	LJ62 BTO	VLW183	LJ03 MMA		
DW430	LJ11 ADV	DW457	LJ61 CFF	HV44	LJ11 EFP	HV71	LJ62 BTY	VLW184	LJ03 MME		
DW431	LJ11 ADX	DW458	LJ61 CFG	HV45	LJ11 EFR	HV72	LJ62 BVE	VLW185	LJ03 MMF		
DW432	LJ11 ADZ	DW459	LJ61 CDX	HV46	LJ11 EEU	HV73	LJ62 BVP	VLW186	LJ03 MMK		
DW433	LJ11 AEA	DW460	LJ61 CDY	HV47	LJ62 BEO	HV74	LJ62 BVY	VLW187	LJ03 MKM		
DW434	LJ11 ABK	DW461	LJ61 CDZ	HV48	LJ62 BGK	HV75	LJ62 BWF	VLW188	LJ03 MKN		
DW435	LJ11 ABN	DW462	LJ61 CEA	HV49	LJ62 BGX	HV76	LJ62 BWP	VLW189	LJ03 MYN		
DW436	LJ11 ABO	DW463	LJ61 CEF	HV50	LJ62 BHY	HV77	LJ62 BFZ	VLW190	LJ03 MXR		
DW437	LJ11 ABU	DW464	LJ61 CEK	HV51	LJ62 BKU	HV78	LJ62 BGZ	VLW191	LJ03 MXS		
DW438	LJ11 ABV	HV25	LJ60 JGY	HV52	LJ62 BKX	HV79	LJ62 BHF	VLW192	LJ03 MXT		
DW439	LJ11 ABX	HV26	LJ60 JGZ	HV53	LJ62 BMZ	HV80	LJ62 BJK	VLW193	LJ03 MXU		
DW440	LJ11 ABZ	HV27	LJ11 EFT	HV54	LJ62 BNE	HV81	LJ62 BJX	VLW194	LJ03 MWX		
DW441	LJ11 ACF	HV28	LJ11 EFU	HV55	LJ62 BNL	HV82	LJ13 FDD	VLW195	LJ53 BEU		
DW442	LJ11 ACO	HV29	LJ11 EFV	HV56	LJ62 BNU	HV83	LJ13 FDE	VLW196	LJ53 BEY		
DW443	LJ11 ACU	HV30	LJ11 EFW	HV57	LJ62 BXD	VLW170	LJ03 MOA	VLW197	LJ53 BFA		
DW444	LJ11 AAE	HV31	LJ11 EFX	HV58	LJ62 BXF	VLW171	LJ03 MOF	VLW198	LJ53 BFE		
DW445	LJ11 AAF	HV32	LJ11 EFY	HV59	LJ62 BYT	VLW172	LJ03 MOV	VLW199	LJ53 BFF		
DW446	LJ61 CFA	HV33	LJ11 EFZ	HV60	LJ62 BYU	VLW173	VLT 173				
DW447	LJ61 CFK	HV34	LJ11 EGC	HV61	LJ62 BZH	VLW174	LJ03 MPF				
DW448	LJ61 CFL	HV35	LJ11 EGD	HV62	LJ62 BZR	VLW175	LJ03 MPU				
DW449	LJ61 CDV	HV36	LJ11 EFE	HV63	LJ62 BZY	VLW176	LJ03 MPV				
DW450	LJ11 AAX	HV37	LJ11 EFF	HV64	LJ62 BAO	VLW177	LJ03 MLL				
DW451	LJ11 AAY	HV38	LJ11 EFG	HV65	LJ62 BAU	VLW178	LJ03 MLN				
DW452	LJ61 CEV	HV39	LJ11 EFK	HV66	LJ62 BCU	VLW179	LJ03 MLV				
DW453	LJ61 CEX	HV40	LJ11 EFL	HV67	LJ62 BND	VLW180	LJ03 MLX				
DW454	LJ61 CEY	HV41	LJ11 EFM	HV68	LJ62 BPV	VLW181	LJ03 MLY				

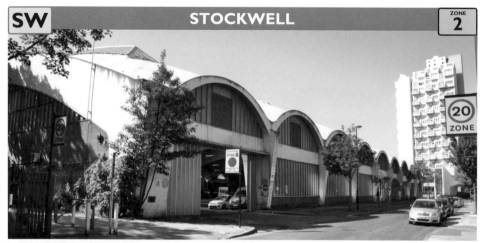

In 2011 the author Will Self nominated **Stockwell Bus Garage** as London's most important building. This is the exit, fronting onto Lansdowne Way on August 31st, 2013.

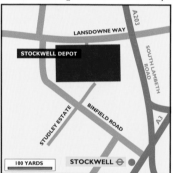

STOCKWELL (SW)
Binfield Road, London SW4 6ST
Operated by: Go-Ahead London
Location: TQ30417669 [51.473431, -0.124235]
Nearest Tube Station: Stockwell (0.2 miles)
Nearest Bus Routes: 22/024/025/026/88/A3 & N2
- South Lambeth Road, Stockwell Station (Stop A)
Bus Routes Serviced: 11/19/87/88/170/196/315/
333/337/639/670/N11/N19/N44 & N87

This Grade 2* Listed building was opened in 1952 and featured the largest area of uninterrupted floor space enclosed by a single roof in Europe – some 73,750 ft². Due to post WWII material shortages, principally steel, the roof was designed as a whale-back structure and constructed in reinforced concrete.

An interior view of **Stockwell Bus Garage** on April 23rd, 2014 with Go-Ahead London bus **WHV26** sitting under the cavernous concrete roof.

Go-Ahead London bus **E162** departing from **Stockwell Bus Garage** onto Lansdowne Way on April 23rd, 2014.

VEHICLE ALLOCATION

DP193	EU53 PXY	E152	SN11 BTZ	LDP291	LX06 EZW	SE54	YX60 EOO	WVL113	LX03 EEB
DP194	EU53 PXZ	E153	SN11 BUA	LT41	LTZ 1041	WHV17	LJ61 NVC	WVL114	LX03 EEF
DP195	EU53 PYA	E154	SN11 BUE	LT42	LTZ 1042	WHV18	LJ61 NVD	WVL115	LX03 EEG
DP196	EU53 PYB	E155	SN11 BUF	LT43	LTZ 1043	WHV19	LJ61 NVE	WVL116	LX03 EEH
DP197	EU53 PYD	E156	SN11 BUH	LT44	LTZ 1044	WHV20	LJ61 NVF	WVL117	LX03 EEJ
DP198	EU53 PYF	E157	SN11 BUJ	LT45	LTZ 1045	WHV21	LJ61 NVG	WVL118	LX03 EEM
DP199	EU53 PYG	E158	SN11 BUO	LT46	LTZ 1046	WHV22	LJ61 NVH	WVL119	LX03 ECV
DP200	EU53 PYH	E159	SN11 BUP	LT47	LTZ 1047	WHV23	LJ61 NVK	WVL120	LX03 ECW
DP201	EU53 PYJ	E160	SN11 BUU	LT48	LTZ 1048	WHV24	LJ61 NVL	WVL121	LX03 ECY
DP202	EU53 PYL	E161	SN11 BUV	LT49	LTZ 1049	WHV25	LJ61 NVM	WVL122	LX53 AZP
DP203	EU53 PYO	E162	SN11 BUW	LT50	LTZ 1050	WHV26	LJ61 NVN	WVL123	LX53 AZR
DP204	EU53 PYP	EH1	LX58 DDJ	LT51	LTZ 1051	WHV27	LJ12 CHH	WVL150	LX53 BJO
DP205	BT04 BUS	EH2	LX58 DDK	LT52	LTZ 1052	WHV28	LJ61 NVP	WVL468	LJ61 NWX
DP209	SN56 AYD	EH3	LX58 DDL	LT53	LTZ 1053	WHV29	LJ61 NVR	WVL469	LJ12 CHC
E1	SN06 BNA	EH4	LX58 DDN	LT54	LTZ 1054	WHV30	LJ61 NVS	WVL470	LJ61 NWZ
E2	SN06 BNB	EH5	LX58 DDO	LT55	LTZ 1055	WHV31	LJ12 CHK	WVL471	LJ61 NXA
E3	SN06 BND	EH21	YX13 BJE	LT56	LTZ 1056	WVL1	LG02 KGP	WVL472	LJ61 NXB
E4	SN06 BNE	EH22	YX13 BJF	LT57	LTZ 1057	WVL2	LG02 KGU	WVL473	LJ61 NXC
E5	SN06 BNF	EH23	YX13 BJJ	LT58	LTZ 1058	WVL3	LG02 KGV	WVL474	LJ61 NXD
E6	SN06 BNJ	EH24	YX13 BJK	LT59	LTZ 1059	WVL4	LG02 KGX	WVL475	LJ61 NXE
E7	SN06 BNK	EH25	YX13 BJO	LT60	LTZ 1060	WVL5	LG02 KGY	WVL476	LJ61 NXF
E8	SN06 BNL	EH26	YX13 BJU	LT61	LTZ 1061	WVL6	LG02 KGZ	WVL477	LJ61 NWL
E9	SN06 BNO	EH27	YX13 BJV	LT63	LTZ 1063	WVL7	LG02 KHA	WVL478	LJ61 NWM
E10	SN06 BNU	EH28	YX13 BJY	LT64	LTZ 1064	WVL8	LG02 KHE	WVL479	LJ61 NWN
E11	SN06 BNV	EH29	YX13 BJZ	LT65	LTZ 1065	WVL9	LG02 KHF	WVL480	LJ61 NWO
E12	SN06 BNX	EH30	YX13 BKA	LT66	LTZ 1066	WVL10	LG02 KHH	WVL481	LJ12 CHD
E13	SN06 BNY	EH31	YX13 BKD	LT67	LTZ 1067	WVL11	LG02 KHJ	WVL482	LJ61 NWR
E14	SN06 BNZ	EH32	YX13 BKE	LT68	LTZ 1068	WVL12	LG02 KHK	WVL483	LJ12 CHF
E15	SN06 BOF	EH33	YX13 BKF	LT118	LTZ 1118	WVL13	LG02 KHL	WVL484	LJ12 CHG
E38	LX06 FKN	EH34	YX13 BKG	LT119	LTZ 1119	WVL87	LF52 ZNV	WVL485	LJ61 NWU
E129	SN60 BZA	EH35	YX13 BKJ	LT189	LTZ 1189	WVL96	LF52 ZNJ	WVL486	LJ61 NWV
E130	SN60 BZB	EH36	YX13 BKK	PVL203	X503 EGK	WVL104	LF52 ZMU	WVL487	LJ61 NVZ
E131	SN60 BZC	EH37	YX13 BKL	PVL232	Y732 TGH	WVL105	LX03 EXV	WVL488	LJ61 NWA
E132	SN60 BZD	EH38	YX13 BKN	SE47	YX60 EOE	WVL106	LX03 EXW	WVL489	LJ61 NWB
E133	SN60 BZE	LDP191	SN51 UAD	SE48	YX60 EOF	WVL107	LX03 EXZ	WVL490	LJ61 NWC
E134	SN60 BZF	LDP204	SN51 UAT	SE49	YX60 EOG	WVL108	LX03 EXU	WVL491	LJ61 NWD
E135	SN60 BZG	LDP287	LX06 FBB	SE50	YX60 EOH	WVL109	LX03 EDR	WVL492	LJ61 NWE
E136	SN60 BZH	LDP288	LX06 FBC	SE51	YX60 EOJ	WVL110	LX03 EDU	WVL493	LJ61 NWF
E137	SN60 BZJ	LDP289	LX06 EZU	SE52	YX60 EOK	WVL111	LX03 EDV	WVL494	LJ61 NWG
E151	SN11 BTY	LDP290	LX06 EZV	SE53	YX60 EOL	WVL112	LX03 EEA	WVL495	LJ61 NWH

The main, Bushey Road, entrance to **Sutton Bus Garage** on October 16th, 2013.

SUTTON (A)
Bushey Road, Sutton SM1 1QJ
Operated by: Go-Ahead London
Location: TQ25456488 [51.369433, -0.199093]
Nearest Station: West Sutton (0.7 miles)
Nearest Bus Routes: 80 & 613 - Sutton Bus Garage/
Bushey Road
Bus Routes Serviced: 80/93/151/154/164/213/413
& N155

The garage was opened in January 1924 by the London General Omnibus Company with a capacity of about 100 buses. It won the Bus Garage of the Year Award for 2004 and in 2013 ran buses branded as "London General".

VEHICLE ALLOCATION

DOE1	LX58 CWN	DOE21	LX58 CXL	DOE41	LX09 BXK	PVL282	PJ02 RCF	SE171	YX61 EKK
DOE2	LX58 CWO	DOE22	LX58 CXN	DOE42	LX09 BXL	PVL283	PJ02 RCO	SE172	YX61 EKL
DOE3	LX58 CWP	DOE23	LX58 CXO	DOE43	LX09 BXM	PVL284	PJ02 RCU	SE173	YX61 EKM
DOE4	LX58 CWR	DOE24	LX58 CXP	DOE44	LX09 BXO	PVL285	PJ02 RCV	SE174	YX61 EKN
DOE5	LX58 CWT	DOE25	LX58 CXR	DOE45	LX09 AXU	PVL286	PJ02 RCX	SOE29	LX09 AZR
DOE6	LX58 CWU	DOE26	LX58 CXS	DOE46	LX09 AXV	PVL287	PJ02 RCY	SOE30	LX09 AZT
DOE7	LX58 CWV	DOE27	LX58 CXT	DOE47	LX09 AXW	PVL288	PJ02 RCZ	SOE31	LX09 BXP
DOE8	LX58 CWW	DOE28	LX58 CXU	DOE48	LX09 AXY	PVL289	PJ02 RDO	SOE32	LX09 BXR
DOE9	LX58 CWY	DOE29	LX58 CXV	DOE49	LX09 AXZ	PVL290	PJ02 RDU	SOE33	LX09 BXS
DOE10	LX58 CWZ	DOE30	LX58 CXW	DOE50	LX09 AYA	PVL291	PJ02 RDV	SOE34	LX09EVB
DOE11	LX58 CXA	DOE31	LX58 CXY	DOE51	LX09 AYB	PVL292	PJ02 RDX	SOE35	LX09 EVC
DOE12	LX58 CXB	DOE32	LX58 CXZ	DOE52	LX09 AYC	PVL293	PJ02 RDY	SOE36	LX09 EVD
DOE13	LX58 CXC	DOE33	LX58 CYA	DOE53	LX09 AYD	PVL294	PJ02 RDZ	SOE37	LX09 EVF
DOE14	LX58 CXD	DOE34	LX58 CYC	DOE54	LX09 AYE	PVL295	PJ02 REU	SOE38	LX09 EVG
DOE15	LX58 CXE	DOE35	LX58 CYE	E58	LX07 BYC	PVL296	PJ02 RFE	SOE39	LX09 EVH
DOE16	LX58 CXF	DOE36	LX58 CYF	E59	LX07 BYD	PVL297	PJ02 RFF	SOE40	LX09 EVJ
DOE17	LX58 CXG	DOE37	LX58 CYG	E60	LX07 BYF	SE167	YX61 EKF	WVL74	LF52 ZPD
DOE18	LX58 CXH	DOE38	LX09 BXG	LDP197	SN51 UAK	SE168	YX61 EKG	WVL76	LF52 ZPG
DOE19	LX58 CXJ	DOE39	LX09 BXH	LDP201	SN51 UAP	SE169	YX61 EKH		
DOE20	LX58 CXK	DOE40	LX09 BXJ	PVL281	PJ02 RBZ	SE170	YX61 EKJ		

Thornton Heath Bus Garage viewed on August 19th, 2014 with Arriva London bus **T139** entering the depot and passing Arriva London buses **DLA376** & **DLA386** parked in the yard.

THORNTON HEATH (TH)
Whitehall Road, Thornton Heath CR7 6AE
Operated by: Arriva London
Location: TQ32166765 [51.392508, -0.114847]
Nearest Station: Thornton Heath (0.9 miles)
Nearest Bus Routes: 64/109/289/N64 & N109 - Thornton Heath Pond (Stop J)
Bus Routes Serviced: 198/250/255/289/410 & 450

This garage was built on the site of Thornton Heath Tram Depot which was opened on October 9th, 1879 by the Croydon Tramways Company and closed by London Transport on December 31st, 1949. Thornton Heath was rebuilt and partially operational prior to the official reopening as an omnibus garage in 1951.

VEHICLE ALLOCATION

DLA256	X508 GGO	DWL6	Y806 DGT	DWS15	LJ53 NGN	PDL113	LJ54 LHO	T128	LJ10 HVH
DLA374	LJ03 MSY	DWL7	LJ51 DDK	DWS16	LJ53 NFE	PDL114	LJ54 LHP	T129	LJ10 HVK
DLA376	LJ03 MTF	DWL8	LJ51 DDL	DWS17	LJ53 NFF	PDL124	LJ56 APZ	T130	LJ10 HVL
DLA377	LJ03 MTK	DWL9	LJ51 DDN	DWS18	LJ53 NFG	PDL125	LJ56 ARF	T131	LJ10 HTZ
DLA378	LJ03 MTU	DWL10	LJ51 DDO	ENX9	LJ12 BYS	PDL126	LJ56 ARO	T132	LJ10 HUA
DLA379	LJ03 MTV	DWL11	LJ51 DDU	ENX10	LJ12 BYT	PDL127	LJ56 ARU	T133	LJ10 HUH
DLA380	LJ03 MTY	DWL16	LJ51 DEU	ENX11	LJ12 BYU	PDL128	LJ56 ARX	T134	LJ10 HUK
DLA381	LJ03 MTZ	DWS1	LJ53 NGZ	ENX12	LJ12 BYV	PDL129	LJ56 ARZ	T135	LJ10 HUO
DLA382	LJ03 MUA	DWS2	LJ53 NHA	ENX13	LJ12 BXY	PDL130	LJ56 ASO	T136	LJ10 HUP
DLA383	LJ03 MUB	DWS3	LJ53 NHB	ENX14	LJ12 BXZ	PDL131	LJ56 ASU	T137	LJ10 HUU
DLA384	LJ03 MYU	DWS4	LJ53 NHC	ENX15	LJ12 BYA	PDL132	LJ56 ASV	T138	LJ10 HUV
DLA385	LJ03 MYV	DWS5	LJ53 NHD	ENX16	LJ12 BYB	PDL133	LJ56 ASX	T139	LJ10 HUY
DLA386	LJ03 MYX	DWS6	LJ53 NFT	ENX17	LJ12 BYC	PDL134	LJ56 AOW	T140	LJ10 HUZ
DLA387	LJ03 MYY	DWS7	LJ53 NFU	ENX18	LJ12 BYD	PDL135	LJ56 AOX	T141	LJ10 HTT
DLA388	LJ03 MYZ	DWS8	LJ53 NFV	ENX19	LJ12 BYF	PDL136	LJ56 AOY	T142	LJ10 HTU
DLA389	LJ03 MZD	DWS9	LJ53 NFX	PDL97	LJ54 BAO	T122	LJ10 HVB	T143	LJ10 HTV
DWL1	Y801 DGT	DWS10	LJ53 NFY	PDL98	LJ54 BAU	T123	LJ10 HVC	T144	LJ10 HTX
DWL2	Y802 DGT	DWS11	LJ53 NFZ	PDL99	LJ54 BAV	T124	LJ10 HVD		
DWL3	Y803 DGT	DWS12	LJ53 NGE	PDL100	LJ54 BBE	T125	LJ10 HVE		
DWL4	Y804 DGT	DWS13	LJ53 NGF	PDL111	LJ54 LHM	T126	LJ10 HVF		
DWL5	Y805 DGT	DWS14	LJ53 NGG	PDL112	LJ54 LHN	T127	LJ10 HVG		

The entrance to **Tolworth Garage** on October 16th, 2013 with London United buses **TA320** & **SDE5** amongst those in view. The wash unit can be seen on the left and the main depot buildings on the right. It opened in 2002 with a nominal capacity of 100 buses.

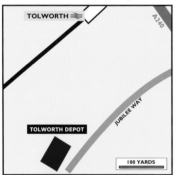

TOLWORTH (TV)
Kingston Road, Tolworth KT5 9NU
Operated by: London United
Location: TQ196965409 [51.375715, -0.280689]
Nearest Station: Tolworth (300 yards)
Nearest Bus Routes: 406/418/965 & K2 - Tolworth, Tolworth (Stop A)
Bus Routes Serviced: 57/131/265/613/662/665/ 965/K2 & K4

The wash plant at **Tolworth Bus Garage**, viewed on September 6th, 2014.

VEHICLE ALLOCATION

DE57	SK07 DXE	DPS653	LG02 FFX	TA208	SN51 SYG	TA286	LG02 FEK	VLE12	PG04 WHR
DE58	SK07 DXF	DPS654	LG02 FFY	TA209	SN51 SYH	TA313	SN03 DZK	VLE13	PG04 WHS
DE59	SK07 DXG	DPS655	LG02 FFZ	TA210	SN51 SYJ	TA315	SN03 DZP	VLE14	PG04 WHT
DE60	SK07 DXH	DPS658	LG02 FGD	TA211	SN51 SYO	TA316	SN03 DZR	VLE15	PG04 WHU
DE61	SK07 DXJ	DPS683	SN03 LEF	TA212	SN51 SYR	TA317	SN03 DZS	VLE16	PG04 WHV
DE62	SK07 DXL	DPS684	SN03 LEJ	TA214	SN51 SYT	TA318	SN03 DZT	VLE17	PG04 WHW
DE63	SK07 DXM	DPS685	SN03 LEU	TA219	SN51 SYY	TA320	SN03 DZW	VLE18	PG04 WHX
DE64	SK07 DXO	DPS688	SN03 LFD	TA220	SN51 SYZ	VLE1	PG04 WHC	VLE19	PG04 WHZ
DE65	SK07 DXP	DPS721	SN55 HLA	TA221	SN51 SZC	VLE2	PG04 WHD	VLE20	PG04 WJA
DE66	SK07 DXR	DPS722	SN55 HLC	TA222	SN51 SZD	VLE3	PG04 WHE	VLE21	PA04 CYC
DE67	SK07 DXS	SDE6	YX08 MEU	TA223	SN51 SZE	VLE4	PG04 WHF	VLE22	PA04 CYE
DPS589	SN51 TCY	SDE7	YX08 MEV	TA224	SN51 SZT	VLE5	PG04 WHH	VLE23	PA04 CYF
DPS592	SN51 TCK	SDE8	YX08 MFA	TA225	SN51 SZU	VLE6	PG04 WHJ	VLE24	PA04 CYG
DPS648	LG02 FFS	SDE9	YX08 MHM	TA236	LG02 FBA	VLE7	PG04 WHK	VLE26	PA04 CYJ
DPS649	LG02 FFT	SDE10	YX08 MFK	TA241	LG02 FBF	VLE8	PG04 WHL		
DPS650	LG02 FFU	TA204	SN51 SYA	TA244	LG02 FBL	VLE9	PG04 WHM		
DPS651	LG02 FFV	TA206	SN51 SYE	TA284	LG02 FEH	VLE10	PG04 WHN		
DPS652	LG02 FFW	TA207	SN51 SYF	TA285	LG02 FEJ	VLE11	PG04 WHP		

Arriva London bus **DW581** exiting from **Tottenham Bus Garage** on July 22nd, 2014.

TOTTENHAM (AR)
Philip Lane, Tottenham, London N15 4JB
Operated by: Arriva London
Location: TQ33688957 [51.588761, -0.072042]
Nearest Tube Station: Tottenham Hale (0.5 miles)
Nearest Bus Routes: 41/76/123/149/230/243/259/
279/318/341/349/476 & W4 (Philip Lane/High Road)
Bus Routes Serviced: 41/67/76/123/149/230/243/
341/N41 & N76

The garage was built in 1913 by the Metropolitan Electric Tramway Company to house the omnibuses utilized to support its tram services.

VEHICLE ALLOCATION

DW298	LJ10 CVE	DW326	LJ60 AXH	DW424	LJ11 ACZ	DW581	LT63 UKC	HV23	LJ60 AWU
DW299	LJ10 CVF	DW327	LJ60 AXK	DW425	LJ61 CEN	DW582	LT63 UKD	HV24	LJ60 AWV
DW300	LJ10 CVG	DW328	LJ60 AXM	DW426	LJ61 CEO	DW583	LT63 UKE	T145	LJ60 AVR
DW301	LJ10 CVH	DW329	LJ60 AXN	DW427	LJ61 CEU	DW584	LT63 UKF	T146	LJ60 AVT
DW302	LJ10 CVK	DW330	LJ60 AXO	DW534	LJ13 CLN	DW585	LT63 UKG	T147	LJ60 AVU
DW303	LJ10 CVL	DW331	LJ60 AXP	DW535	LJ13 CLO	DW586	LT63 UKH	T148	LJ60 AVV
DW304	LJ10 CVM	DW332	LJ60 AXR	DW536	LJ13 CLV	HV1	LJ09 KRU	T149	LJ60 AVW
DW305	LJ10 CVN	DW333	LJ60 AXS	DW537	LJ13 CLX	HV2	LJ09 KOE	T150	LJ60 AVX
DW306	LJ10 CVO	DW334	LJ60 AXT	DW538	LJ13 CLY	HV3	LJ09 KOU	T151	LJ60 AVY
DW307	LJ10 CVP	DW335	LJ60 AXU	DW539	LJ13 CEV	HV4	LJ09 KOH	T152	LJ60 AVZ
DW308	LJ10 CUO	DW336	LJ60 AWW	DW540	LJ13 CEX	HV5	LJ09 KOV	T153	LJ60 AWA
DW309	LJ10 CUU	DW401	LJ11 AEO	DW541	LJ13 CFA	HV6	LJ09 KOW	T154	LJ60 AWC
DW310	LJ10 CUV	DW402	LJ11 AEP	DW542	LJ13 CFD	HV7	LJ60 AWY	T155	LJ60 AVC
DW311	LJ10 CUW	DW403	LJ11 AET	DW543	LJ13 CFE	HV8	LJ60 AWZ	T156	LJ60 AVD
DW312	LJ10 CUX	DW404	LJ11 AEU	DW544	LJ13 CFF	HV9	LJ60 AXA	T157	LJ60 AVE
DW313	LJ10 CUY	DW405	LJ11 AEV	DW545	LJ13 CFG	HV10	LJ60 AXB	T158	LJ60 AVF
DW314	LJ10 CVA	DW406	LJ11 AEW	DW546	LJ13 CFK	HV11	LJ60 AXC	T159	LJ60 AVG
DW315	LJ10 CVB	DW407	LJ11 AEX	DW547	LJ13 CFL	HV12	LJ60 AXD	T160	LJ60 AVK
DW316	LJ10 CVC	DW408	LJ11 AEY	DW548	LJ13 CFM	HV13	LJ60 AXF	T161	LJ60 AVM
DW317	LJ10 CVD	DW409	LJ11 AEZ	DW549	LJ13 CDV	HV14	LJ60 AXG	T162	LJ60 AVN
DW318	LJ60 AXX	DW410	LJ11 AFA	DW550	LJ13 CDX	HV15	LJ60 AWF	T163	LJ60 AVO
DW319	LJ60 AXY	DW417	LJ11 AEK	DW551	LJ13 CDY	HV16	LJ60 AWG	T164	LJ60 AVP
DW320	LJ60 AXZ	DW418	LJ11 AEL	DW552	LJ13 CDZ	HV17	LJ60 AWH	T165	LJ60 AUO
DW321	LJ60 AYA	DW419	LJ11 AEM	DW553	LJ13 CEA	HV18	LJ60 AWM	T166	LJ60 AUP
DW322	LJ60 AYB	DW420	LJ11 AEN	DW554	LJ13 CEF	HV19	LJ60 AWN	T167	LJ60 AUR
DW323	LJ60 AYC	DW421	LJ11 ACV	DW555	LJ13 CEK	HV20	LJ60 AWO	T168	LJ60 AUT
DW324	LJ60 AYD	DW422	LJ11 ACX	DW579	LT63 UKA	HV21	LJ60 AWP		
DW325	LJ60 AYE	DW423	LJ11 ACY	DW580	LT63 UKB	HV22	LJ60 AWR		

A general view of **Twickenham Depot** on September 6th, 2014. The garage was rebuilt in 1986/87 and an additional bay, constructed at the time, is clearly visible on the right.

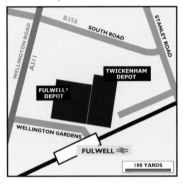

TWICKENHAM (TF)
The Old Tram Depot, Stanley Road, Twickenham, Middlesex TW2 5NT
Operated by: Abellio
Location: TQ14817191 [51.434862, -0.347518]
Nearest Station: Fulwell (Adjacent)
Nearest Bus Routes: 33/281/481 & 681 - Fulwell, Fulwell (Stop C)
Bus Routes Serviced: 117/235/290/481/490/969/H20/H25/H26/K1/K3/R68 & R70

For a potted history of Fulwell Depot, please see Page 38.

NB Both London United* and Abellio utilize this depot with the former occupying the west end and Abellio the east. (*See Page 38)

VEHICLE ALLOCATION

8447	RD02 BJK	8112	DK04 SUU	8510	LJ08 CZT	8548	YX10 FFK	8749	RN52 FVR
8448	RD02 BJO	8116	MX56 HYR	8511	LJ08 CZU	8549	YX10 FFL	8750	RN52 FVS
8449	RD02 BJU	8117	MX56 HYS	8512	LJ08 CZV	8550	YX10 FFM	8751	RN52 FXD
8450	RD02 BJV	8118	YX13 EHE	8513	LJ08 CZX	8551	YX10 FFN	8752	RN52 FYO
8451	RD02 BJX	8119	YX13 EHF	8514	LJ08 CZY	8567	YX11 HPA	8753	RN52 FZA
8478	KP02 PWV	8120	YX13 EHG	8515	LJ08 CZZ	8568	YX11 HPC	8788	YX12 GHA
8479	KP02 PVE	8121	YX13 EHH	8529	YX10 FEF	8569	YX11 HPE	8789	YX12 GHB
8480	KP02 PUK	8122	YX13 EHJ	8530	YX10 FEG	8570	YX11 HPF	8790	YX12 GHD
8481	KP02 PVU	8123	YX13 EHK	8531	YX10 FEH	8571	YX11 HPJ	8791	YX12 GHF
8482	KM02 HGF	8124	YX13 EHL	8532	YX10 FEJ	8572	YX61 BXG	8792	YX12 GHG
8483	KP02 PUJ	8125	YX13 EHM	8533	YX10 FEK	8573	YX11 HPL	8793	YX12 GHH
8484	KM02HGE	8126	YX13 EHN	8534	YX10 FEM	8574	YX11 HPN	8806	YX13 EFM
8485	KU52 YKO	8127	YX13 EHO	8535	YX10 FEO	8575	YX11 HOA	8807	YX13 EFN
8486	KU52 YKR	8460	RL02 FOT	8536	YX10 FEP	8577	YX61 GAA	8808	YX13 EFO
8487	KU52 YKS	8461	RL02 FOU	8537	YX10 FET	8578	YX61 GAO	8809	YX13 EFP
8033	BU05 HFN	8462	RL02 FVM	8538	YX10 FEU	8579	YX61 GAU	8810	YX13 EFR
8041	V301 MDP	8463	RL02 FVN	8539	YX10 FEV	8580	YX61 GBE	8811	YX13 EFS
8101	LJ56 VSP	8464	RL02 ZTB	8540	YX10 FFA	8581	YX61 GBF	8812	YX13 EFT
8102	LJ56 VST	8467	HX04 HTP	8541	YX10 FFB	8582	YX61 GBO	8813	YX13 EFU
8103	LJ56 VSU	8468	HX04 HTT	8542	YX10 FFC	8743	RN52 EYK	8814	YX13 EFV
8104	LJ56 VSV	8469	HX04 HTU	8543	YX10 FFD	8744	RN52 EYL	8815	YX13 EFW
8105	LJ56 VSX	8470	HX04 HTV	8544	YX10 FFE	8745	RN52 FPA	8816	YX13 EFY
8106	LJ56 VSY	8507	LJ08 CZP	8545	YX10 FFG	8746	RN52 FPC	8817	YX13 EFZ
8110	SN04 EGD	8508	LJ08 CZR	8546	YX10 FFH	8747	RN52 FRD		
8111	SN04 EFJ	8509	LJ08 CZS	8547	YX10 FFJ	8748	RN52 FRF		

UXBRIDGE

The entrance to **Uxbridge Bus Garage** on July 20th, 2013.

UXBRIDGE (UX)
Bakers Road, Uxbridge, Middlesex UB8 1RJ
Operated by: Metroline
Location: TQ05688423 [51.546962, -0.477681]
Nearest Tube Station: Uxbridge (adjacent)
Nearest Bus Routes: Uxbridge Bus Station (adjacent)
Bus Routes Serviced: 331/607/A10/U1/U2/U3/U4/
U5 & U10

Metroline bus **DC1540** outside of **Uxbridge Bus Garage** on Route U2 on March 12th, 2014.

VEHICLE ALLOCATION

DC1540	LK03 NLE	DE1583	LK08 FNF	DE1803	YX10 BFL	TE1575	LK08 FMU	TP1534	LK03 UFS
DC1541	LK03 NLF	DE1584	LK08 FNG	DE1804	YX10 BFM	TE1576	LK08 FMV	TP1535	LK03 UFT
DC1542	LK03 NLG	DE1585	LK08 FNH	DE1805	YX10 BFN	TE1577	LK08 FMX	TP1536	LK03 UFU
DC1543	LK03 NLJ	DE1586	LK08 FKT	DE1806	YX10 BFO	TE1578	LK08 FMY	TP1537	LK03 UFV
DC1544	LK03 NLL	DE1587	LK08 FKU	DE1807	YX10 BFP	TE1579	LK08 FMZ	TP1538	LK03 UFW
DC1545	LK03 NLM	DE1588	LK08 FKV	DE1808	YX10 BFU	TE1580	LK08 FNA	TP1539	LK03 UFX
DC1546	LK03 NLT	DE1589	LK08 FKW	DE1809	YX10 BFV	TE1581	LK08 FNC	VW1560	LK55 ACU
DC1547	LK03 NFY	DE1590	LK08 FLC	DE1810	YX10 BFY	TE1582	LK08 FND	VW1561	LK55 AAE
DC1548	LK03 NFZ	DE1591	LK08 FLD	DE1811	YX10 BFZ	TP433	LK03 GFZ	VW1562	LK55 AAF
DC1549	LK53 FDC	DE1592	LK08 FLE	DE1812	YX10 BGE	TP440	LK03 GGX	VW1563	LK55 AAJ
DC1550	LK53 FDE	DE1593	LK08 FLF	DE1813	YX10 BGF	TP446	LK03 GHF	VW1564	LK55 AAN
DC1551	LK53 FDF	DE1594	LK08 FLG	DE1814	YX10 BGK	TP1525	LK03 UFD	VW1565	LK55 AAU
DC1552	LK53 FDG	DE1595	LK08 FLV	DE1815	YX10 BGO	TP1526	LK03 UFE	VW1566	LK55 AAV
DC1553	LK53 FDJ	DE1596	LK08 FLW	DE1816	YX10 BGU	TP1527	LK03 UFG	VW1567	LK55 AAX
DC1554	LK53 FDM	DE1597	LK08 FLZ	DE1895	YX60 BZN	TP1528	LK03 UFJ	VW1568	LK55 AAY
DC1555	LK53 FDN	DE1798	YX10 BFA	DE1896	YX60 BZO	TP1529	LK03 UFL	VW1569	LK55 AAZ
DC1556	LK53 FDO	DE1799	YX10 BFE	TE1571	LK08 FNE	TP1530	LK03 UFM	VW1570	LK55 ABF
DC1557	LK53 FDP	DE1800	YX10 BFF	TE1572	LK08 FMA	TP1531	LK03 UFN		
DC1558	LK53 FDU	DE1801	YX10 BFJ	TE1573	LK08 FMO	TP1532	LK03 UFP		
DC1559	LK53 FDV	DE1802	YX10 BFK	TE1574	LK08 FMP	TP1533	LK03 UFR		

The Camberwell New Road exit of **Walworth Depot** on September 12th, 2014 with Abellio buses **9504** & **9449** in view. When solely a tram depot it was known as Camberwell but, with the introduction of buses in 1950, the name was changed to avoid confusion with the bus garage on the opposite side of the road.

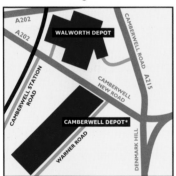

*SEE PAGE 24

WALWORTH (WL)

301 Camberwell New Road, London SE5 0TF
Operated by: Abellio
Location: TQ32387691 [51.475568, -0.095708]
Nearest Station: Denmark Hill (0.7 miles)
Nearest Bus Routes: 36/185/436 & N136 - Warner Road (Stop H)
Bus Routes Serviced: 35/40/172/188/343/381/484/ N35/N343 & N381

Two tram depots were opened on this site by the Pimlico, Peckham & Greenwich Street Tramways Company in 1871 and 1873. They were enlarged prior to sustaining bomb damage during WWII and then substantially rebuilt before closure to trams by London Transport on October 7th, 1951. The depot was then used exclusively as an omnibus garage.

The less-than auspicious entrance off Camberwell Road to **Walworth Depot** on August 31st, 2013. The entrance to the garage building can be identified by the sign board visible above the wall.

Go-Ahead London bus **PVL311** passing the Camberwell Road entrance to **Walworth Depot** on August 31st, 2013.

VEHICLE ALLOCATION

2401	SN61 DFL	9006	BX54 DHO	9049	LF55 CYY	9439	LJ09 CBY	9747	YN51 KVD
2402	SN61 DFO	9007	BX54 DHP	9050	LF55 CYX	9440	LJ09 CCA	9754	YN51 KVL
2403	SN61 DFP	9008	BX54 DHV	9051	LF55 CYW	9441	LJ09 CCD	9756	YN51 KVO
2404	SN61 DFU	9009	BX54 DHY	9052	LF55 CYV	9442	LJ09 CCE	9761	YN51 KVU
2405	SN61 DFV	9010	BX54 DHZ	9053	LF55 CZB	9443	LJ09 CCF	9813	LG52 ZXB
2406	SN61 DFX	9011	BX54 DJD	9054	BX55 XNG	9444	LJ09 CCK	9814	LG52 URZ
2407	SN61 DFY	9012	BX54 DJE	9055	BX55 XNJ	9445	LJ09 CCN	9815	LG52 XWE
2408	SN61 DFZ	9013	BX54 DJF	9056	BX55 XNK	9446	LJ09 CCO	9816	LG52 XYK
2409	SN61 DGE	9014	BX54 DJJ	9057	BX55 XNL	9447	LJ09 CCU	9818	LG52 XYP
2410	SN61 DGF	9015	BX54 DJK	9058	BX55 XNM	9448	LJ09 CCX	9820	LG52 XYN
2411	SN61 DGO	9016	BX54 DJO	9059	BX55 XNN	9449	LJ09 CCY	9822	LG52 XYZ
2412	SN61 DGU	9017	BX54 DJU	9060	BX55 XNO	9450	LJ09 CCZ	9824	LG52 XZS
2413	SN61 DGV	9018	BX54 DJV	9061	BX55 XNP	9451	LJ09 CDE	9825	LG52 XZR
8053	X313 KRX	9019	BX54 DJY	9062	BX55 XNR	9452	LJ09 CDF	9826	LG52 XYL
8330	YX11 AHA	9020	BX54 DJZ	9063	BX55 XNS	9453	LJ09 CDK	9827	LG52 XZT
8331	YX11 AHC	9034	BX55 XMH	9064	BX55 XNT	9454	LJ09 CDN	9828	LG52 XYJ
8332	YX11 AHD	9035	BX55 XMJ	9065	BX55 XNU	9455	LJ09 CDO	9829	LG52 XWD
8333	YX11 AHE	9036	BX55 XMK	9069	BX55 XNZ	9456	LJ09 CDU	9830	KN52 NCE
8334	YX11 AHF	9037	BX55 XML	9070	LF06 YRC	9457	LJ09 CDV	9832	KN52 NDD
8335	YX11 AHG	9038	BX55 XMM	9428	LJ09 CAA	9458	LJ09 CDX	9833	KN52 NDE
8336	YX11 AHJ	9039	BX55 XMO	9429	LJ09 CAE	9459	LJ09 CDY	9834	KN52 NDO
8337	YX11 AHK	9040	BX55 XMP	9430	LJ09 CAO	9460	LJ09 CDZ	9835	KN52 NDG
8340	YX11 AHO	9041	BX55 XMR	9431	LJ09 CAU	9461	LJ09 CEA	9836	KN52 NDJ
8341	YX11 AHP	9042	BX55 XMS	9432	LJ09 CAV	9462	LJ09 CEF	9837	KN52 NDY
8342	YX11 AHU	9043	BX55 XMT	9433	LJ09 CAX	9463	LJ09 CEK	9838	KN52 NDZ
9001	BX54 DHJ	9044	BX55 XMU	9434	LJ09 CBF	9464	LJ09 CEN	9839	KN52 NEJ
9002	BX54 DHK	9045	LF55 CZA	9435	LJ09 CBO	9465	LJ09 CEO	9840	KN52 NEO
9003	BX54 DHL	9046	BX55 XMW	9436	LJ09 CBU	9466	LJ09 CEU	9841	KN52 NEU
9004	BX54 DHM	9047	BX55 XMZ	9437	LJ09 CBV	9741	YN51 KUW	9842	KN52 NEY
9005	BX54 DHN	9048	LF55 CYZ	9438	LJ09 CBX	9744	YN51 KVA	9843	KN52 NFA

Waterloo Bus Garage on September 17th, 2013. It was opened during the 1980s as a Red Arrow garage and currently only operates on Mondays to Fridays.

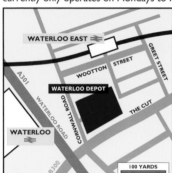

WATERLOO (RA)
Cornwall Road, London SE1 8TE
Operated by: Go-Ahead London
Location: TQ31327993 [51.503001, -0.109617]
Nearest Station: Waterloo East (300 yards)
Nearest Bus Routes: 59/68/168/171/172/176/N68/N171 & X68 - Waterloo Station, Waterloo Rd (Stop D)
Bus Routes Serviced: 507 & 521

Go-Ahead London buses **MEC33** and **MEC10** parked inside **Waterloo Bus Garage** on March 8th, 2014.

The wash plant at **Waterloo Bus Garage** on September 17th, 2013.

VEHICLE ALLOCATION

EB1	LC63 CYA	MEC10	BG09 JKJ	MEC21	BD09 ZRC	MEC32	BD09 ZVX	MEC43	BT09 GOJ
EB2	LC63 CXY	MEC11	BD09 ZPR	MEC22	BD09 ZRE	MEC33	BD09 ZVY	MEC44	BT09 GOK
MEC1	BG09 JJK	MEC12	BD09 ZPS	MEC23	BD09 ZRF	MEC34	BD09 ZVZ	MEC45	BT09 GOP
MEC2	BG09 JJL	MEC13	BD09 ZPT	MEC24	BD09 ZRG	MEC35	BD09 ZWA	MEC46	BT09 GOU
MEC3	BG09 JJU	MEC14	BD09 ZPU	MEC25	BD09 ZRJ	MEC36	BD09 ZWB	MEC47	BT09 GOX
MEC4	BG09 JJV	MEC15	BD09 ZPV	MEC26	BD09 ZRK	MEC37	BD09 ZWC	MEC48	BT09 GPE
MEC5	BG09 JJX	MEC16	BD09 ZPW	MEC27	BF59 NHJ	MEC38	BD09 ZWE	MEC49	BT09 GPF
MEC6	BG09 JJY	MEC17	BD09 ZPX	MEC28	BD09 ZVT	MEC39	BD09 ZWF	MEC50	BT09 GPJ
MEC7	BG09 JJZ	MEC18	BD09 ZPY	MEC29	BD09 ZVU	MEC40	BD09 ZWG		
MEC8	BG09 JKE	MEC19	BD09 ZPZ	MEC30	BD09 ZVV	MEC41	BD09 ZWH		
MEC9	BG09 JKF	MEC20	BD09 ZRA	MEC31	BD09 ZVW	MEC42	BT09 GOH		

Waterside Way Bus Garage on September 19th, 2013 with the wash plant in view on the left.

WATERSIDE WAY (PL)
Waterside Way, London SW17 0HB
Operated by: Go-Ahead London
Location: TQ26337125 [51.426166, -0.184204]
Nearest Station: Haydons Road (0.7 miles)
Nearest Bus Routes: 493 - Waterside Way (Stop SR)
Bus Routes Serviced: 39/485/493 & G1

Go-Ahead London bus LDP222 parked in the yard at Waterside Way Bus Garage on September 19th, 2013.

The small office and amenities block at Waterside Way Bus Garage on September 19th, 2013.

VEHICLE ALLOCATION

LDP151	Y851 TGH	LDP220	SK52 MPO	LDP265	LX05 EYS	LDP294	LX06 EZK	SE184	SN12 AUY
LDP211	SK52 MMU	LDP221	SK52 MLU	LDP266	LX05 EYT	SE175	SN12 AUM	SE185	SN12 AVB
LDP212	SK52 MMV	LDP222	SK52 MLV	LDP267	LX05 EYU	SE176	SN12 AVO	SE186	SN12 AVC
LDP213	SK52 MMX	LDP223	SK52 MLX	LDP268	LX05 EYV	SE177	SN12 AUP	SE187	SN12 AVD
LDP214	SK52 MOA	LDP224	SK52 MLY	LDP269	LX05 EYW	SE178	SN12 AUR	SE188	SN12 AVE
LDP215	SK52 MOF	LDP225	SK52 MLZ	LDP270	LX05 EYY	SE179	SN12 AUT	SE189	SN12 AVF
LDP216	SK52 MOU	LDP226	SK52 MMA	LDP271	LX05 EXZ	SE180	SN12 AUU	SE190	SN12 AVG
LDP217	SK52 MOV	LDP227	SK52 MME	LDP272	LX05 EYA	SE181	SN12 AUV	SE191	SN12 AVJ
LDP218	SK52 MPE	LDP263	LX05 EYP	LDP292	LX06 EZZ	SE182	SN12 AUW	SE192	SN12 AVK
LDP219	SK52 MPF	LDP264	LX05 EYR	LDP293	LX06 EZJ	SE183	SN12 AUX	SE193	SN12 AVL

A general view of **West Ham Bus Garage** on August 20th, 2014. The building was designed with sustainability in mind and incorporates a laminated timber roof structure, a living green roof, rainwater harvesting and natural ventilation. The site was originally occupied by a Parcelforce building and this was demolished in 2007 to facilitate the construction of the depot. It replaced Stratford and Waterden Road garages which were both removed to make way for the Olympic Park.

WEST HAM (WH)
Stephenson Street, Canning Town, London E16 4SA
Operated by: Stagecoach London
Location: TQ39048248 [51.522566, 0.003046]
Nearest DLR Station: Star Lane (0.4 miles)
Nearest Bus Routes: 276 & 323 - Manor Road, Star Lane (Stop L)
Bus Routes Serviced: 15/69/86/97/104/115/147 /158/238/241/262/323/330/473/488 & D3

West Ham Garage was opened in February 2008 and replaced two depots in Stratford. It was fully operational by November 2009 and officially opened on July 14th, 2010. With a nominal capacity for 320 vehicles it is the largest bus garage in the UK and is the training centre and head office for Stagecoach London.

Looking north towards **West Ham Bus Garage** on August 20th, 2014. The white column supports the Northwind 100 Wind Turbine which, combined with the efficiencies incorporated into the depot building, reduces the CO_2 output from the depot by around 27%.

Looking south towards the wash plant at **West Ham Bus Garage** on August 20th, 2014, with Stagecoach London buses 17910 & 18260 parked in the yard.

VEHICLE ALLOCATION

10101	LX12 DAU	17755	LX03 BTZ	17928	LX03 OTD	18258	LX04 FZC	19964	ALD 933B
10102	LX12 DBO	17757	LX03 BUE	17929	LX03 OTE	18259	LX04 FZD	19965	ALD 941B
10103	LX12 DBU	17798	LX03 BWM	17930	LX03 OTF	18260	LX04 FZE	19966	ALD 968B
10104	LX12 DBV	17799	LX03 BWN	17931	LX03 OTG	18261	LX04 FZF	19967	ALM 50B
10105	LX12 DBY	17802	LX03 BWV	17932	LX03 OTH	18262	LX04 FZG	19968	ALM 60B
10106	LX12 DBZ	17815	LX03 BXK	17933	LX03 OTJ	18263	LX04 FZH	19969	ALM 89B
10107	LX12 DCE	17816	LX03 BXL	17934	LX53 JXU	18264	LX04 FZJ	19970	ALM 71B
10108	LX12 DCF	17817	LX03 BXM	17935	LX53 JXV	18265	LX04 FZK	36340	LX09 ACY
10109	LX12 DCO	17818	LX03 BXN	17936	LX53 JXW	18266	LX05 BVY	36344	LX09 ADV
10110	LX12 DCU	17820	LX03 BXR	17937	LX53 JXY	18267	LX05 BVZ	36345	LX59 ANF
10111	LX12 DCV	17821	LX03 BXS	17938	LX53 JYA	18268	LX05 BWA	36346	LX59 ANP
10112	LX12 DCY	17822	LX03 BXU	17939	LX53 JYB	18269	LX05 BWB	36347	LX59 ANR
15074	LX09 AEY	17824	LX03 BXW	17940	LX53 JYC	18270	LX05 BWC	36348	LX59 ANU
15076	LX09 AFA	17825	LX03 BXY	17941	LX53 JYD	18271	LX05 BWD	36349	LX59 ANV
15078	LX09 AFD	17834	LX03 BYJ	17942	LX53 JYE	18272	LX05 BWE	36350	LX59 AOA
15079	LX09 AFJ	17846	LX03 BYZ	17943	LX53 JYF	18273	LX05 BWF	36351	LX59 AOB
15080	LX09 AFK	17848	LX03 BZA	17944	LX53 JYG	18274	LX05 BWG	36352	LX59 AOC
15081	LX09 AFL	17848	LX53 JYL	18204	LX04 FWP	18275	LX05 BWH	36353	LX59 AOD
15083	LX09 AFU	17849	LX53 JYN	18205	LX04 FWR	18276	LX05 BWJ	36354	LX59 AOE
15084	LX09 AFV	17850	LX03 BZD	18206	LX04 FWS	18277	LX05 BWK	36355	LX59 AOF
15086	LX09 AFZ	17865	LX03 NFK	18220	LX04 FXH	18454	LX05 LLP	36356	LX59 AOG
15087	LX09 AGO	17889	LX03 OPY	18232	LX04 FXY	18456	LX55 EPC	36357	LX59 AOH
15088	LX09 AGU	17890	LX03 OPZ	18233	LX04 FXZ	18457	LX55 EPD	36358	LX59 AOJ
15089	LX09 AGV	17891	LX03 ORA	18236	LX04 FYC	18458	LX55 EPE	36359	LX59 AOK
15090	LX09 AGY	17903	LX03 ORV	18237	LX04 FYD	18459	LX55 EPF	36360	LX59 AOL
15091	LX09 AGZ	17909	LX03 OSC	18238	LX04 FYE	18460	LX55 EPJ	36361	LX59 AOM
15092	LX09 AHA	17910	LX03 OSD	18239	LX04 FYF	18461	LX55 EPK	36362	LX59 ECF
15095	LX09 AHE	17911	LX03 OSE	18240	LX04 FYG	18462	LX55 EPL	36363	LX59 ECJ
17454	Y454 NHK	17912	LX03 OSG	18241	LX04 FYH	19859	LX12 CZN	36364	LX59 ECN
17489	LX51 FMJ	17913	LX03 OSJ	18242	LX04 FYJ	19860	LX12 CZO	36365	LX59 ECT
17490	LX51 FMK	17914	LX03 OSK	18243	LX04 FYK	19861	LX12 CZP	36366	LX59 ECV
17495	LX51 FMU	17915	LX03 OSL	18244	LX04 FYL	19862	LX12 CZR	36367	LX59 ECW
17528	LX51 FOM	17916	LX03 OSM	18245	LX04 FYM	19863	LX12 CZS	36368	LX59 ECY
17529	LX51 FON	17917	LX03 OSN	18246	LX04 FYN	19864	LX12 CZT	36369	LX59 ECZ
17530	LX51 FOP	17918	LX03 OSP	18247	LX04 FYP	19865	LX12 CZU	36370	LX59 EDC
17545	LY02 OAU	17919	LX03 OSR	18248	LX04 FYR	19866	LX12 CZV	36371	LX59 EDF
17551	LY02 OBC	17920	LX03 OSU	18249	LX04 FYS	19867	LX12 CZW	36372	LX59 EDJ
17556	LY02 OBH	17921	LX03 OSV	18250	LX04 FYT	19868	LX12 CZY	36373	LX59 EDK
17557	LY02 OBJ	17922	LX03 OSW	18252	LX04 FYV	19869	LX12 CZZ	36374	LX59 EDL
17580	LV52 HFN	17923	LX03 OSY	18253	LX04 FYW	19870	LX12 DDA	36375	LX59 EDO
17586	LV52 HFU	17924	LX03 OSZ	18254	LX04 FYY	19871	LX12 DAO		
17588	LV52 HFX	17925	LX03 OTA	18255	LX04 FYZ	19961	WLT 324		
17589	LV52 HFY	17926	LX03 OTB	18256	LX04 FZA	19962	WLT 652		
17749	LY52 ZFH	17927	LX03 OTC	18257	LX04 FZB	19963	WLT 871		

Westbourne Park Bus Garage on July 26th, 2014 with Tower Transit buses **DN33779** & **DN33780** in the exit road. It opened in 1981 and its adjacency to the A40 Westway flyover can clearly be seen.

NB PART OF THE DEPOT IS UNDER THE A40 WESTWAY

WESTBOURNE PARK (X)
Great Western Road, London W9 3NW
Operated by: Tower Transit
Location: TQ24948188 [51.521445, -0.200732]
Nearest Tube Station: Westbourne Park (200 yards)
Nearest Bus Routes: 28/31/328/N28 & N31 - Westbourne Park (Stop A)
Bus Routes Serviced: 23/70 & 295

Routemaster buses parked on the north side of **Westbourne Park Bus Garage** on July 26th, 2014.

A view of the roof, formed by the underside of the A40 flyover, at **Westbourne Park Bus Garage** on July 26th, 2014.

VEHICLE ALLOCATION

DML44313	YX12 AAJ	DML44327	YX12 DJD	DNH39111	SN12 APY	DNH39125	SN12 ATO	VN37957	BN61 MXH
DML44314	YX12 AEA	DML44328	YX12 DJE	DNH39112	SN12 APZ	DNH39126	SN12 ATU	VN37958	BN61 MXC
DML44315	YX12 AED	DN33776	SN12 AVR	DNH39113	SN12 ARF	DNH39127	SN12 ATV	VN37959	BN61 MXF
DML44316	YX12 AEF	DN33777	SN12 AVT	DNH39114	SN12 ARO	DNH39128	SN12 ATX	VN37961	BN61 MXL
DML44317	YX12 AEU	DN33778	SN12 AVU	DNH39115	SN12 ARU	DNH39129	SN12 ATY	VN37988	BF62 UYB
DML44318	YX12 AOF	DN33779	SN12 AVV	DNH39116	SN12 ARX	DNH39130	SN12 ATZ	VN37989	BF62 UYA
DML44319	YX12 AFV	DN33780	SN12 AVW	DNH39117	SN12 ARZ	DNH39131	SN12 AUA	VN37990	BF62 UYC
DML44320	YX12 AMK	DN33781	SN12 AVX	DNH39118	SN12 ASO	DNH39132	SN12 AUC	VN37991	BF62 UYE
DML44321	YX12 ARZ	DN33782	SN12 AVY	DNH39119	SN12 ASU	VN37943	BK10 MFZ	VN37992	BF62 UYG
DML44322	YX12 AXU	DN33783	SN12 AVZ	DNH39120	SN12 ASV	VN37952	BN61 MWZ	VN37993	BF62 UYD
DML44323	YX12 AVJ	DN33784	SN12 AWA	DNH39121	SN12 ASX	VN37953	BN61 MXB	VN37994	BF62 UYH
DML44324	YX12 AYF	DN33785	SN12 AWB	DNH39122	SN12 ASZ	VN37954	BN61 MXA	VN37995	BF62 UYJ
DML44325	YX12 AZW	DN33786	SN12 EHB	DNH39123	SN12 ATF	VN37955	BN61 MXE	VN37996	BF62 UYK
DML44326	YX12 DHZ	DN33787	SN12 EHC	DNH39124	SN12 ATK	VN37956	BN61 MXD		

Willesden Junction Bus Garage viewed on May 10th, 2014.   *Allison Smith*

WILLESDEN JUNCTION (WJ)
46 Station Road, London NW10 4XB
Operated by: Metroline
Location: TQ21588306 [51.533149, -0.247045]
Nearest Station: Willesden Junction (300 yards)
Nearest Bus Routes: 228 & 266 - Willesden Junction (Stop M)
Bus Routes Serviced: 18/187/206/226/228 & N18

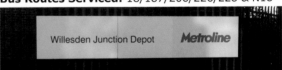

VEHICLE ALLOCATION

DE1612	YX58 DWM	DE1636	YX58 FOH	DE1661	YX09 AEN	VW1849	BF60 UUG	VW1873	BF60 VHY
DE1613	YX58 DWN	DE1637	YX58 FOJ	DE1662	YX09 AEO	VW1850	BF60 UUK	VW1874	BF60 VJC
DE1614	YX58 DWO	DE1638	YX58 FOK	DE1663	YX09 AEP	VW1851	BF60 UUH	VW1875	BF60 VJK
DE1615	YX58 DWP	DE1639	YX58 FOM	DE1664	YX09 AET	VW1852	BF60 UUL	VW1876	BF60 VJJ
DE1616	YX58 DWU	DE1640	YX58 FON	DEL1970	YX12 AOS	VW1853	BF60 UUN	VW1877	BF60 VJE
DE1617	YX58 DWV	DE1641	YX58 FOP	DEL1971	YX12 AOT	VW1854	BF60 UUM	VW1878	BF60 VHZ
DE1618	YX58 DWY	DE1642	YX58 FOT	DEL1972	YX12 AFU	VW1855	BF60 UUO	VW1879	BF60 VJG
DE1619	YX58 DWZ	DE1643	YX58 FOU	DEL1973	YX12 AFK	VW1856	BF60 UUR	VW1880	BF60 VJD
DE1620	YX58 FPA	DE1644	YX58 FOV	DEL1974	YX12 AZG	VW1857	BF60 UUP	VW1881	BF60 VJL
DE1621	YX58 FPC	DE1645	YX58 FRC	DEL1975	YX12 AFO	VW1858	BF60 UUT	VW1882	BF60 VJU
DE1622	YX58 FPD	DE1646	YX58 FRD	DEL1976	YX12 AVT	VW1859	BF60 UUS	VW1883	BF60 VJV
DE1623	YX58 FPE	DE1648	YX58 HVB	DEL1977	YX12 AYK	VW1860	BF60 UUX	VW1884	BF60 UVB
DE1624	YX58 FPF	DE1649	YX58 HVM	DEL1978	YX12 ATN	VW1861	BF60 UUY	VW1885	BF60 UVA
DE1625	YX58 FPG	DE1650	YX09 AEA	DEL1979	YX12 ATK	VW1862	BF60 UUV	VW1886	BF60 UVD
DE1626	YX58 FPJ	DE1651	YX09 AEB	DEL1980	YX12 APK	VW1863	BF60 UUZ	VW1887	BF60 UVG
DE1627	YX58 FPK	DE1652	YX09 AEC	VW1782	LK59 FCY	VW1864	BF60 VHP	VW1888	BF60 UVH
DE1628	YX58 FPL	DE1653	YX09 AED	VW1841	BK10 MFO	VW1865	BF60 VHR	VW1889	BF60 UVC
DE1629	YX58 FPN	DE1654	YX09 AEE	VW1842	BF60 UUA	VW1866	BF60 VHV	VW1890	BF60 UVE
DE1630	YX58 FPO	DE1655	YX09 AEF	VW1843	BF60 UUB	VW1867	BF60 VHU	VW1891	BF60 VJM
DE1631	YX58 FPT	DE1656	YX09 AEG	VW1844	BF60 UTZ	VW1868	BF60 VHW	VW1892	BF60 VJN
DE1632	YX58 FPU	DE1657	YX09 AEJ	VW1845	BF60 UUD	VW1869	BF60 UUW	VW1893	BF60 VJO
DE1633	YX58 FPV	DE1658	YX09 AEK	VW1846	BF60 UUC	VW1870	BF60 VHT	VW1894	BF60 VJP
DE1634	YX58 FPY	DE1659	YX09 AEL	VW1847	BF60 UUE	VW1871	BF60 VHX		
DE1635	YX58 FOF	DE1660	YX09 AEM	VW1848	BF60 UUJ	VW1872	BF60 VJA		

The Pound Lane entrance to **Willesden Bus Garage** on May 10th, 2014. *Allison Smith*

WILLESDEN (AC)
287 High Road, Willesden, London NW10 2JY
Operated by: Metroline
Location: TQ21998470 [51.548275, -0.238189]
Nearest Tube Station: Dollis Hill (0.6 miles)
Nearest Bus Routes: 52/98/260/266/302/460 &
N98 - Willesden Bus Garage (Stop WN)
Bus Routes Serviced: 6/52/98/260/302/460 N52 &
N98

Metroline buses **VP571** & **VP548** parked in the yard at **Willesden Bus Garage** on May 10th, 2014.
Allison Smith

The High Road entrance to **Willesden Bus Garage** on June 22nd, 2013 with staff on Metroline bus **VP511** effecting a crew change.

VEHICLE ALLOCATION

VP473	LK03 GKU	VP504	LK53 LXX	VP531	LK04 CUA	VP558	LK04 CVW	VW1401	LK62 DVO
VP474	LK03 GKV	VP505	LK53 LXY	VP532	LK04 CUC	VP559	LK04 CVX	VW1402	LK62 DVP
VP475	LK03 GKX	VP506	LK53 LXZ	VP533	LK04 CUG	VP560	LK04 EKU	VW1403	LK62 DVR
VP476	LK03 GKY	VP507	LK53 LYA	VP534	LK04 CUH	VP561	LK04 EKV	VW1404	LK62 DVU
VP477	LK03 GKZ	VP508	LK53 LYC	VP535	LK04 CUJ	VP562	LK04 EKW	VW1405	LK13 BHW
VP478	LK03 GLF	VP509	LK53 LYD	VP536	LK04 CUU	VP563	LK04 EKX	VW1406	LK13 BHX
VP479	LK03 GLJ	VP510	LK53 LYF	VP537	LK04 CUW	VP564	LK04 EKY	VW1407	LK13 BHY
VP480	LK03 GLV	VP511	LK53 LYG	VP538	LK04 CUX	VP565	LK04 EKZ	VWH1360	LK62 DHX
VP481	LK03 GLY	VP512	LK04 CPY	VP539	LK04 CUY	VP566	LK04 ELC	VWH1361	LK62 DHZ
VP482	LK03 GLZ	VP513	LK04 CPZ	VP540	LK04 CVA	VP567	LK04 ELH	VWH1362	LK62 DJY
VP483	LK03 GME	VP514	LK04 CRF	VP541	LK04 CVB	VP568	LK04 ELJ	VWH1363	LK62 DJZ
VP484	LK03 GMF	VP515	LK04 CRJ	VP542	LK04 CVC	VP569	LK04 ELU	VWH1364	LK62 DKE
VP489	LK03 GMY	VP516	LK04 CRU	VP543	LK04 CVD	VP570	LK04 ELV	VWH1408	LK62 DWA
VP490	LK03 GMZ	VP517	LK04 CRV	VP544	LK04 CVE	VP571	LK04 ELW	VWH1409	LK62 DWD
VP491	LK03 GNF	VP518	LK04 CRZ	VP545	LK04 CVF	VP572	LK04 ELX	VWH1410	LK62 DWE
VP492	LK03 GNJ	VP519	LK04 CSF	VP546	LK04 CVG	VP573	LK04 EMF	VWH1411	LK62 DWF
VP493	LK03 GNN	VP520	LK04 CSU	VP547	LK04 CVH	VP574	LK04 EMJ	VWH1412	LK62 DWJ
VP494	LK03 GNP	VP521	LK04 CSV	VP548	LK04 CVJ	VP575	LK04 EMV	VWH1413	LK62 DWM
VP495	LK53 LXM	VP522	LK04 CSX	VP549	LK04 CVL	VP576	LK04 EMX	VWH1414	LK62 DWO
VP496	LK53 LXN	VP523	LK04 CSY	VP550	LK04 CVM	VP577	LK04 ENE	VWH1415	LK62 DWU
VP497	LK53 LXO	VP524	LK04 CSZ	VP551	LK04 CVN	VP578	LK04 ENF	VWH1416	LK62 DWV
VP498	LK53 LXP	VP525	LK04 CTE	VP552	LK04 CVP	VP579	LK04 ENH	VWH1417	LK62 DWY
VP499	LK53 LXR	VP526	LK04 CTF	VP553	LK04 CVR	VP580	LK04 ENJ	VWH1418	LK62 DXF
VP500	LK53 LXT	VP527	LK04 CTU	VP554	LK04 CVS	VPL186	Y186 NLK	VWH1419	LK62 DXG
VP501	LK53 LXU	VP528	LK04 CTV	VP555	LK04 CVT	VW1398	LK62 DVH		
VP502	LK53 LXV	VP529	LK04 CTX	VP556	LK04 CVU	VW1399	LK62 DVJ		
VP503	LK53 LXW	VP530	LK04 CTZ	VP557	LK04 CVV	VW1400	LK62 DVL		

Wood Green Bus Garage viewed on May 3rd, 2014.

WOOD GREEN (WN)
Jolly Butchers Hill, High Road, Wood Green,
London N22 8HF
Operated by: Arriva London
Location: TQ30909045 [51.597956, -0.110871]
Nearest Tube Station: Wood Green (200 yards)
Nearest Bus Routes: 121/141/144/184/221/232/
243/329/W3 & W4
Bus Routes Serviced: 29/141/144/221/329/617 &
N29

The garage was opened as a horse tram depot in 1895 by the North Metropolitan Tramways & Omnibus Company. It was converted to electric working in 1904 and subsequently extended, becoming part of London Transport on July 1st, 1933. It was utilized as a trolleybus depot from May 8th, 1938 and solely as a bus garage from November 7th, 1961.

Arriva London buses **DW439** & **HV127** parked inside of **Wood Green Bus Garage** on May 3rd, 2014.

Arriva London bus **HV111** departing from **Wood Green Bus Garage** on September 17th, 2013.

VEHICLE ALLOCATION

DW414	LJ11 AEE	DW501	LJ62 BKN	HV108	LJ13 FCF	T216	LJ61 CGV	VLW80	LF52 USU
DW415	LJ11 AEF	DW502	LJ62 BMO	HV109	LJ13 FCG	T217	LJ61 CGX	VLW81	LF52 USV
DW416	LJ11 AEG	DW503	LJ62 BNA	HV110	LJ13 FCL	T218	LJ61 CGY	VLW82	LF52 USW
DW465	LJ61 CCV	DW504	LJ62 BZV	HV111	LJ13 FCM	T219	LJ61 CGZ	VLW83	LF52 USX
DW466	LJ61 CCX	DW505	LJ62 BAA	HV112	LJ13 FBE	T220	LJ61 CHC	VLW84	LF52 USY
DW467	LJ61 CCY	DW506	LJ62 BBZ	HV113	LJ13 FBF	T221	LJ61 CFM	VLW85	LF52 UPV
DW468	LJ61 CCZ	DW507	LJ62 BDF	HV114	LJ13 FBG	T222	LJ61 CFN	VLW86	LF52 UPW
DW469	LJ61 CDE	DW508	LJ62 BDO	HV115	LJ13 FBP	T223	LJ61 CFO	VLW114	LJ03 MJV
DW470	LJ61 CDF	DW509	LJ13 CCE	HV116	LJ13 FBL	T260	LJ61 LKL	VLW115	LJ03 MGX
DW471	LJ61 CDK	DW510	LJ13 CCF	HV117	LJ13 FBN	VLW50	LF02 PLO	VLW116	LJ03 MGY
DW472	LJ61 CDN	DW511	LJ13 CCK	HV118	LJ13 FBO	VLW51	WLT 751		
DW473	LJ61 CDO	DW512	LJ13 CCN	HV119	LJ13 FBU	VLW52	LF02 PSO		
DW474	LJ61 CDU	DW513	LJ13 CCO	HV120	LJ13 FBV	VLW53	LF02 PSU		
DW475	LJ61 CBX	DW514	LJ13 CCU	HV121	LJ13 FBX	VLW54	WLT 554		
DW476	LJ61 CBY	DW515	LJ13 CCV	HV122	LJ13 FAM	VLW55	LF02 PSY		
DW477	LJ61 CCA	HV84	LJ13 FDF	HV123	LJ13 FAO	VLW56	LF02 PSZ		
DW478	LJ61 CCD	HV85	LJ13 FDG	HV124	LJ13 FAU	VLW57	LF02 PTO		
DW479	LJ61 CCE	HV86	LJ13 FDK	HV125	LJ13 FBA	VLW58	LF02 PTU		
DW480	LJ61 CCF	HV87	LJ13 FDL	HV126	LJ13 FBB	VLW59	LF02 PTX		
DW481	LJ61 CCK	HV88	LJ13 FDM	HV127	LJ13 FBC	VLW60	LF02 PTY		
DW482	LJ61 CCN	HV89	LJ13 FDN	HV128	LJ13 FBD	VLW61	LF02 PVE		
DW483	LJ61 CCO	HV90	LJ13 FDO	HV129	LJ13 FEO	VLW62	LF02 PVJ		
DW484	LJ61 CCU	HV91	LJ13 FDP	HV130	LJ13 FEP	VLW63	LF02 PVK		
DW485	LJ61 CAA	HV92	LJ13 FCN	HV131	LJ13 FET	VLW64	LF02 PVL		
DW486	LJ61 CAE	HV93	LJ13 FCO	T201	LJ61 CHD	VLW65	LF02 PVN		
DW487	LJ61 CAO	HV94	LJ13 FCP	T202	LJ61 CHF	VLW66	LF02 PVO		
DW488	LJ61 CAU	HV95	LJ13 FCU	T203	LJ61 CHG	VLW67	LF52 UTC		
DW489	LJ61 CAV	HV96	LJ13 FCV	T204	LJ61 CHH	VLW68	LF52 UTE		
DW490	LJ61 CAX	HV97	LJ13 FCX	T205	LJ61 CHK	VLW69	LF52 USE		
DW491	LJ61 CBF	HV98	LJ13 FCY	T206	LJ61 CHL	VLW70	LF52 UTG		
DW492	LJ61 CBO	HV99	LJ13 FCZ	T207	LJ61 CHN	VLW71	LF52 UTH		
DW493	LJ61 CBU	HV100	LJ13 FDA	T208	LJ61 CHO	VLW72	WLT 372		
DW494	LJ61 CBV	HV101	LJ13 FDC	T209	LJ61 CHV	VLW73	LF52 UTL		
DW495	LJ61 CKA	HV102	LJ13 FBY	T210	LJ61 CHX	VLW74	LF52 UTM		
DW496	LJ61 CKC	HV103	LJ13 FBZ	T211	LJ61 CGF	VLW75	LF52 USM		
DW497	LJ61 CKD	HV104	LJ13 FCA	T212	LJ61 CGG	VLW76	LF52 USN		
DW498	LJ61 CKE	HV105	LJ13 FCC	T213	LJ61 CGK	VLW77	LF52 USO		
DW499	LJ62 BKD	HV106	LT63 UKJ	T214	LJ61 CGO	VLW78	LF52 USS		
DW500	LJ62 BKG	HV107	LJ13 FCE	T215	LJ61 CGU	VLW79	LF52 UST		

Arriva London bus **LT4** parked inside the main depot building at **Ash Grove Bus Garage** (AE) on August 5th, 2014. (See Page 6)

Arriva Shires bus **6170** passing **Garston Bus Garage** (GR), its home depot, on July 22nd, 2014 whilst working the No.258 Route to South Harrow.

STORAGE, MAINTENANCE AND TOUR BUS GARAGES

This short section notes the three garages that at the end of 2014 were primarily engaged in maintenance or storage duties and not supplying buses for TFL routes. Also listed are the three garages utilized for the supply and maintenance of tour buses operating in London.

London United buses **DP10** & **DP123** parked in the yard at **Twickenham Bus Garage** (NC) on August 13th, 2013. (See Page 109)

CN — BEDDINGTON FARM — ZONE 5

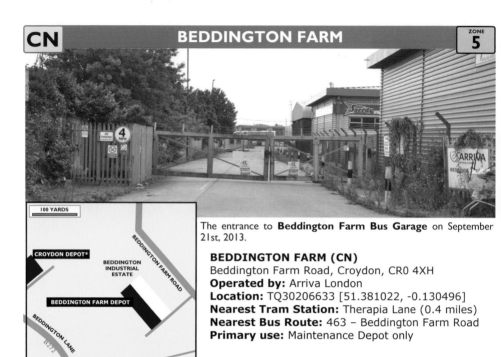

The entrance to **Beddington Farm Bus Garage** on September 21st, 2013.

BEDDINGTON FARM (CN)
Beddington Farm Road, Croydon, CR0 4XH
Operated by: Arriva London
Location: TQ30206633 [51.381022, -0.130496]
Nearest Tram Station: Therapia Lane (0.4 miles)
Nearest Bus Route: 463 – Beddington Farm Road
Primary use: Maintenance Depot only

*SEE PAGE 30

PV — PERIVALE (EAST) — ZONE 4

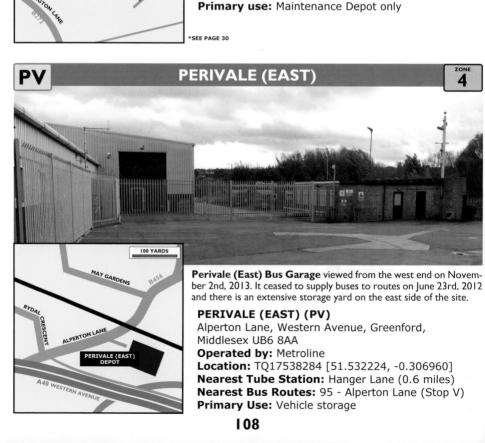

Perivale (East) Bus Garage viewed from the west end on November 2nd, 2013. It ceased to supply buses to routes on June 23rd, 2012 and there is an extensive storage yard on the east side of the site.

PERIVALE (EAST) (PV)
Alperton Lane, Western Avenue, Greenford, Middlesex UB6 8AA
Operated by: Metroline
Location: TQ17538284 [51.532224, -0.306960]
Nearest Tube Station: Hanger Lane (0.6 miles)
Nearest Bus Routes: 95 - Alperton Lane (Stop V)
Primary Use: Vehicle storage

108

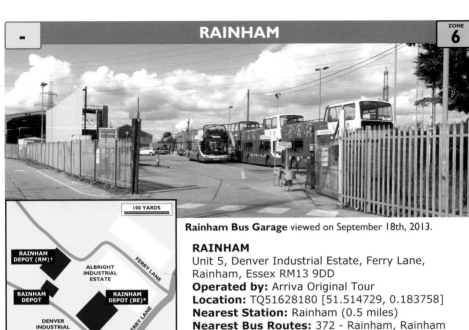

RAINHAM

Rainham Bus Garage viewed on September 18th, 2013.

RAINHAM
Unit 5, Denver Industrial Estate, Ferry Lane,
Rainham, Essex RM13 9DD
Operated by: Arriva Original Tour
Location: TQ51628180 [51.514729, 0.183758]
Nearest Station: Rainham (0.5 miles)
Nearest Bus Routes: 372 - Rainham, Rainham
(London) (Stop B)
Primary Use: Maintenance and garaging of tour
buses

*SEE PAGE 76   †SEE PAGE 77

TWICKENHAM

Twickenham Bus Garage on August 17th, 2013.

TWICKENHAM (NC)
The Skills Centre, Twickenham Trading Estate,
Rugby Road, Twickenham TW1 1DQ
Operated by: London United
Location: TQ15767439 [51.456671, -0.335170]
Nearest Station: Twickenham (0.7 miles)
Nearest Bus Routes: 481 - Twickenham,
Twickenham Trading Estate (Stop K)
Primary use: Maintenance Depot only

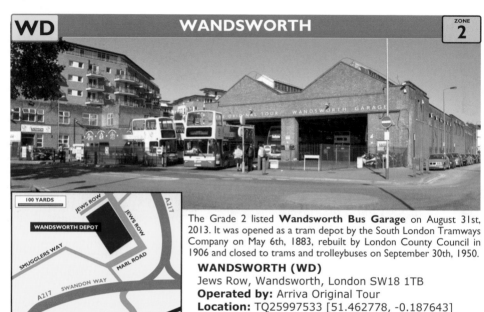

The Grade 2 listed **Wandsworth Bus Garage** on August 31st, 2013. It was opened as a tram depot by the South London Tramways Company on May 6th, 1883, rebuilt by London County Council in 1906 and closed to trams and trolleybuses on September 30th, 1950.

WANDSWORTH (WD)
Jews Row, Wandsworth, London SW18 1TB
Operated by: Arriva Original Tour
Location: TQ25997533 [51.462778, -0.187643]
Nearest Station: Wandsworth Town (300 yards)
Nearest Bus Routes: 28/44/N28 & N44 - Wandsworth, Swandon Way (Stop TC)
Primary use: Garaging tour buses

Wimbledon Bus Garage viewed on September 19th, 2013.

WIMBLEDON (-)
St Martins Way, Summerstown, London SW17 0AR
Operated by: Big Bus Company
Location: TQ26077206 [51.433921, -0.186564]
Nearest Station: Earlsfield (0.7 miles)
Nearest Bus Routes: 44/77/270 & N44 - Burntwood Lane (Stop SD)
Primary use: Garaging tour buses

Arriva London buses **LT178**, **LT182**, **DW227**, **VLW95** & **LT220** parked inside **Clapton Bus Garage** on August 5th, 2014. (See Page 27)

Atlas Road (AS)-allocated Tower Transit bus **VMW32422** crossing the Grand Union Canal as it approaches Westbourne Park Bus Garage on July 26th, 2014.

AND FINALLY ...

THE BUS GARAGE THAT CLOSED DURING 2014

Lee Valley Bus Garage on July 22nd, 2014. It was opened in 2005 to accommodate the articulated buses being deployed on Route 149, but was compulsorily purchased for the National Grid in 2014. It closed on March 1st and was replaced by the nearby **Edmonton Depot**. (See Page 35)

PROPOSED SITE FOR NEW GARAGE IN 2015

The proposed site of a garage for Tower Transit at 78 Picketts Lock Lane, N9 0AX viewed on July 22nd, 2014. It is located at TQ36279379 (51.626426, -0.032691389).

INFORMATION UPDATE

Former Metrobus garages **Croydon** (C) (See Page 30) and **Orpington** (MB) (See Page 66) are now managed by London General in the Go-Ahead Group.